DIRTY DAYS

DIRTY DAYS

TRUE NEW YORK CITY BAR AND ROCK STORIES

KEVIN PATRICK CORRIGAN

EDITED BY
SHAMUS O'CALLAHAN

Iron Molly Entertainment, Inc

Special Thanks

DIRTY DAYS

TRUE NEW YORK CITY BAR AND ROCK N' ROLL STORIES

Special Thanks:

Steven O'Connell
Peter Vandall
Annie J. Corrigan
Nora Leahy
Monica Blessing
Rosa Cho
Stacey Meyrowitz
John Yorke
Jim Florentine
Red Lion
Back Fence
Kenny's Castaways
The Bitter End
Lion's Den
Rock n' Roll Cafe
The 4th Floor Band
Weedkiller Band
Begorrah Band
Bleecker Street

Credits / Contact

DIRTY DAYS (1971 - 2004)

True New York City Bar And Rock Stories

(C.) Iron Molly Entertainment, Inc
Astoria, NY 11103

Publisher:
Iron Molly Entertainment, Inc

For speaking engagements, readings, live music performances.
www.kevinpcorrigan@gmail.com

Library of Congress Cataloging-in-Publication has been applied for.

ISBN/SKU 978-1-0879-2948-4
EISBN 978-1-0879-2949-1

Contents

**Dedicated to my
friend Bleecker
Street Legend
"The Dude"**
Peter May

Quote

"I started writing a funny New York City bar story book. I was soon reminded of how close we all are to God and our Demons, War and Peace, Blind Faith and Laughter."

Kevin Patrick Corrigan
Dirty Days

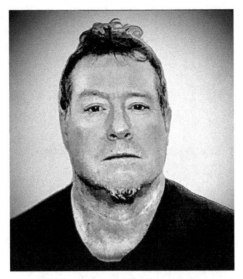

Kevin Patrick Corrigan 2021
Author

New York City

Mayors Of New York City from 1971 - 2004

John Lindsey (1966 - 1973)

Abe Beame (1974 - 1977)

Ed Koch (1978 - 1989)

David Dinkins (1990 - 1993)

Rudy Guilliani (1994 - 2001)

Mike Bloomberg (2002 - 2013)

1

Times Square 1971

CHAPTER 1

TIMES SQUARE 1971

A half naked woman stood in the middle of Times Square flashing her exposed breast.

"Look at that lady in her underwear! She is showing her boobies!" I shouted.

The lady had on lingerie. Being seven years old at the time I had no idea what lingerie was.

All four of my sisters and my mother turned to where I was pointing.

My mother's face seemed to swell red like she got hit with a waffle iron. She began yelling in her thick Irish accent, "Heads down right now! Everybody! Let's go! Stare at the floor! No looking up 'til New Jersey! If anybody looks up you will get it when we get home!"

All my sisters' eyes went to the floor right away. I snuck one last peek at the lady. She was hoisting up her breasts and waving toward us.

"Let's go Kevin! Look at the floor!" My mother barked.

Reluctant, I listened.

It wasn't a good idea to not listen to my mother.

This was my first memory of Times Square.

It was 1971. I was a little boy stuck in traffic with my family in the back of our blue Chevy station wagon.

Before my mother told us to look at the floor I was leering out the back window at all the nonstop action. It was a fishbowl of chaos. I was mesmerized.

-Bums were everywhere.

-Dirty red and pink faced people drank on every corner.

-It was the middle of the day and I saw people lying on the ground sleeping.

-I saw people pushing each other.

-I saw a tug of war over a bottle in a brown paper bag.

-At every light five guys tried to wash our car's windows.

-Women walked around practically naked.

-I saw a guy being chased by the cops.

Afraid to look up my mind raced, I thought, 'What is this place? If Ma don't want us to see what's happening than this might be the hell I hear about in church on Sundays'.

Curiosity filled my mind. I needed to see more but knew if I was caught looking up, it would not be good for me. I could feel my Mother's eyes on the top of my hair. With my head down I couldn't see anything, but I could hear.

I heard women cackling.

They were cooing the word "sugar" over and over again.

"Hey sugar! Nice sugar! You need some sugar? Sugar?"

'Is there a sugar store out there?' I wondered. 'I like sugar on my corn flakes'.

I wanted to look up so bad. I had no other choice but to keep listening.

-I heard angry car horns.

-I heard glass smashing.

-I heard people screaming and laughing.

-I heard the phrases, "Did you pay for that?! Fuck You! Get out of Vietnam! Ten cent movies! Live sex! Come on in!"

I knew what "Fuck you" meant from the schoolyard.

I knew you had to pay for things from my parents teaching me.

I knew what Vietnam was from seeing teenagers on my block leaving for it as their mothers cried in the street.

But, what was live sex?

What was it?

I asked myself, "Was live sex a play? Was it an animal like live stock? Was live sex a game?"

My only brother Brian was two years old. He had yet to figure out the hardcore dynamic of an "Off The Boat" Irish-farm-raised mother born in 1935.

My oldest sister Eileen was about nine. She was holding Brian in the second row seat between sisters Shelia and Patricia.

In 1971 a child's car seat was the oldest sibling's lap. Eileen's head was down for fear of her life.

Brian had wide opened eyes. His head swiveled looking all around. It didn't matter that he was a baby. My Mother wasn't having any of that.

A dirty oil rag was in the front seat between my parents. My Mother threw it over Brian's head like he was a ring toss peg. Even he wasn't going to be allowed to look. He tried to pull it off but couldn't because Eileen was holding his arms. Brian feverishly shook his head trying to shake free of the oil rag.

Later on in life I realized we were driving through the area of New York City where the "Tunnel Bunnies" worked. It was a stretch of streets that started in Times Square and ran ten blocks to the Lincoln tunnel entrances for New Jersey.

It was a place where packs of half-naked hookers walked around looking for clients. There could be ten of them at an intersection at one time.

The clients would pull their cars over. The Tunnel Bunnies would take care of business right there.

Being a kid I had no idea what was going on just feet away from my wholesome family station wagon.

It seemed like forever with my head down. My mother was facing us. She watched us like a hawk school-marme. I could feel the heat getting hotter from her stare burning the top of my skull.

After a few minutes stuck still in traffic, I noticed I could see the close-up action from my side eye. My curiosity was getting the better of me. I had to get a full peek. The commotion of the street was a lure calling out to me to defy my mother. I needed to look.

My sister Mary was in the back section of the station wagon with me. She was scared. I could see from my peripheral vision more ladies in their underwear.

My mother saw that I could see.

"Put your faces to the floor! As close to the floor as possible! Mary and Kevin lie down back there. Face to the ground! Let's go!"

Her Irish brogue always got thicker when she was mad.

She sounded like she was in a cow field in Ireland shouting away a fox.

Mary and I laid flat-faced. Our noses were touching the floor.

I heard the underwear ladies whistling and making woohoo noises outside.

I wanted to peek.

I needed to peek.

I was terrified to peek.

The thought of getting the Irish wrath when I got home held my face down.

I began to think, 'Was a two second glimpse worth the fury of my mother?'

I listened to an underwear lady say, "You want a date sugar?"

A million thoughts raced in my mind like symbols spinning on a slot machine, 'Should I peek? Don't peek! Was it smart to peek? Peak you chicken! You will not be allowed out of the house for a month if you peek! Sneak a Peek! No peek! Yes peek! You're crazy to peek! You're crazy not to peak!'

The mind spin was out of control. Ten seconds of undecided thoughts spun in my brain before finally stopping on, 'Go for it! Have a peek!'

I heard a new and different underwear lady coo, "Oooh... You're a handsome one."

I started to think on how to pull the peek off.

With my nose on the floor I realized I couldn't see my mother in my side eye. The second row seat was shielding me from her. If I couldn't see her than she couldn't see me. Even at a young age I understood that law of physics.

I side-eyed around for five seconds. It was official. If I turned over my mother wouldn't be able to notice from where she was. The back seat was a wall of cover.

It was a great discovery.

To be safe I calculated once more the angle of my mother's eye sight from my position to hers. For certain she couldn't see me.

I whispered to Mary with a facedown side-eye, "I'm gonna peek. Ma won't be able to see me if I turn to look up."

Mary whispered back with her facedown side-eye. She was scared for me, "No... Don't do it. Ma will kill you."

Mary was closest to me in age. We were a year apart. We always stayed together on family outings.

"I'm going for it," I mouthed to Mary.

Her eyes bugged outward with fright.

Something fantastic was happening right outside the station wagon. I was determined to witness it. I turned my body from face down to face up with a silent ease.

Traffic was still halted. I could see another half-naked woman an inch from the side back window of the station wagon. She was wearing underwear that went up her big butt crack. I wondered where the bottom half of her underwear was. I could see her entire ass. There were pock marks all over it. She was reaching in the window of the car stopped two feet from us.

"Hey handsome. So what do you say? Do you want a date?" She asked.

Amazed, I thought, 'What is going on? A woman in her underwear is asking a man stopped in traffic if he wanted a date. This must be a good place to find a wife. I got to come here when I'm older.'

The underwear lady continued talking, "Come on Sugar! You want some sweetness tonight?"

Everyone in my family station wagon could hear the underwear lady. Including my mother.

"John could you turn up the radio please!?" My mother asked my father.

My mother never asked my father to turn the radio louder, especially a Met game. Something was up.

My father went to High School in Manhattan. He was oblivious to the chaos. He made the radio louder. Ralph Kiner was calling the play by play of a New York Mets baseball game.

"Tom Seaver is pitching a great game...."

Ralph's voice could be heard through the small radio speaker on the wagon's dash. His voice going head-to-head with the half-naked lady's sales pitch.

I decided I better turn back around. The way my mother asked for the radio to go louder was no nonsense. I knew if I got caught peeking I was doomed.

I shimmied around slow and easy. The image of the big giant pock-marked butt crack etched into my mind forever.

Mary looked at me with a facedown side-eye. She was relieved I didn't get caught.

We weren't allowed to raise our heads until we were in the Lincoln tunnel.

The Mets game ended about two minutes after we got into New Jersey. The Mets won. My father turned the radio to the Yankee game. Three innings later we pulled onto my street in Old Bridge, New Jersey. Phil Rizzuto the Yankee announcer was telling a crazy story. He was calling somebody a Huckleberry when my father turned the car off.

My Mother made Irish soda bread with raisins that night. We ate it warm with melted butter. It was delicious.

I kept saying to myself, "I have to go back to that place when I get older. I have too."

Saint Patrick's Day 1979 (Warning Very Graphic)

CHAPTER 2

SAINT PATRICK'S DAY 1979

(Warning Very Graphic)

Eight years passed to Saint Patrick's Day 1979.

I was half-a-man of fifteen years old on my own in Times Square with some high school friends. We were all freshman.

The decadence of 1970's New York City was seen the instant we got off the bus at The Port Authority station. The first eye catching sight was flashing neon that read "Girls, Girls, Girls". My friends and I were drawn to the sign like steel to magnets.

The place was called *Show World* on the northwest corner of 42nd Street and 8th avenue. Another sign on the building read "7 Live Bedroom Acts" and "Live Sex".

My friends and I stood looking at the door of *Show World* not knowing what to do. It was scary and enticing. I now knew how Adam felt about the apple.

"We got to go in there," one friend said, half drooling.

"Let's go to a bar first. Get buzzed," I replied, pulling my guys up 8th avenue.

In 1979 the drinking age was 18 years old in New York and New Jersey. In 1979 New York City, the legend of the un-written rule was true, "If you can reach the bar and act alright. You can get a drink".

I was six foot two at 15. I was also 145 pounds. I was a skinny wiry kid. My friends were also tall. We walked north on 8th avenue to 44th street where an orange pink neon sign was lit with the words 'Smith's Bar'. We stopped to look through the window. It was pretty busy. We agreed to go inside.

The place was packed with Saint Patrick's Day revelers wall to wall. There were other groups of teenagers in the bar milling about too. White headed Irish old men were seated everywhere. Irish music was blasting. Everybody was singing along. It was great. We bought two pitchers of beer for four or five dollars.

We were kids and had planned on coming to New York City for the Saint Patrick's Day parade for months. I saved my paper route money for this day. The other guys did the same from their jobs in deli's and food stores. We were set.

It was March in New York City. It wasn't freezing but it was cold. From the window of *Smith's Bar* we could see women outside wearing their underwear under coats. I wondered if any of the half-naked women were the ones I saw when I was younger.

"Look, hookers!" My buddy pointed out.

"Those are hookers man! Wow! Hookers! I never saw a hooker before," another enthralled buddy said.

It made sense now why my mother made us put our heads down years ago. Hookers were everywhere. Sex was everywhere. At fifteen I knew what sex was, unlike when I was seven. Energy of the sickest was all around. It was a combination of danger and joy. I loved it.

We drank and sang Irish tunes in *Smith's* for over two hours. At noon we had a good buzz going. It was time to go to the parade.

We walked further north on 8th avenue.

After two blocks we went into a deli to grab beers. In 1979 New York City nobody bothered you drinking in public. As long as the booze was covered by something. The deli guys would give you a small brown paper bag the perfect size for a can of beer, or pint bottle of hard booze. We marched brown bags in hand.

We passed thousands of people wearing green. Almost everyone in green was carrying brown bagged beers too. If we passed five thousand people, four thousand nine hundred and ninety eight of them had brown paper bags in their hands. The two that didn't were holding lit marijuana joints.

In 1979 New York City nobody bothered you if you walked down the street smoking weed. The smell of weed, hot pretzels, piss, puke, hot dogs, happiness, and regret were everywhere in Times Square.

We were somewhere around Central Park when we heard bag pipes coming from the east. Hearing bag pipes in the streets of New York City on Saint Patrick's Day is like receiving a sacrament from the Lord.

My friends weren't as excited to hear them as I was. Saint Patrick's Day was just another day to drink for them. For me it was personal. My mother always made me remember I was Irish. It was very important to her. She was an Irish immigrant who came to America at nineteen years old. She always made Saint Patrick's Day a big deal in our house. I knew corn beef, mash potatoes, homemade rice pudding and Irish soda bread would be waiting for me when I got home. I had chills hearing the pipes.

We watched the parade for about ten minutes until my restless friend spoke, "Let's get out of here. Let's go to a peep show. Let's go back toward the Port Authority where all the hookers are walking around and look at them."

I was the only one who cared about the parade. I knew I was going to have to recount it for my mother when I got home. I had a good enough visual of the parade for my memory. I saw plenty of bag pipers, drunken cops, step dancers, and plastered firemen to recount for my mother later on.

"Ok. Let's get out of here. We'll go to Times Square and get peeps," I said.

We walked south on 7th avenue through the heart of Times Square before crossing over to 8th avenue to the Port Authority.

Every step we took was a new scene of mayhem. We saw drunk women yelling at each other. We saw bums lying in their own piss and people selling weed out in the open.

The closer we got to 42nd street and 8th avenue the more porno shops and peep shows there were. My buddies had their sights set on *Show World* with live nude girls, sex shows, and peep movie booths. None of us had any idea what we were in for.

In 1979 big cities all across America were literally falling apart. In Times Square it was evident. The sorrow of addiction and homelessness was oozing out at every nook and cranny. Abandoned buildings were strewn about. It was rough. Two hundred police officers were stationed there every night. They didn't even put a dent in the crime. The corner of 42nd Street and 8th avenue was declared the most dangerous place in America; right where *Show World and The Port Authority* stood. We arrived not knowing what to do.

"Fuck it! Let's just go in," I said. "If they throw us out. They throw us out."

I was the first in the door.

The others followed.

Nobody in Show world questioned the five fifteen year old kids walking in at once.

I noticed other groups of teenage kids inside. Some of them I recognized from being in *Smith's Bar* earlier. I quickly realized nobody was going throw us out.

To be a part of the action in *Show World* you had to buy tokens from a guy who stood at a podium that was four feet higher than the floor. He looked like a giant.

I reached up to hand him a five dollar bill.

He said nothing when he handed me my tokens. The others did the same.

Each token was worth a quarter.

We stood in disbelief at how easy it was to be there. A pounding Boomp, Boomp, Boomp beat of some type of music I never heard before mixed in with orgasmic moans of women in ecstasy. The moans echoed throughout the place.

There was a guy shouting into a microphone as the moans and the beats pulsed, "You drop it. We mop it! Let's go fellas! Live sex upstairs! Yeah that's right! You drop it! We mop it!"

We decided to split up to explore this palace of perversion and carnal lust. We set a meeting spot on the corner of 42nd and 8th in a half hour. None of us had watches. I looked around for a clock. There was no clock.

I looked up in the sky to ask the token guy, "Do you know what time it is?"

Never looking up from counting bills, he growled, "No." We all chuckled at each other seeing how much of a fuck this guy didn't give.

"Screw it! Guess how long a half an hour is. See you later," I said to my friends.

We all separated.

There were signs that pointed behind the token guy that read 'Live Nude Girls'. Two of my guys walked toward that hallway. One guy went upstairs to the live sex show.

I walked downstairs toward the sign that read twenty five cent movies. I figured I would start at the bottom of this wonderland and work my way up. The last one of my guys decided to go downstairs too.

Grown men with quiet concentrative looks on their faces were everywhere. We were teenage metal heads in blue jeans. The grown men were dressed in suits and construction worker outfits.

We weren't the only teenagers in *Show World*. Other groups of kids from New York and New Jersey were walking around too. All the teens dressed the same. Either a velour shirt with a denim jacket. Or, a black concert t-shirt from a metal band worn under a not buttoned up flannel shirt.

At the bottom of the stairs I saw walls and walls of phone booth type apparatuses. I went to the left. My friend went to the right.

We nodded, 'See you later'.

Outside the one-man booths were posters of the titles and a synopsis of what the movie was about inside. I browsed the pictures. Titles like "French Whore", "Mandingo Time", "Two On One Fever", and "Blondes Likes It Hard" were plastered on the booths.

I thumbed over the signs the way one would a card catalog at the library or looking at LP's in a record bin. Both extinct practices now.

I scanned the posters for a few minutes. I saw my friend go in a booth. I snuck over to see what he was seeing.

"Southern Belle Rides the North Pole" was his choice.

The picture outside his booth had a hot blonde in cutoff jeans. She was on her knees in front of a guy dressed in a Civil War era Union Soldier's uniform. The Union soldier had his junk out.

In January of 1979 a TV show called "The Dukes of Hazard" aired for the first time. Everybody watched it. There was only a handful of TV channels back then. The entire country watched the same shows.

All my friends and I had a crush on Daisy Duke from that show. She wore the highest cutoff shorts ever on TV. Later that summer all the girls in my neighborhood wore their shorts like Daisy Duke. Daisy Duke caused a lot of teenage pregnancy in 1979. The day after "The Dukes of Hazard" first aired every guy in my school was talking about Daisy's cutoff shorts.

I knew the Daisy Duke themed movie poster subliminally called my buddy to pick "Southern Belle rides The North Pole".

I made a mental note to see that movie later.

I walked toward the back of the room. I looked at a title, "Barnyard Heaven".

The poster had a picture of a grinning naked guy holding a live chicken and a girl smiling in front of a horse. The tag line was, "A hard day's work in the barnyard gets off".

'What was this about?' I thought.

I had no idea what to think. My curiosity was ignited. I decided this was my choice. The door opened outward. I stepped in the booth. I pulled the door closed behind me.

The floor was sticky. I thought someone must had spilled a soda on the ground. There was a coin operated machine and a small white movie screen inside. The booth wasn't giant but it wasn't that tight.

I put a token in the slot. It was like putting money in a washing machine at the laundromat.

The white screen came alive. I heard the sound of a film

projector. A sound I heard many times in school when watching health and education movies. I looked at the screen in anticipation of what was "Barnyard Heaven".

The first image I saw was a close up shot of a guy's face. He looked like he was in his glory. It was a silent movie but I could tell he was moaning in ecstasy. His shoulders were moving like he was rowing a boat.

I had never seen a porno movie before. I thought, 'What's this guy doing?'

The movie cut from the close-up shot to a head-to-toe full wide shot. I was astonished to see a naked guy holding a live wing-flapping chicken. He was moving it up and down on his junk. The movie then cut to a close up of the chicken. The guy was fucking the chicken ass.

I instantly started to dry heave. I began gagging violently. I fought hard not to puke. Deep gags hit my throat. I tried breathing deep which caused me to hyperventilate. I looked at the ceiling fighting to hold my cookies. I battled my stomach to stay down. I felt I wasn't going to win. I moved my head toward the floor. I retched three times then projectile vomited onto my sneakers.

I tried to move my feet to avoid the puke stream but couldn't. They were stuck to the floor.

I coughed and gagged. I tried to be quiet in my disgust. I still had so much to see. I didn't want to get thrown out for causing a commotion. It took about twenty seconds to regain my composure. My Chuck Taylors were soaked with puke.

This couldn't be real. This had to be a camera trick. I looked back at the screen. The movie cut to a close up of the guy in his ecstasy. Then the movie cut to a close up of the chicken's ass. He was for sure penetrating the poor bird.

I was about to walk out of the booth with the film still playing when the movie cut to a close up of a horse. I couldn't not look. I watched the horse swinging his head up and down. He looked happy.

After a five second close up of the horse. The movie cut to a wide shot. I saw the whole horse. His head was screen left and his hind quarters was screen right. There was a girl on her knees with no clothes on in the middle section of the horse. She was facing away from the camera. You could see her ass. It was real nice. She was moving her hands and bobbing her head up and down.

I thought, 'Is she milking the horse? Can you milk a horse?'

The movie then cut to a close-up shot of the girl's face. My stomach shot again to my neck. The horse's penis was in her mouth.

I jumped back slamming against the wall. It made a loud thud. My feet slipped on the wet puke floor like I was on an ice pond. I would have fell but the tight booth's design held me up. I could not believe what I saw.

"That's fucking disgusting", I wretched out as I puked on my sneakers once more.

After a few more deep breaths I began to regain my composure. The blasting Boomp Boomp music "Thank God" muffled my gasps, wretches, and slamming against the wall thuds.

Eyes up I spoke soft to myself, "Do not get thrown out of here. You still have so much more to see."

I took in all the sounds and flashing lights.

I continued speaking to myself looking at the ceiling, "Relax Kev. You got to walk out of this booth right now. This movie was a bad idea."

The live microphone guy was on a rant.

He barked more furious, "You drop it. We mop it! Come on fellas! That's right boys!"

The piped-in orgasmic moaning was spinning my mind. I felt dead and alive. I fought my stomach to stay put.

I inhaled two more breaths.

"Don't be a pussy. Look back. It can't be real. It's got to be a camera trick. This can't be real."

I mustered the courage to look back at the screen.

To my utter disbelief it was true and real. The horse's junk was in her mouth. This hot chick was sucking this huge horse cock monstrosity and she was loving it. The horse was loving it too.

I couldn't hold back my gut from erupting up my throat again. I didn't think I had anything left in my stomach but I did. It came out fast. I put my hands over my mouth so not to ralph on the screen. The puke hit my hands splattering all over my face. It cascaded down onto my Black Sabbath t-shirt and open green flannel. I was now covered in puke.

I looked to the top of the booth. I could see the ceiling. The flashing of neon red and green lights were pulsating above. To double check if what I just saw was real and not a camera trick I had to look back at the screen. There it was. A giant horse cock inside a girl's mouth.

'Why? And how? Could a person's life get to the point where they have a horse's penis in their mouth? What kind of world do I live in?' I thought.

The whole movie was about two or three minutes. A sign came up, "To continue movie from this point you have fifteen seconds to put in another token."

There was no way I was going to put in a token. I wanted out of there.

The screen went blank white. I looked down at my shirt. I started to wipe away the puke. I took off my green flannel. I used it to wipe my face and body clean. I rubbed the barf on the floor to the side with my puke-soaked sneakers. It was mostly beer but here and there was a smattering of English muffin and street pretzel. I composed myself. I pushed the door open.

My friend was out of the "Southern Belle rides The North Pole" movie. He saw me. He came over giggling like a school boy, because he was. His face went from laughing to mild concern when he saw my flushed red face and wet concert shirt.

"What happened to you man? Did you puke? You didn't drink that much today?"

"I just watched a guy fuck a live chicken and a girl blow a horse. I couldn't take it so I puked on myself."

"No way! You are full of shit! A guy can't fuck a chicken. No way."

"The chicken isn't as bad as the girl sucking a horse's cock."

"Really? I don't believe you. I'm going in," he said pushing me aside.

He was a determined person on a mission to prove me wrong.

"There is no way a guy can fuck a live chicken. You are full of shit," he said looking at me as he pulled the door closed.

"It's slippery in there. Be careful," I warned.

The door clicked shut.

I composed myself and walked over to the Southern Belle movie. I went in the booth. The floor was sticky but not as sticky as "Barnyard Heaven".

I put my token in the slot. The movie started. The girl was beautiful. I thought of what a lucky guy the Union soldier was. They had normal sex on a bale of hay. I didn't have to puke. The movie was over after two or three minutes. I left the booth.

I went back to "Barnyard Heaven" to check on my buddy. The door was still closed.

He walked in ten seconds before I walked into "Southern Bell Rides the North Pole". I could see the shadows of his sneakers moving from side to side at the bottom of the booth's door.

A minute later he came out. He was flush red. His velour pullover shirt and blue denim jacket were wet. The collar of the jacket was pulled up like the 'Fonz'. I saw a piece of hot dog on it.

"You got a piece of dirty water dog on your collar," I pointed out.

"That was fucked up. How can someone put a horse's cock in their mouth? I wouldn't want to be the next guy kissing her," he stammered.

"Wipe yourself off. Let's go upstairs. I don't want to get thrown out for puking."

I looked at the floor of the "Barnyard Heaven" booth. It was drenched with two guys worth of puke.

We walked out of the 25 cent movie floor. We went up the stairs to the next level. The token booth guy was taking money and handing out tokens to another group of teens trying to act older.

"You drop it! We mop it," was barked for the three hundredth time over the sound system.

I realized nobody in this place gave a shit about anything. It was a vortex of lust and sin. My buddy nodded toward the "Live Sex Show" sign that pointed to the next floor up.

"You go. I'm going to work my way up there. I want to see what this "live nude girls" thing is about on this floor," I told him.

It was best we split up. I didn't want to be attracting attention. Two teenagers walking side by side with wet puke stained shirts is not a compelling sight for the house. He went up the stairs toward the live sex show. I walked past the token guy to where the "Live Nude Girls" sign pointed.

The music was loud. It sounded like drums from the

jungle. The sound of girls moaning to the jungle beats was energizing. I felt alive even though I just puked on myself.

The floor was laid out different from the 25 cent movie floor. There were three semicircles of booths. Each semicircle had about fifteen booths. There was a flashing red neon sign on top of each semicircle that read, "Live Nude Girls".

I thought about what happened to me in the last booth downstairs. I walked back toward the middle of the semi-circle. I picked a booth and went inside. The door opened out toward me like the booth before. I went inside.

Just like the movie booths there was a coin-operated machine. Instead of the blank white screen there was a window. On the other side of the window was a black barrier.

It was dark inside. A small amount of light was coming from the open ceiling of the roofless booth. Neon flashes illuminated the coin-operated machine with blasts of light. I had no idea what was going to happen. I put the token in the slot. I heard the mechanism click. The black barrier on the other side of the window started to rise. The moving barrier sounded like an automatic garage door opening. I watched with the utmost curiosity. The barrier rose up exposing the other side.

"Wow!" I said to myself.

There stood a naked women on a stage. It was the first time I ever saw a live naked woman. She has short blonde hair and looked Russian. I looked at all the parts of this woman. I only ever saw a naked women in my friend's father's Playboy books. We would steal them for peeks when he was at work.

The woman wasn't that attractive. You could tell her face was pretty at one time. She wasn't fat but she wasn't skinny. She didn't look happy being there. She looked bored and listless.

I felt things I never felt before in my body. I watched in awe at the naked lady. She moved her hips from side to side in an uninspired lethargic way. I looked at her eyes. I became sad.

She wasn't a happy person. The first naked lady I ever saw was depressed.

I looked around. I could see the faces of other guys in the semicircle of booths. One guy held up a dollar. The girl saw the bill. She gyrated a little faster over to him. I watched her pull the window up. The guy could reach in now. He handed her a dollar. She put her womanhood up to his open window. He touched her. She let him graze it for about two seconds before she backed away and pushed the window back down.

I thought about waving a dollar and getting a touch but the movies I saw in High School about sexually transmitted diseases popped in my head. I figured I better keep my hands to myself. I didn't want my fingers to fall off. I need them to make music and write in the future.

After about two minutes I heard the clicking mechanism sound. The black barrier started to go down. The time for that token was up. I hurried to put in another token. The barrier went back up.

I looked at the naked woman's face again. She was so sad. It kind of soured it for me. I knew she wasn't having a good time standing there naked. I tried to rush that thought out of my head and look at tits and ass and the good stuff. I did that for a few seconds but my gaze was always drawn back to her sorrowful face.

To my left a guy waved a five dollar bill. The girl almost tripped over herself going to him. She let him touch her womanhood for about 10 seconds. She faked like she was enjoying it. The click sound went off again. My token time was up.

As the barrier lowered I leaned down following the bottom of the barrier until the last glimpse of naked lady was seen before the window closed shut.

I decided I would go see what was going on upstairs at the "Live Sex Show" floor. I pushed the booth door out. I left the first naked woman I ever saw in my life, forever.

I went up the stairs to the "Live Sex" floor. One large semi-circle of booths spanned the length of the room. It was different from the "Live Nude Girls" floor with the three semi circles of booths. I found an empty one. I pushed the door and went inside. I put a token in the coin-operated machine. The barrier slid up. I couldn't believe what I saw. A Puerto Rican guy was banging a hot Black chick.

I could see the faces of the guys across the giant semi-circle stage. I saw two of my buddies in booths that were three away from each other. My friend who puked on himself was to the left and another of my guys was to the right. They were looking in amazement at the "Live Sex Show".

The barrier was lowering on my fellow puke buddy. I watched him bend down to follow the gate's decent until it closed for the last peep. I saw his eye get a last glance. A few seconds later his gate rose up again. His eyes were glowing. He was so enamored. My barrier started to go down. I looked at the action also following the bottom edge of the barrier until my last glance of banging could be seen. This went on for token after token. I lost track of time.

My friends across the stage in their booths never noticed me. They were in their own pubescent wonderland. I wanted to get their attention. I decided to wave. The guy banging saw me waving. I distracted him from his thrusting. He looked at me with a pissed off face.

My friends noticed the banging guy looking away in anger. They were curious to see what he was looking at. That bought their eyes on me. They started waving back at me with their thumbs up laughing. The banging guy noticed the other two guys waving. He made another face. He shut his eyes, got his concentration right, and went back to work plowing the hot chick.

I saw the barrier of my puke friend's booth go down. It took a little bit till it went up again. I started waving making faces toward my puke buddy's booth. The barrier rose up full. It wasn't my friend in the booth this time. It was an older guy in a suit. He looked like Walter Matthau. He saw me waving. He smiled and waved back with a cutesy grin. I looked away. He kept trying to get my attention. I could see him puckering his lips in my side-eye. I ignored him.

My door went down. I went into my pocket for more tokens. I wanted to see the climax of this spectacle despite a sixty year old pervert blowing kisses at me from across the sex show stage. I rifled through my pockets. They were empty except for my bus ticket home. I was out of tokens. Not only was I out of tokens. I was out of money.

"Damn!" I screamed.

I turned to get out of the booth. I pushed the door to leave. It didn't move. I pushed again. Nothing.

I pushed a little harder. It didn't budge.

I started to get a little nervous.

Was I locked in?

The music seemed to pulse louder. I stopped pushing for a second.

Was I trapped?

I pushed again, and again, and again, against the door. It didn't open.

I felt the walls closing in. I began to panic. My mind started to roam to the dark side.

Was this one of those Times Square Shanghai's I've heard about? Was the Walter Matthau look alike coming for me?

"Fuck! They got me prisoner in this booth," I shouted out loud.

I pushed harder against the door. The entire semicircle of booths filled with leering men started to shake back and forth.

I heard the banging guy scream, "What the Fuck Now!?"

I pushed even harder against the door. It didn't budge again.

I was now in a slight panic. I screamed my friend's names to come rescue me.

The music pounded louder.

I pushed with all my might against the door.

I was strong as an Ox at Fifteen. I decided I was going to knock this whole semicircle of booths to the ground and escape the Shanghai.

"Fuck it!" I howled.

I faced the entrance of the booth with my back pressed against the shuttered peep window. I extended my arms touching both side walls. I pushed outward. The entire semicircle of booths began rocking. I decided I was going to hold myself up by pushing on the walls while leaning back against the peep window. Then I would spider climb the walls and go over the open roof.

I tested the fragility of the peep walls. I realized I could knock all these booths over. But before I destroyed the entire semicircle of peep booths I was going to give one more turn and push of the door knob.

I gripped it hard.

I felt it moving from the other side. Someone was trying to get in.

I yelled for my buddies over the loud pulsating beats and piped-in orgasmic moans.

The mic guy for the 500th time barked, "You drop it. We mop it! Come on fellas! Come on boys!"

The door knob moved again. Someone was coming in. I stepped back as far as I could which was only about nine inches.

I raised my fist ready to swing.

I formulated a quick plan.

Whoever opens the door gets an automatic punch to the nose. Their eyes would well up. They won't be able to see.

I'll run past the would-be-abductor to the street swinging at anything that moves.

Fists up adrenaline raged through my body. I cracked my neck in anticipation of a fight.

The door moved inward.

In that split second I realized I was pushing the door outward like every other booth I was in that day. This was an inward door. I felt like a major dick.

I still had my fists up ready to chuck haymakers.

I still had no idea who was on the other side.

I hoped it wasn't somebody from the house.

Dukes ready to fire.

The person revealed himself.

Hallelujah!

It was my buddy who also puked on himself. I put my hands down. I was so relieved to see him. He somehow heard my calls over the loud thumping beats and moans.

"What is wrong with you?" He chuckled as I sighed a giant sigh.

The token guy on the four foot podium was off his perch. He also heard my calls and shouts. He also saw the semi-circle of peep booths rocking back and forth. He was coming at us hard and fast. He was about five feet tall and five feet wide. He looked like he could handle himself.

"Time to leave!" The token guy yelled loud. "Let's go Leprechauns! You two guys got puke all over yourself. You're screaming and wrecking my booths and ruining the show! Time to Go! You know where the door is!"

My puke buddy and I left with no incident. We waited for the rest of the guys outside on 42nd Street and 8th avenue.

The other guys soon came out with smiles and tales of naked ladies and sex. We compared stories on the bus ride back to Jersey. My Mom's corned beef was great when I got home. I told her of all the nice bag pipers I saw that day.

Three Card Monty 1979

CHAPTER 3

THREE CARD MONTY 1979

Street hustles were everywhere in New York City during the 70's and 80's. One hustle was called *Three Card Monty*.

The first time I saw a *Three Card Monty* Crew operate I was 15 with a pack of buddies from my neighborhood. We were walking around Times Square after taking the 7 train from Shea Stadium after a Mets baseball game in Queens.

A crowd was gathered in the middle of the sidewalk between 47th and 48th street on 7th Avenue. We were curious so we went over to investigate. We saw some rough looking guys playing cards.

A Dealer was behind a small folding table with three cards facing up on it. The Queen of Hearts, the King of Spades, and the Jack of Diamonds. We watched the action. A bettor placed five dollars on the table. He pointed to the King of Spades. The Dealer flipped the cards face down. He shuffled them, then laid them out. The bettor pointed to the card he thought was the King of Spades. The Dealer turned the card face up. It was the King of spades.

'Wow pretty easy', we all looked in thought at each other.

The Dealer never shut up. He looked like a hardcore tough guy who just got out of jail. He was funny like a stand-up comedian. He had a comment for everything. He was very entertaining. I liked listening to him.

I noticed another tough guy next to The Dealer watching everything. The bettor was cleaning up. He won three games in a row. He walked away from the table counting his money.

"Another winner! Who's the next lucky one? Step up place a bet!" The Dealer barked.

We started going into our pockets to play. We were pushing each other to be first. It looked so easy to win.

My one friend was a tough kid who liked to fight. He won the pushing battle. He put five dollars down.

"Ok. Go easy on me buddy!" The Dealer chuckled. He laid the cards out.

The Jack of Diamonds, Queen of Hearts, and the King of Spades were displayed for all to see.

"Pick a card champ," The Dealer said.

My friend pointed to the Jack of Diamonds. The Dealer turned the cards and shuffled pretty fast. I followed along. The dealer laid the cards out.

I thought to myself, 'The far left card.'

My friend pointed to the far left card. The dealer turned it over.

We all cheered, "Jack of Diamonds!"

I noticed three other tough looking guys appear out of nowhere. One next to the dealer and two on each side of the table. I began to get an uneasy feeling. I stepped to my betting friend.

"Come on you're up. Let's get out of here," I whispered in his ear.

I noticed the guy who won the three hands in a row was standing right next to me. Almost on top of me. I watched the eyes of the guys on the side of the table. They were side-eyeing the guy who won the three hands in a row. They were signaling each other back and forth with glances. I realized they were all together.

"Come on double or nothing," The Dealer said.

My friend didn't hesitate putting the ten dollars down. He also didn't notice we were surrounded. The Dealer faced the cards up. My friend again pointed to the Jack of Diamonds. The Dealer turned the cards faced down. He shuffled pretty fast again. He laid the cards out and asked, "Which one's the winner boss?"

I followed along. I thought it was the center card. My friend did too. He pointed to the center card. The dealer turned the center card over, Jack of diamonds. My friend was now fifteen dollars up.

I noticed the tough looking guys getting tighter on us. We were totally surrounded. They were all working together.

I grabbed my betting friends shoulder, "Come on man! Let's get out of here."

The Dealer butted in sweet talking all nice to me, "I need a chance to get my money back pal. Come on, your friend is on a roll. He could wipe me out. He is good."

I could see the devil behind The Dealers smiling eyes. He wasn't aggressive. He was chatty and pleasant. He was funny. You couldn't help but like him. My insides still felt uneasy. The Dealer pulled out two twenty dollar bills. My friend's eyes lit up.

The Dealer gave the butter up, "You got twenty dollars right there. The fifteen you just won and your original five. You are good man. Get out another twenty and we'll do a straight up forty dollar for forty dollar game. You win you walk with fifty-five dollars of my money. I win. I have twenty five dollars of yours. The game is over. You go back to where you came from."

I started to do the math. It didn't add up, did it? I was perplexed with the quick street calculations.

My friend had bet in his eye. I knew he was going to go for it. He was reeled in The Dealer's net. I was still calculating numbers in my head. I noticed the other tough looking guys were even tighter on us. We were fifteen year old kids. These guys were in their twenties and thirties. They looked like they fought every day. We were tough kids and unafraid to fight. But, I didn't think we would win against these guys for one second. We would have needed weapons. Which none of us had.

"Let's do it!" My friend blurted out.

I could see my friend counting the fifty-five dollars in his head. A giant amount of money for a teenager in 1979. I still tried to do the math that The Dealer was spewing. My friend pointed again to the Jack of Diamonds. The Dealer turned the cards face down. He shuffled them. This time he shuffled them a lot faster. He was blazing. His hands looked like a maestro on fast forward with the cards. It was surreal the way The Dealer's hands moved. I couldn't follow along. The dealer put out the cards. I had no idea which card was my guys.

"For the big marbles. Which card is the Jack of diamonds?" The Dealer asked.

I guessed the center one. So did my friend. He pointed. The Dealer flipped the center card over. It was not the Jack of Diamonds.

"Oh, Queen of Hearts! The dirty whore!" The Dealer shouted. He grabbed the money quick.

My friend was down twenty five bucks now. All the money he had. He was shocked. I saw rage fill his face. He was pissed.

"Turn the other cards over. I want to see the Jack of Di-amonds," my friend shouted, sensing foul play.

My friend went to reach for the cards. The Dealer swiped them up. The guy who won the three games in a row was now on top of me. I got ready to start swinging. My friend was a known hot head and one of the toughest guys I knew. He was afraid of no one. They knew we were about to fight.

"Show me the fucking cards!" My friend screamed, lunging for The Dealer.

The tough guy next to The Dealer jumped in front of my friend. He pointed down the street and yelled, "Cops!"

I looked. I didn't see any cops. In that one-second glace down the block the Dealer scooped up the little folding table. Like the wind, the dealer and all the tough looking guys were gone, gone, gone in a blink. They melted into the thick crowd on 7th avenue. The guy who won the three hands in a row was nowhere to be seen either.

My friend was out twenty-five bucks. He was conned.

One good thing came out of that encounter. Nobody I was ever with got raked in by the *Three Card Monty* Guys ever again. I always pulled them away from the allure.

4

White Rose Bar - Ozzy/ Motorhead Paladium 1981

CHAPTER 4

THE WHITE ROSE BAR MAY 2nd, 1981

OZZY AND MOTORHEAD CONCERT PALLADIUM NYC

One thing that bought me into the city all the time was heavey metal. I always had a dream to write music and stories then perform them on the stages of New York City. Two bands that influenced me were Motorhead and Black Sabbath. On May 2nd, 1981 Motorhead and Ozzy Osbourne, (the ex-singer at the time of Black Sabbath) were performing at the Palladium in New York City.

I bought my ticket Months before the show. I remember saying to my friend after reading the ticket, "Ozzy Osbourne and *Motorhead*! What the fuck is a Motorhead?"

"I don't know. Let's go to 'Rock n' Roll Heaven' and find out," my friend said.

Rock n Roll Heaven was a record store/booth owned by a guy named Johnny Z. The store was located in a place where you could buy anything called The International Flea Market. It was on Route 18 in East Brunswick, New Jersey. Johnny Z was always working at his store and he knew everything about heavy metal music.

Aside:

"Rock N' Roll Heaven" was small in terms of space but huge in terms of impact on a generation. Johnny Z later started Megaforce records. The record label that was the epicenter for the heavy metal music genre. Johnny Z was responsible for giving Metallica its start on their international recording career, as well as many other metal bands. It all started at his tiny record booth in New Jersey.

When we walked into "Rock N Roll Heaven". Johnny Z gave us a big, "What's up fellas?"

"We're going to see *Ozzy* in the city in a few months. The opener is a band called *Motorhead*. You know anything about *Motorhead*?" I asked Johnny.

Johnny was roving around listening to me. By the time I was done talking he had four different *Motorhead* albums in his hands.

"*Motorhead* is fucking great! I guarantee you're going to love them," Johnny Z said. He was very enthusiastic handing us the records. We looked at them in awe. The first was called, 'Overkill". It had crazy art work on the cover. My friend and I nodded, 'cool' to each other.

The next album was called "Bomber". It had a picture of a wild looking plane. We nodded, 'very cool'. The third album was called, 'The Ace of Spades'. It had a picture of three dirty looking guys dressed as Mexican bandits from the 1800's. They looked like fucked up dudes. My friend and I kept nodding, 'very, very cool'.

The fourth record was an EP Called, 'Motorhead'. It had an evil logo with the words 'Motorhead' on it. We nodded more excited, 'very, very, very cool' at each other.

EP stands for Extended Play Record. An EP has half the number of songs as a full album. It is also half the price of a full album.

My friend and I stared mesmerized at all the album covers. We flipped the albums over to gaze at the back covers. We read the songs titles and checked out band pictures. We studied the artwork like we were making vaccines to save America. This quiet contemplation and study lasted a half hour. Johnny Z didn't care how long you took looking at albums. He knew part of the record buying process was to be lost in the 'album zone'.

There were fifteen other kids in "Rock n Roll Heaven" doing the same thing we were doing. They were looking at records from bands called, *Saxon, Manowar, Raven, Tank*, and *Rose Tattoo* to name a few. It was always quiet as a library when teenagers would browse through albums at "Rock N Roll Heaven".

My friend and I had a conference. We had maybe eight bucks between us. We decided to buy the EP called 'Motorhead". It was worth the risk to put out a little money on an EP, to see what the band was about, than to spend a lot of money on a full album and not liking it.

My friend and I did share the same thought, *'Motorhead* had to be good if they were playing with Ozzy'. We bought the EP for something like three or four bucks.

We hitchhiked back to Old Bridge and put the album on the record player in my buddy's basement. The songs on the record were, "Motorhead", "On Parole", "Beer Drinkers and

Hell Raisers", and "City Kids". We put the needle on the record and 'Pow'! We were hooked. We played the entire record at least twenty times that day.

The next day we hitch hiked back to "Rock n' Roll Heaven" for more *Motorhead*. We bought "The Ace of Spades" and the "Overkill" album. Johnny Z made a point to tell us that most of the songs on 'The Ace of Spades' album were probably going to be performed by *Motorhead* at the *Ozzy* show. He also pointed out the songs on the 'Overkill' album that were probably going to be played at the show.

Later that day in my friend's basement we put the needle on the 'Ace of Spades' record and POW again! We were on a lifelong hook by the magnetic force that is *Motorhead*. We played the "Ace of Spades" album six times that night. For the next three months we crammed *Ozzy's* "Blizzard of Oz", *Motorhead's* "Ace of Spades" and *Motorhead's* "Overkill" into our heads so we would know every word of every song at the Palladium.

May 2, 1981: DAY OF SHOW:

The White Rose Bar was in old grime and crime New York City. It sat on the corner of 29th street and 9th avenue. On May 2nd, 1981 the White Rose was packed with young metal heads on their way to see *Ozzy Osbourne* and *Motorhead* at The Palladium on 14th street. I was a teenager with a group of friends.

We stepped over countless bums and passed many hookers on our march to The White Rose Bar from The Port Authority in Times Square. We were going to booze-up there before the concert.

In that area of New York City after dark in 1981 you had to travel in packs. If you got separated from your pack you were going to be mugged. The White Rose Bar was the place my friends and I always visited when in Manhattan for events.

I first stumbled upon The White Rose Bar as a fifteen year old in 1979. I was with a group of friends from High School. We were wandering around the streets by Madison Square Garden looking for a place to drink before a New York Knick basketball game. The drinking age was eighteen in New York City at that time. It didn't matter anyway. Nobody checked ID's back then. Nobody gave a shit about anything in New York City back then. We always got served.

It was the neon rose glowing out front of The White Rose that spell bound our teenage minds. It looked so cool. It lured us in from a block away like flies to decaying meat. We went inside and were at home.

Most of the regulars were late fifties and early sixty year old World War II vets. These guys saw so much in their lives they didn't give a rat's ass about a bunch of teenagers under-age drinking. Just don't be a dickhead and everything will be all right. From that day on it was ritual to go to there.

In 1981 New York City, if you weren't walking around with a gun out, you could pretty much do whatever you wanted. Drink in public. Smoke pot in public. Take a leak in public. Bang in public. The streets of New York City in 1981 smelled of marijuana, cigarettes, piss, hot pretzels, sex, and vomit.

When we walked in The White Rose the day of the *Ozzy* show, Patsy Cline's "I Fall To Pieces" was cranking on the juke box. Other black concert tee-shirt wearing teenagers, also going to see the show, mixed in with the white haired daily boozers.

The Bartender was right to the point, "What you having gents?"

"Three pitchers of Schaefer."

"How many glasses?"

"Eight."

We passed the test. We were getting served. We were all 16 and 17 years old. The Schaefer was on its way.

The slogan for Schaefer beer since the 1950's was, "Schaefer is the one beer to have when you were having more than one". We planned on having more than one.

Growing up in the New Jersey/New York City area in the 70's and 80's we watched Mets and Yankee baseball games on regular TV. Schaefer beer was a sponsor of both teams for a long time. The Schaefer circle of sports was something I loved to watch. The Schaefer Brewery in Brooklyn closed up in the early 1980's, not long after this outing. We never realized this was one of the last times we would be able to get real Schaefer beer on tap in New York City.

All our fathers had cases of Schaefer beer stored somewhere in the house for family gatherings. My cousins and I would sneak sips at those occasions. The first beer I ever tasted was a Schaefer.

We took our pitchers to an empty booth. The place was filling up with other *Ozzy* and *Motorhead* fans from Jersey, Queens, and the Bronx. We were lucky we got a booth. My buddies and I were pumped to see *Ozzy*. We had three Schaefer pitchers and a booth to drink in. There's nothing like a New York City bar booth with your friends. Especially, before an *Ozzy* and *Motorhead* show.

The jukebox at The White Rose was blasting Johnny Cash, Patsy Kline, The Dubliners, old Irish folk, Merle Haggard, and Bob Seger. Everybody knew the words to most of the songs. The bar sang as one that day.

Before you knew it the entire bar was talking to each other. The main topic was songs, "The Ace Of Spades" by *Motorhead* and "Revelation (Mother Earth)" by *Ozzy*. My buddy Tony was playing air guitar and head banging so fast I thought his brains were going to spill on the beer soaked floor. He screamed, "The Ace of Spades! The Ace of Spades!" between the Irish and country songs on the juke box. The bartender didn't give a fuck about Tony's outburst. Soon the pitchers started piling high 3, 6, 9, 12, and 15.

After fifteen pitchers it was time to leave The White Rose. We had a good thirty minute walk to the Palladium at 14th street on the east side. The White Rose was at 29th street on the west side.

In the streets I saw at least forty kids from Old Bridge I knew from School. They were doing the same thing we were. Carrying beers in brown paper bags on their way to see *Ozzy* and *Motorhead*.

We had front row seats in the balcony. The seats were great. We snuck beers in. Everybody snuck in beers or bottles of booze to events back then. The venues didn't care about anything as long as you weren't stabbing or shooting anybody. Weed was always openly passed around at concerts back then.

When *Motorhead* came on the entire place went crazy. Everybody was head banging, fist-pumping, and singing along. Johnny Z was 'Dead on Right' with which songs *Motorhead* would play. We were prepared.

The crowd was one that day. For the whole show there was a sea of humanity singing along to every song. It seemed that almost everybody at the show also crammed the album into their heads. The entire place sang every lyric. It was awesome. It's instances like that I know God exists.

Ozzy came on stage about 15 minutes after *Motorhead*. He was wearing a white fringed outfit with a blue shirt. He seemed so happy to be there. He kicked ass. The band was awesome. Rudy Sarzo on bass, Tommy Aldridge on drums, Lindsay Bridgewater on keys, and Randy Rhoads on guitar.

My shirt, sopping wet from head banging to Motorhead, got more drenched when Ozzy started playing. I was dripping like I just walked out of the ocean. I had to take my shirt off because I was overheating. I was a teenager having the time of my life. I knew every lyric to every song Ozzy and *Motorhead* sang that night. When I left the Palladium my voice was hoarse like I performed the show. I love that day to this day!

Aside:

The White Rose bar and The Palladium are long gone now. Although, The White Rose still lives on in the form of BILLYMARK'S WEST Bar, at the same location, 29th Street and 9th avenue New York City. BILLYMARK'S WEST Bar is one of the greatest, and last, old time bars left from those dirty days. The White Rose's booths are still there; right where we left them in 1981. You can still feel the energy emanating out through the worn wood.

5

Saint Patrick's Day 1985

SAINT PATRICK'S DAY

MARCH 17th 1985

New York City the mecca of beer, brawls, and barf every March 17th was where I belonged. I was with my childhood friend Captain Al Batenko.

Our Saint Patrick Day drinking began at 11am after a quick bus ride under the Hudson River to the Port Authority bus station. The smelll of hot pretzels and violence mingled in the air. Drunks clad in green paraded up and down 8th avenue laughing. We headed to Smith's Bar 44th street and 8th avenue. A place where people are to the point and beer is cheap. It was a Saint Patrick's Day tradition for us to go there.

In 1985, Smith's bar and 8th avenue was rough. Today Smith's Bar is at the same location. It's no longer rotten and rough anymore. Neither is that part of 8th avenue. In 1985, 8th avenue around Times Square was still a place where streetwalking hookers strolled free. Three card Monte con men were also still everywhere. People were getting mugged openly by "snatch-and-grab" kids.

We were twenty-one years old and had been drinking in Smith's for six years at this point in our lives. The stench of five week old mop water greeted us at the door. The smokey, murky air, left little room for oxygen. Four or five professional drinkers, heads on tables, were passed out - resting to rise - only to drink again. Hookers in lingerie grabbed at the free corned beef and cabbage buffet like suckling pigs at a sow. Hopelessness was everywhere. We zeroed in on two empty stools.

The bartender's greeting was the standard neighborhood straight to the point, "What do you want?"

"Two bud drafts", I replied.

To my left sat a hard-looking quite large fella. From the gaze in his eye I could tell he was lonely.

After our first beer, I noticed in the mirror behind the bar that the large fella was listening to our conversation. After our third beer he broke the ice.

"No way Reggie Jackson! Pete Rose is the best player in baseball," the large fella said.

"Come on," I replied, "He sucker punched Bud Harrelson in the '73 playoffs. I'm a Met fan!"

The tone was set, baseball. The anchor of every drunken New York City bar conversation in 1985. For the next hour we talked women, football, and more baseball. We cracked jokes. I found out the large fella was originally from Ohio. He worked for a trucking outfit on the west side.

There seems to be a mysterious bond between strangers sitting side by side drunk in a bar on Saint Patrick's Day at one in the afternoon. We drank, and we drank, and we drank, finally hitting that point in inebriation where every issue brought to the floor is of the upmost seriousness. The point where the happiness of being drunk gets sucked out of you like the beer in your empty glass. Where the smallest, most remote insignificant matter becomes an immense situation.

The three of us started talking about life and family. Two subjects closest to even the most ruthless of people's hearts.

My large barroom companion began telling a story that took my complete attention. He spoke of his tour in Vietnam. How he enlisted at eighteen because he didn't get along with his father.

In the 1960's most 18 year old kids were hoping to avoid the draft. This guy enlisted.

I listened to his story. He told us of this terrible relationship with his old man. So tragic and oppressive it made him want to go to a war. A burning curiosity made me ask how his relationship with his father became so unbearable.

He replied, "My father was a World War II hardass."

The subject of his father before the war made him uneasy. He continued talking about Vietnam. How he killed. How he got shot. He showed us the scar. He told us of his Army buddies who saved his life and how he returned the favor.

I was eleven years old at the end of Vietnam. I asked how he felt about the reason for the war. His answers was to the point.

"I couldn't give a shit," he said, looking me square in the eye.

I noticed my beer was empty. I knew I was in for something way different from the "Mets are better than the Yankees" bar room bull. This called for a refill and a shot of comfort on the side. The three of us downed shots of Southern Comfort symbolizing our unity in the Saint Patrick's Day drunken world.

The large fella looked into his emptied shot glass. I wanted to change the subject but I knew he wasn't done.

The awkward moment became interrupted by the commotion from a one legged man rising to his foot. He looked to be in his late sixties, early seventies. The gristly man in a state of total blind drunkenness began shouting, "Fucking Jap took my life away. I am the walking dead in hell!"

Al and I seemed to be the only ones in the room to notice this outburst. We watched on. You could tell all the regulars at Smith's were used to this guy's rants. The bartender did nothing. He kept on pouring drinks.

The one legged man stood up. He began balancing himself. He grabbed a crutch then dragged himself to the bar.

"Give me another one. I'm outta here. Mother fucking Japs," he barked in a harsh raspy cigarette voice.

The bartender poured the shot. Took the money. Rang it up.

I watched the one legged man down the double of house whiskey. He gave a gut grinning smile. He straightened himself up and headed for the door.

I noticed the varsity style jacket he wore. It was an authentic Jersey City Giants jacket. It was the real thing from the 30's or 40's when Jersey City was host of the New York Giants minor league Baseball team. He opened the door to the street. You could hear the sounds of 8th avenue enter the room - car horns and buses rattling uptown. The smell of hot pretzels wafted inside joining with the dirty-water mop stench. It was a relieving aroma.

Before he left the one legged man threw one finale outburst, "I'm dead! They took it away. I did nothing! I was the best!"

The door shut. The one legged man turned uptown into the daylight.

The large fella didn't react to the one legged man's screaming. He continued to speak as if on cue, "My war was here. I joined one war to leave another."

His voice became monotone. He didn't take his eyes off

his beer glass. At this point he was talking to himself. I think he knew we were listening.

"My war was here... Coward!"

Al and I listened speechless to this conversation turned monologue.

"My whole tour I couldn't stop thinking about my old man. His thought constantly filled my mind. Even after a firefight where I killed. I never wrote or called. My family never knew what was going on with me."

The large fella drank his full beer to the halfway mark with one slurp. He put his glass on the bar. He stared at it for a few seconds clenching his jaw. He turned to look at me. Making eye contact was hard to handle. I looked back direct and listened.

"It was a Sunday afternoon when I returned home to Ohio. My family was in the backyard barbecuing when I arrived."

The large fella became silent again. He didn't take his eyes off mine. We stared at each other. Tears filled his eyes.

He began to struggle choking on his words, "My father's sight made me cringe..."

He breathed in deep. A hard uneasy silence stung me. A steady flow of tears began to stream down his twitching cheeks. His big hands couldn't wipe them all away.

He was fighting to get the words he needed to speak out, "Nobody noticed me. There they all were. My whole family. I stood watching. Thinking how time had stood still at home. Then came the moment I knew the war would be over. My father from the corner of his eye noticed me."

This very large grown man began to openly sob. It started to get to me. My eyes misted up.

I wiped my eyes waiting for him to finish the story. It took five second for him to compose himself before he continued, "When my father and I looked at each other. I didn't know how to react. I felt dizzy. The unpeaceful times I spent with him flew through my mind. He began to charge toward me. I stood firm and tall not knowing what to expect when he reached me. A punch, a push, I didn't know. I just stood there. When he was upon me. He put out his arms and with the might of the almighty he..."

A giant hic-up sucked in all his air. The large fella began deep choking on his words. He couldn't talk anymore. Tears were everywhere. Despite his sobbing. I asked. I had to know.

"He what? What did he do?"

Dead in my eye he looked. An unexpected smile appeared.

"He hugged me! He fucking hugged me."

Happy tears poured from his eyes. He kept talking.

"He told me he prayed every night for my safe return. He wouldn't let me go. My father wouldn't let me go. Do you believe it? He wouldn't let me go. We were all safe."

Glassy eyed my Ohio friend smiled the happiest smile.

"Do you know my father is my best friend in the whole world now."

The large fella stood up straight and proud. He wiped his eyes. A cold silence hit the air. The large fella stretched his back. He sucked in a giant sniffle then walked past us to the bathroom.

Uneasy, Al and I couldn't look at each other for a good minute. When our Ohio bar friend returned there was an intolerable sobering kind of mood. Al and I finished our beers. We gave our goodbyes and good lucks. I told the bartender to back the large fella up. Al and I walked out. We never saw the guy ever again. A mad scurry of green clad Saint Patrick's Day drunks bounced all about. We camouflaged ourselves in the green parade that staggered toward the Port Authority.

6

Mackey's Wake 1989

CHAPTER 6

MACKEY'S WAKE 1989

I filled my belly with potatoes and chicken in anticipation of the boozing. I put on my suit. I left Jersey City about 6pm for Brooklyn. The funeral home was a few blocks from the subway stop.

This point in my life I was working as a dock worker and a bartender in New Jersey. I was also writing allot. Mostly angry young man songs and poems. I was living on Gates Avenue in Jersey City.

Most nights I was in Manhattan in the East Village. A bartender acquaintance from one of the places I hung out and performed had died. Although I didn't know him long. I felt I needed to go to his wake. He was an older guy and he always was very nice to me. He was very wise and he loved to share it.

The closest Irish bar to Mackey's wake was going to be the holding room for the mourners. This wasn't a planned set upon thing. This was an occurrence for all New York City wakes. The closet Irish bar to the funeral home gets slammed.

I saw the shamrock in the window of a dive bar. It was named Shanessy's or Hennessey's. I couldn't tell the name because three quarters of the neon sign was out. I didn't care there was a shamrock in the window. I went inside.

The first people I saw was a hack comedian and a few waitresses I knew from open mic nights on the Lower East side of Manhattan. We had a few drinks and shots. Then we left for the funeral home.

I stood with the hack comedienne and the waitresses in line to pay our respects. It's always weird when you're at a funeral or wake with people you only know from a bar. You see them in a different light. Like when you find out your second grade teacher doesn't live in the classroom.

The place was packed. It took a half hour to get to Mackey's body.

I knelt down, did the sign of the cross, and said my prayer in thought, "God, I know you took Mackey up with you. I know you know what a great guy he was. I always looked for advice from him on work matters, and sometimes music, and girls. He always took time to think before he spoke to me. He was a great person. Please look after his soul."

I stood in the back of the funeral parlor for a few minutes. It was jam packed like a rush hour subway train. The hack comedienne, the waitresses, and I, went back to the Irish Bar.

I found myself pretty drunk an hour later. I headed toward the subway with the hack comedienne. He asked if he could borrow a twenty. Looking in my wallet I saw two twenties. I grabbed one. I gave it him. He never had any good jokes, but I knew he was good for the loan.

The hack got off at the last stop in Brooklyn. I had another 15 minute ride to midtown Manhattan for the PATH train to Jersey City. I closed my eyes for a second.

The next time I opened my eyes the train was pulling out of the uptown Harlem 125th Street station. I saw where I was. I was pissed at myself for falling asleep. I missed my stop by miles.

Falling asleep on a New York City subway train is a dangerous thing to do. You could wake up with your pockets cut out and all your money gone. If you slept on the train in 1989 it was easy to become a victim of a cut and grab posse. They were everywhere.

I thought, 'At the next station I'll get a train heading back downtown.'

The station came quick. I got off. The doors shut behind me. The train pulled away.

I looked where to go. I noticed a sign that said, "Downtown trains are not stopping at this station. You must walk to the next station on 125th street, or get on the next uptown train and change in the Bronx."

I was a little hung over from my half hour snooze. It was still early about 9pm. I walked up the stairs heading to the street. I didn't want to wait for another train to go further uptown to change in the Bronx only to come back downtown. At night in 1989 you never knew when, or if, a train would come. I at least wanted to be going in the direction of home.

New York City in 1989 was turbulent. Homelessness was a scourge. Crack had people robbing people everywhere. The subway trains were covered in graffiti. Neighborhoods were unofficially segregated. If you were in the wrong place at the wrong time, you could end up dead.

A white guy in a suit tends to attract attention in the neighborhood I was now walking through. Most of the people in this area are nice hard working people. But, there was a true element of discontentment and thuggery in these New York City streets during dark hours in 1989. I wasn't in a good place.

I began to walk toward 125th street. Everybody seemed to stop their conversations when I past.

In my life so far I got along with everybody. I told myself, "You got good karma from treating all souls equal. It's all gonna be OK."

I wasn't afraid. I just didn't want to fight anybody. I had no where to go if I lost in this neighborhood.

The people I walked by didn't know me and they hated me. I felt glares from everywhere. I saw people make faces in the reflections of cars and gated shops on my stroll. I heard the whispers, "Pig" and "5-O".

I had traveled about five blocks when I stopped for a traffic light to change. A few cars passed. I crossed the street. I felt like I was being watched, because I was. 'My karma will carry me through this neighborhood', I thought, 'I have always been good to all people. I better keep on moving'.

I arrived at the 125th street subway stop. I walked into the station. I had to buy a token to get back on the train. I looked in my wallet. I saw my last twenty. I grabbed the bill. It didn't feel like money.

"Fuck!" I said, out loud.

It wasn't money. It was a flyer for an anti-establishment punk show that looked like a twenty dollar bill. It was worthless. I gave the bad comic my last twenty.

I recalculated the way home to myself. I could keep walking the almost one hundred blocks toward the PATH train to Jersey City. Or, I could jump the turnstile here and get on the next train downtown.

I decided I was going to jump.

I jumped the turnstiles many times in the 80's. Nobody cared backed then. The key to jumping a turnstile is timing. Once you hear the train squeal to a stop and the doors pop open. That's when you jump and run.

I stood next to the turnstile trying to be invisible. I looked around for cops. There were none in uniform. I hoped that there were none in plain clothes. An old guy put a token in the turnstile and walked to the tracks. The only person on my side of the turnstile was the token booth guy. I knew he wasn't coming out from that booth to chase me. I waited in my funeral suit. I estimated the time to get from where I was to the opened subway door a few seconds from hopping.

About a minute went by when I heard what sounded like a huge mob screaming and hollering. I looked to the stairwell that I just came down, where the sound was emanating. The noises and hollers were drawing closer and louder. I was waiting for them to reveal themselves.

I see one teenage kid. Than another. Than a hundred teenage kids running down the stairs. They were coming right at me. They were screaming and yelling. They were wearing school colors of some sort. A basketball game must have just let out somewhere up above. Hundreds of kids were teeming from the stairs toward the turnstiles.

The first of the kids to reach the turnstiles were maneuvering their bodies into a position to jump over them. The first one saw me standing there. He stopped in his tracks. So did everyone behind him.

Like water crashing into a dam, a back log of kids piled up in front of the turnstiles. The kids kept on coming. The first ones up against the turnstile were getting pushed harder and tighter against the steel. None of the kids would jump over. The place was packed with teenagers as far as your eyes could see. They all stared at me. I stared back. The crush on the first kids was getting worse. They were in pain.

After four seconds I see the ocean of two hundred teenagers part. One very big kid clears his way through. He walks right up to my face. He was about six-foot-four. I had to look up at him. He looked like a linebacker for the Football Giants. He was definitely the toughest kid in his neighborhood. He stared me up and down. He spoke, "If we jump the turnstile? You gonna bust us!?"

I looked him up and down. I looked at all the kids staring at me in quiet. The first kids were in pain from the growing crush pushing their stomachs into the steel turnstile.

"They think I'm a cop." I said to myself.

I looked back into the eyes of this big kid.

My goon Irish face reeked of NYPD. But, I was the furthest thing from one.

At this point in history there was no reason for white guy to be in this neighborhood at this time of night, unless they were a cop. I had to answer him back.

"I'll tell you what. I'm going to turn my back. And what I don't see. I don't see."

I turned my body to face away from the kids. The screaming and hollering began again. A mad scurry of two hundred teenagers jumping the turnstile echoed through the station. It took two minutes for them all to hop. When the last one jumped. I looked around. I saw the token booth guy watching me. I shrugged my shoulders. He shrugged his. I jumped over the turnstile in my funeral suit. It was 1989 New York City. Nobody gave a fuck about anything.

When I got to the PATH Train Station for Jersey City I jumped that turnstile too. I didn't get caught. I made it home. I have never fallen asleep on a subway train ever again.

How Bleecker Street Became To Be For Me 1990

CHAPTER 8

COW FIELDS, RUGBY, AND NEW YORK CITY

HOW BLEECKER STREET CAME TO BE FOR ME (1991)

As a kid I spent many summers in Ireland. I stayed on my Grandparents farm in Longford in the center of the country. The place where my mother grew up. I loved herding the cows to be milked each morning and night. I loved driving the tractor to cut hay. I'm a kid from New Jersey but I know how to work a farm. I also know how to be a Bog man. I was taught by the best, my Grandfather and my Uncle Dick.

In the summer of 1979, my Cousin, Richard from Longford, was in a pick-up sports group that played Irish Football, Irish Hurling, and Rugby. One day I went with him to a cow pasture to play Rugby with other kids from the area.

American football is derived from Rugby. They let me

play. It was a brutal-nonstop-fast-violent game. I loved it automatically. I had my head handed to me by the Irish kids that day. They all wanted to take a shot at "The Yank from America". And, they did. I went back to my Grandfather's farm battered and bruised.

Back home in America I played pop warner and freshman high school football. My coaches were good. I knew how to tackle and hit people. Some of my favorite times were playing pick-up football games with the kids from my neighborhood. We would play tackle football on any open area we could find. We would practically kill each other. It was great.

My Uncle Patty Joe from Donegal was an ex-rugby player. He came for a visit the day after my beating in the cow pasture. I told him I almost got killed in the game by the kids from Longford.

"We're not going to have any of that," Patty Joe said to me.

Patty Joe had a rugby ball in his car. He got it. We went out to the back garden. That day Uncle Patty Joe taught me some skills, rules, and moves of Rugby.

I practiced every day in the cow fields. A week passed. I went back to play with the Longford kids. This time the story was different.

I always knew how to tackle from my Sayre Woods South Rebels pop warner football experience. The week before I didn't know any Rugby techniques. Now I did. When I went back to play I was just as good as any of the Irish kids. "The Yank from New Jersey" had a few hits in store for them. This time the other kids went home with the bruises. It was a great time. I fell in love with Rugby.

Years past to the fall of 1985. I was attending William Paterson College in Northern New Jersey. I was dating a beautiful Spanish nursing student from Seton Hall University, also in North Jersey. I was living in Clifton, New Jersey, a few miles between each school.

One Tuesday my girlfriend's car was out of commission. She asked me to drive her back and forth to Seton Hall from where she lived in Bayonne, New Jersey. I picked her up in the morning. I dropped her off at Seton Hall then drove to classes at my school a few miles away.

Later that day I returned to pick her up. I was sitting parked in front of the school waiting for her. I noticed a team of guys playing Rugby on the front lawn. I watch for a little while. I wanted to play so bad. I had to check it out. I mustered up the courage to approach a guy who looked like the coach. He saw me coming. He spoke first. I was amazed how friendly he was.

"My name is Jack. I'm the coach. You interested in playing Rugby?"

"I am. I played in Ireland."

"You're from Ireland?" He questioned, eyes lighting up.

"No. My mother is. I'm from here, New Jersey. I played with my cousin in Ireland when I would spend my summers there."

"You want to play with us. We could always use a big guy like you."

I thought for a second, 'I did want to play but I don't go to this school. Well, my school didn't have a Rugby team. I wouldn't be cheating on them. So, why not?'

"What days do you practice? And, what days do you play?" I questioned.

"We practice Tuesday and Thursdays at 4pm. We play on Saturdays. Why don't you come out? We could use a big guy like you," Jack replied.

I was mulling how to pull this off. An inner voice in my head began to speak. I heard it say, "Go for it! Don't tell anybody you don't go here."

"I'm gonna do that. I'll see you Thursday."

I kept it a secret I was only on campus to pick up my girlfriend whose car broke down.

I walked to the front gate of the school. I was supposed to be there ten minutes earlier. My girl was waiting. I told her I was joining the Seton Hall Rugby team. She was puzzled.

"You don't go to school here. How are you going to do that?"

"I'm not going to tell anyone. I know you won't tell anyone. I'll see what happens."

I went to practice that Thursday and never looked back. I became the starting Wing Forward for the Seton Hall Rugby team for two years. I led the team in scoring for a little while. Sometimes I scored two or three times a game. One day I was even on the front page of The Setonian, the Seton Hall school newspaper. My girlfriend laughed when she saw it, "I pay a lot of money to go here. I'm never on the front page of the school newspaper. I've never even been mentioned in the school newspaper."

Seton Hall Rugby had a good team when I was there. We won a few tournaments and most of our games. I made many friends. I would go to parties at Seton Hall and not my own school. No one ever found out I didn't go there.

Fast forward five years to the fall of 1990. I was a college graduate with a degree in Communications, Radio and Television writing and production. My life had drifted toward the arts. I was a young "idealist" following my dream of writing books and films that would, "Save the world". I was a full-fledged member of the underbelly of the New York City art scene.

I was living in Jersey City, New Jersey. A few minutes train ride from Manhattan. I was hanging around the Lower East Side most nights. I had jobs at trucking companies and bars to pay rent. I was writing a lot, anything: short stories, screen plays, poetry. I never perused a network Radio or TV job, though, I was filming and directing Independent comedy films.

I was part of an art collective called "*The New Underground*". My buddy Wayno Draino was an artist. He was the main *New Underground* guy. The people I was hanging out with were freaky artist and weirdos. I loved it. We were going to art galleries, music shows, and poetry readings almost every night. If there was an open bar art gallery show, or a good band on a stage, we were there.

The bar I was working at suddenly closed. The owner took off with all the money. I called Wayno Draino.

"Hello!" Wayno wailed into the phone.

"Wayno! It's Kev! The bar I work at just closed. I'm broke. I need a job."

"Bleecker Street! Let's go to Bleecker Street," Wayno said. "We'll go see Peter May. He knows everybody in all the bars over there."

Peter May, a legendary downtown rocker and musician, lived in the basement of the historic Back Fence Bar on Bleecker Street. Peter May was living an acclaimed life. I knew him from *The New Underground*. Peter May's band "*Mayhem*" would play our parties. Wayno was right. Peter May knew everybody.

About 7 O'clock on a Monday evening, Wayno and I arrived at The Back Fence. Ernie Jr. was bartending. He knew us. He knew we were looking for Peter May. He waved us to go downstairs. Few people had clearance to go to the basement of The Back Fence. We did.

We carefully went down the steep basement steps, turning the corner past the stacked burlap bags of peanuts in their shells, and burlap bags of sawdust. The Back Fence was a throwback bar. Each day they would put fresh sawdust on the floor. They always had shelled peanuts in bowls on the bar and the tables. There was one rule.

"Put the shells on the floor. Not on the bar! Or, the tables!"

If a customer put peanut shells on the bar they would get the wrath of the bartender. The shells were a pain in the ass to wipe up.

The Back Fence was a great place. Live music played every night. It opened right after World War II ended on VJ Day September 2, 1945. The Beat generation of the 50's, the hippie generation of the 60's, countless bohemians and blue collar people drank together at The Back Fence for decades. Bob Dylan, Joan Baez, Joan Osborne, Mama Cass, and countless other stars of the American music scene had performed at The Back Fence.

We made our way to the back of the basement, zigzagging past rows of empty kegs. Peter May was sitting at a tiny table watching a little black and white TV. He was smoking a cigarette. Leon, the Back Fence cat, was sitting on the TV staring back at Peter May. Leon was the best mouser in the village. No rats or mice every dared to breech The Back Fence. If they did. They died. Peter May saw Wayno and I, "Hey Dudes! What's going on?" He was smiling.

I didn't realize that this meeting was the culmination of a lot of fates in my life so far. A meeting that was about to start a big chapter.

I had a nickname at the time, it was "Bocko". Peter May always called me Bocko. He very rarely called me Kevin. Wayno called me Kev.

"Hey, Bocko! Hey, Wayno! What brings you guys here?"

"Kev needs a job, Dude. We know you know everybody on Bleecker Street. He's been a bartender for a few years. Do you think you could find him a job?" Wayno asked, right to the point.

I always wore my Seton Hall Rugby jacket back then. It was a blue fitted baseball coach type winter windbreaker. It was my only jacket. It always stood out among the freaks, metal heads, hippies, punks, and weirdos in the Lower East Side crowd I hung with. The temperature in New York City was starting to drop in the fall of 1990. I started wearing the jacket again after a hot summer.

"Did you play Rugby?" Peter May asked, pointing at the back of my coat. "I always see you in that jacket. Is that just a jacket you wear, or did you really play Rugby?"

"I played Rugby for Seton Hall University in college," I replied, very proud.

"Good! Let's go! I have someone I want you to talk to," Peter May said, getting up.

Peter May glided his way through the empty kegs, burlap bags of peanuts, and sawdust. He climbed the steep stairs leading to the bar. Wayno and I followed. We walked through the Back Fence bar. Marc West, another legendary Bleecker Street musician, was singing Motown. I stopped for a second to listen. Peter May grabbed my jacket and began pulling me. He yelled, "Come on! I know he's over there now. I don't want to miss him."

"Miss who?" I questioned.

"The guy who is going to hire you!"

We walked out of The Back Fence to Bleecker Street. We crossed Thompson Street walking about sixty Feet until we were at the front door of The Red Lion Pub. There was a big guy at the front door. Peter May gave him a high five, "These guys are with me. Is Alan here?"

"Yeah. He's right inside the door there," the big guy pointed. He gave a friendly nod.

We walked in. The place was very busy. A band was

playing right next to the door. If I took two steps to my left I would be on stage with them. Peter May walked over to a middle-aged man with a thick bushy mustache and a big mop of reddish blonde hair. The man was sitting at the bar a few feet inside the door.

Peter May tapped his shoulder, "Hey Alan, my friend here is a Rugby player and he needs a job."

I could tell Peter May had some clout because the mustached man looked me up and down in consideration, instantly.

"You're pretty big. Where did you play?" He asked.

"I played for Seton Hall University."

I turned my back pointing to the words "Seton Hall Rugby" on my jacket.

Peter May introduced the man, "This is Alan. He owns this bar, The Red Lion. He runs a Rugby team called The Village Lions."

The plot was beginning to thicken why Peter May brought me here.

"Are you any good? What position do you play?" Alan asked.

Alan had a heavy Irish accent. I realized he was an "Off the boat" Irish bar owner. The toughest kind of bar owner in New York City. I knew he was probably rough and shrewd.

With pride I responded, "I played wing forward. I led the team in scoring once."

"You led the team in scoring as a wing forward?" Alan questioned, suspicious.

A wing forward is both a running back and what a lineman would be in American football. A wing forward played in the scrum but also could run with the backs. A good wing forward would be the first to break out of the scrum after the ball. In college, I was fast and in great shape. I was always around the ball. That is how I was able to score so much.

Alan crossed examined me further.

"How can a wing forward lead the team in scoring? You really led the team in scoring?"

I took exception.

"Yes. I led the team in scoring," I didn't like Alan's suspicious tone. "I was fast out of the scrum. I followed the backs like a banshee follows gold. I was always around the ball, and the play."

Alan's eyes opened up feeling my sincerity.

"I'll tell you what!? We have a game on Saturday at Randall's Island. You can start in the B game after the A game is over. If you're any good. I'll give you a job. Be here at 10am on Saturday Morning."

I shook his hand, "I'll see you then."

I looked to Wayno and Peter May. I nodded to leave. We went outside to Bleecker Street. In 1990 every night was like a Saturday Night on Bleecker Street. People and music were everywhere. Wayno was smiling.

"I told you Peter May would know someone," Wayno said. "Let's go drink in Thompkins Square Park."

"No way! I ain't going drinking. I got to get in shape. I haven't played rugby or anything in a few years," I said. "I'm going to get killed on Saturday if I go drinking this week. I'm officially on the wagon. I have five days to get in shape."

Wayno was disheartened. He had a plan we would drink all night and carouse the Lower East Side.

I turned to Peter May, "Thanks Dude! I'm going to get that job."

"Come on let's just finish our drinking for the night. Tomorrow you can go on the wagon," Wayno tried to con me.

"Sorry Wayno. I'm going home right now."

"Come on! Dick Donavan is doing a comedy show at Beowulf. Otto and George are headlining!" Wayno pleaded.

"I'll go with you Wayno," Peter May chimed in.

"There you go, Wayno. 'The Dude' will be your drinking buddy for the night. I'm heading back to Jersey City. Got to get in shape."

"Ok," Wayno said, dejected.

"Thanks again, Peter. I'll see you guys."

I gave everybody a hand slap. I headed toward the train. I took three steps. I started jogging. I trotted down Bleecker Street against the traffic. I made a right on 6th avenue. I jogged to the 9th street PATH station seven short blocks away. I was out of breath when I got there.

I took the PATH train to Journal Square station in Jersey City. I got off the train. I began to wait for the bus. I looked at myself in the bus stop billboard's reflection. I saw my blue Seton Hall Rugby jacket. I started doing jumping jacks.

I thought, 'No bus for the rest of the week'.

I started to jog away. I ran as fast as I could pace myself back to my Greenville neighborhood four miles away. I lived on Gates Avenue and Kennedy Boulevard by the border of Jersey City and Bayonne.

It took over an hour to get home. I would jog for a bit, walk for a bit, and then jog again. I did as many pushups as I could when I arrived home. Not that many, but not that few.

I was still in shape because I was in my twenties. I would always exercise to keep fit. I had a beautiful girlfriend. I always wanted to be attractive to her. Working out to keep up appearances for a girlfriend, who loved me anyway, was not an exercise scheme that would keep me upright in a Rugby game. I had a fitness problem going into Saturday's match.

I called my girlfriend. She was the same girl I was going out with in my Seton Hall Days. She was a nurse now. I figured I might need her skills on Saturday after the game. I told her I was going to play Rugby again in order to get a job. She was in disbelief.

"Rugby again? What's with you and Rugby?" She asked. She was laughing. She was supportive.

I woke up the next morning. It was Tuesday. I had three days to work out, Tuesday, Wednesday and Thursday. I wouldn't do any hard work out on Friday the day before the game. That would be my recovery day. I jogged to Bayonne Park a mile from my house.

I ran up the hill at the back of the Park as many times as I could, about ten. I did wind sprints. I did pushups. I was dying. I had to walk home. I couldn't jog. I felt like Rocky Balboa at the beginning of the montage in "Rocky I".

The next day, I was surprised to be twice as strong as the day before. Muscle memory was activating. I always exercised and played sports in my life. I did twice as many sprints and twice as many hills. I threw myself on the ground a few times to simulate contact. I decided to do a few more hills. I stopped to get my breath at the top of the hill after eight hard ones. I heard someone call out to me, "Are you working out for a war? Wow! Keep up the hard work!"

It was the "Pope of Jersey City", Coach Bobby Hurley Senior. The winningest basketball coach in American High School basketball history. He was in a Saint Anthony's High School shirt and sweat pants. He happened to be standing on the top of the hill for my last run up. He was working out in the park too. He lived in the same neighborhood I did. I didn't know him but I saw him all the time. Coach Hurley is the most respected man in Jersey City. I took it as a sign to have him prod me onward. I was pumped. I was going to get that Red Lion job.

I jogged home thinking about Coach Hurley telling me to keep up the hard work. I felt good. I did a bunch of push-ups when I got home.

For Thursday's workout I was stronger than Wednesday's. Not twice as strong, but stronger. I set my goal to do fifty 40 yard sprints. I did the fifty though most were not full sprints. I knew I had done my best. I left nothing behind in my three days of hard workouts.

Friday night I laid in bed playing the game in my head. I hadn't tackled anyone in years. The only hitting contact I had since playing for Seton Hall was a few bar fights at the place I worked. I hoped I still had it. I let no negative thoughts in my head. I rehearsed in my mind hitting other players with hard shoulder tackles. I didn't sleep much that night. I woke Saturday morning tired. I headed to Greenwich Village.

I borrowed my roommate Joe Tet's white softball cleats. Joe Tet was in his own world. He would wear his baseball glove when he listened to Yankee games on the radio in our apartment. When the announcer would call a ground ball to short, Joe Tet would pretend to scoop it up and throw the guy out. The cleats were crappy but I was happy to have them. If I wore sneakers to play in the game, I would slide all over the field and suck.

I still had my white Rugby shorts and my blue and white striped Seton Hall Rugby jersey I used for college games. I wore them under a purple sheen glossy pair of work out pants. These wacked out 80's sports pants were my only athletic type gym clothes. I would wear the blinding psychedelic purple pants to freak parties on the Lower East Side. They were always a hit. I wasn't sure if they were going to be a hit with this Rugby crowd. I didn't care though. I needed a job.

During the game I knew I was going to look like a dick in those white low top softball cleats. Rugby players in the scrum most always wore black high top cleats.

I arrived early at 9:30am. I stared at The Red Lion. The front door of the bar opened. Alan, the owner, dragged the biggest cooler I had ever seen out the door. The cooler was six feet long. It was enormous. It was more like a coffin. It was stuffed with beer.

Alan noticed me standing there with my cleats over the shoulder. He looked down at my purple gym pants. By the way he looked at me I could tell he either didn't remember me, or he was trying to suck in the menagerie of colors, lines, and shapes I was wearing.

"Who sent you?" He asked.

"Peter May introduced me to you on Monday. You said I could play in the B-game. If I did any good. You would give me a job."

Alan thought for a second. He had a puzzled look. It was now official. I could tell he had no recollection of our meeting.

I was disappointed, though a calm feeling came over me. The butterflies flew out of my body. I could now save face and walk away. I did my best. I tried. I definitely would be in one piece that night. I took a step to walk away. The voice in the back of my head rose up and screamed, "Stay! You need to stay! Push this guy."

I turned around toward Alan. I shifted my shoulders pointing to the back of my jacket.

"Remember! I had on this Seton Hall Rugby jacket."

I turned my back at him. He looked at my jacket.

"Oh, that's right! You're the big shot wing forward who supposedly led Seton Hall in scoring," Alan blurted out, like a smart ass.

"That's right," I said, a small distant annoyance in my voice.

"Good. I'm glad you made it. Grab the other side of this cooler. A van is coming by in a minute."

Side by side Alan and I pulled the enormous cooler out the door of The Red Lion to the curb.

"I have to get ice. Watch the cooler," Alan said.

"Ok."

I was happy to watch the cooler. I was outside The Red Lion looking after hundreds of dollars of beer.

I thought to myself, 'This is good. He trusts me with his beer. I'm gonna get this job'.

Alan came out with a giant bucket of ice. He dumped it

in the cooler. He handed me the bucket, "Go inside to the ice machine in the back of the bar. Fill it up."

"Yes Sir, Alan."

I went inside the bar. I filled the bucket. I went back out front to where Alan was. A few other guys had showed up. They all knew each other.

Alan grabbed the ice bucket from me.

"I'm sorry.　I don't remember your name," he politely said.

"Kevin."

He introduced me to one of the guys.

"This is Kevin. He's going to be playing in the B-game. He's trying out for the team."

"I'm Chris Ratay," the guy replied, shaking my hand.

The guys that were showing up were very clean-cut. I wasn't clean cut at this time in my life. I had a hard, scruffy face. I had long brownish blonde hair. It was a mullet. After graduating college I grew my hair long. It grew from a rat tail at first into a full blown mullet after two years. At the time it was the way to go. At least that's what I thought. I still had a hot girlfriend. She didn't mind the mullet. That was all that mattered to me.

I planned to tie my mullet into a pony tail for the match. I knew it was going to be yanked often during the game. I was expecting that. I noticed all the guys wore black Rugby shorts. They were carrying black high top cleats over their shoulders. I was going to be the sore toe with my white shorts, white low top softball cleats, and long mullet hair. I erased those thoughts. I needed a job.

More and more guys started to arrive. I noticed a trend after meeting the first guys. Most of the team were foreigners. They were from all over the globe, England, Australia, Ireland, New Zealand, Wales, France, and Argentina. They all looked tired and hung over.

I listened to the foreign guys talk. They all spoke of working at The Red Lion the night before. They spoke of different tourist girls they picked up and how they didn't get to sleep until 6 or 7am. It was now almost 10am. Not much sleep for these guys.

I noticed the foreign guys were all coming from out the door of the building above The Red Lion. The picture widened to what was going on. Alan was importing players from all over the world, giving them jobs, and a place to stay in New York City. In exchange they would play on his Village Lions Rugby team.

The guys that were American looked rested. They were all around my age. I found out they all played college Rugby like myself. They all looked very clean cut. None of the American guys worked in bars. They all worked on Wall Street and had banking type jobs. Everybody was very nice to me. I was though the freak outsider in purple sheen pants.

One Wall Street guy asked me, "What do you do?"

"I'm a writer."

"Who you write for?"

"I'm putting a book together right now."

"That's cool," he said.

We were in Greenwich Village, New York City. The place where many American writers got their start. After I told the guys I was a writer putting a book together. They realized I was broke and needed a job from Alan. It didn't take a genius to figure it out. All the guys were very nice and understanding. Right away they made me feel accepted, welcome, and good. No one judged me. It was a good feeling. They were all good guys.

A van pulled up. It mixed in with the cars that were also arriving in front of the Red Lion on Bleecker Street. Alan started barking orders for everybody to get in a vehicle. I noticed about twenty five guys and four rides.

Some guys were talking about sharing a cab to Randall's

Island. I had enough money for two fifty cent Gray Papaya's hot dogs on 8th street and my train ride home to Jersey City. I wasn't getting into a cab. I didn't want anybody to think I was a cheap skate when I didn't chip in for the ride. I slipped in the back of the van along with five hung over guys from New Zealand. The van began to reek of the last night's booze oozing from the New Zealanders pours.

Randall's Island is in the middle of the East River between Queens, The Bronx, and Manhattan. It is a giant recreation space with tennis courts, softball fields, and Rugby pitches. There is an old soccer stadium on the island where concerts are held. The New York City Fire department also trained recruits on Randall's Island. I had been there once for a Rugby tournament with Seton Hall.

We arrived at Randall's island pulling right up to a Rugby field. There were three or four fields with goal posts next to each other. There were other rugby teams getting ready to play on those fields. The giant soccer stadium loomed in the background.

I jumped out of the van as fast as I could. I think I got drunk from breathing in booze fumes from the New Zealand guys. The team gathered. Alan handed out black and white striped rugby shirts. Everyone grabbed one. I was the only one with white shorts. I didn't care. Everybody started to stretch out. I was asked by Alan to grab the bag of balls from the back of the van. I hadn't touched a rugby ball in years.

I said to myself, "What the fuck am I doing here? I'm gonna get killed. I am no way in shape for this and I look like a clown."

I wore white rugby shorts, while everyone else wore black rugby shorts. I had on white low top softball cleats. Everyone else had on black excellent looking high top rugby cleats. I had long hair, looking like I should be in Motley Crue. Everyone else had trimmed tight short haircuts, looking like cops and accountants.

I was now carrying a big bag of Rugby balls out to a field. I had nowhere to run to escape. I was on an Island. I was past the point of no return. I opened the bag of balls. I started to throw them to the guys. I began playing catch with a guy from France who looked like he should be on the waterfront doling out work, or leading The French resistance. His name was Terry. His nose was smashed in, his ears were cauliflower from years of playing rugby. He asked me.

"What position you play?"

"Wing forward."

"Oui good," he said, while under handing the ball to me.

I watched the foreign guys warm up. I realized they weren't a joke.

We all ran around and got loose. I was feeling pretty good. Alan called for the A and the B teams to separate. I was now able to see which guys I was going to be playing with. A full squad of rugby players is fifteen guys. The A-team was all foreigners, except one American from Queens named Dennis. The French guy Terry was the captain of the A-team. The B-team consisted of ten American guys and five foreigners. I would say out of thirty five guys on The Village Lions, twenty five were foreigners.

The captain of the B-team was a guy named Alejandro from Buenos Aries, Argentina. He had a thick accent and a vicious hangover. He worked the night before at Alan's other bar on Sullivan Street called "Sing Sing".

"Sing Sing" was a Karaoke bar around the corner from The Red Lion.

I didn't know it at the time but Alejandro would go on to be a great friend of mine.

Alejandro was the Karaoke host at "Sing Sing". I never understood how he would be the choice to be the host. His accent was thick. Nobody could understand him. Alan would later change the name of "Sing Sing" to "The Lion's Den" and it would become one of New York City's great rock clubs.

"What position you play?" Alejandro asked. His accent was so thick. I asked him to repeat himself.

"I didn't understand you."

"What position do you play?"

"Strong side Wing forward."

"Ok. You play strong side wing forward today."

We formed a practice scrum. We started to work on plays. I had forgotten a lot of the rules of rugby. They came back slow. I couldn't believe I was going to be playing Rugby in order to get a job. But here I was.

The A-game was first. I watched from the sideline. I forgot how violent Rugby was. The teams were killing each other. We were playing The Manhattan Rugby Club. The Village Lions A-team was hung over. I watched the action. The foreign Village Lions guys knew how to play. I was very impressed.

The Village Lions were up by one score midway. The game was close until three minutes into the second half. All the booze had sweated out of The Village Lion's by then. The A-team was no longer hung over. They went on a tear. They won by four scores. They could have won by more but took it easy for the last part of the game. It was now time for the B-game.

I never let nerves get the better of me but they were there. It was the nerves of competition. I hadn't competed in anything for a few years. I was slumming around The Lower East Side with a bunch of freaks, writing poems, making weirdo films, and penning angry young man songs. I jogged out to the field. There was maybe five minutes between games. The Manhattan and Village Lions A-teams shook hands. They went to the enormous cooler to drink. The B-teams got right to it.

The B-teams met in the middle of the field to discuss

ground rules and do the coin toss. We looked at the other team. They looked at us. We were about to try to kill each other. Alejandro, the captain, did the talking. The ref asked him to repeat himself twice his Argentinian accent too thick for him to understand. The rules were set. We were to play two thirty minute halves.

I lined up for the kickoff. We won the toss. I was praying for the ball to get kicked away from me. The whistle blew, Manhattan kicked. It was a high ball. It was coming right at me.

I said, "Fuck! Here we go."

I could hear the tromping footsteps of fifteen guys running to kill. The high kick gave Manhattan a chance to get almost under the ball. They were closing in full force.

I thought, 'If I drop the ball. No job. I might as well jump in the East River a hundred yards away and end it right then'.

I knew I was going to get creamed. The other team was running as fast as they could. They were about five feet from me with a full head of steam when I caught the ball. I turned my back toward the Manhattan guys. I braced for impact. Three guys hit me at once. I didn't go down. I held the ball. I waited two seconds for my team to maul around me. They did. I held onto the ball until Alejandro the scrum half came over. He took the ball from me. He flashed it out to the backs. The maul broke up.

A 'maul' is different from a 'scrum'. A scrum is organized and set up. A maul happens when whoever is close to the ball is fighting for it. Mauls are brutal.

The game was on. I had my first taste of punishment being hit by three guys at once. I was all right. I followed the ball like a madman. I was winded but not as bad as I thought I would be. Adrenaline and poverty fueled me.

My backfield guy kicked the ball to the other side of the field to gain some distance. I ran like the devil to hit the guy with the ball. I just took a shot. Now it was time for me to give one. The guy with the ball tried to run away from me. My high school football training had me zone right in. I nailed the guy. The ball popped out. My guys were right there.

When I played Rugby for Seton Hall, we were good. We were a bunch of American guys who liked to hit each other. This Village Lion B-team of ten Americans and five foreigners played a different type of Rugby than my Seton Hall team. They knew the game really well. Not only did they know how to hit. They knew strategy. It was cool.

I didn't stop running for ten minutes. Every time I felt tired I thought about sleeping in the street. I thought about an empty refrigerator. Those thoughts fueled me.

I was having a great game. Making tackles all over the field. I had two tackles that stopped Manhattan from scoring. I was running with the ball like a thief made of boulders. I never went down. I would plant my feet hard into the ground. I waited for my team to maul around me. They always did. Alejandro would take the ball from me, flash it out to the backs.

It was a zero to zero game at almost halftime. We were pushing a threat to score around the goal line. The ball came lose. Alejandro grabbed it. I broke away from the maul. Alejandro pitched the ball to me. I was four yards from the goal line. I got hit by two guys. I wasn't going to go down. I thought about the smile on my landlord's face when I paid the rent. I had the strength of a drunken gorilla. I dragged the two guys with me into the end zone for a score. The first score of the game. I was pumped. My teammates jumped on me in celebration. Alejandro gave me a hug.

Halftime was called a few minutes later. Alan came out to speak to us. He looked at me. He kind of nodded but he said nothing directly to me. He gave his strategic remarks. Before you knew it half time was over. It was time to play again.

I was hoping they would sub in for me. There were other guys that needed to play. Four or five players were going to be switched out. I was praying I was to be one of them. I proved myself. I scored. I had a bunch of tackles. I wanted to be taken out. I thought, 'I did enough to get the job'.

Terry the French A-team captain came over to me. He said I was doing great. He told me he liked my hard hits. I was too tired to say anything. I gave a thank-filled heavy breathed nod.

I learned how to tackle from years of playing pop warner and high school football. I came from a great football system in Old Bridge, New Jersey. We always had hours of tackling practice. My coaches were excellent. Our teams in pop warner and high school were always very good. I never thought I would have to use that tackling knowledge and training to get a job, but here I was using every bit of it.

We kicked off to Manhattan in the second half. I was spent. Adrenaline, poverty, and rage kept me going. We were up by one score. One of our backs made a muff. The other team took advantage of it and scored. I was happy I wasn't anywhere near that play. The game was tied. It stayed that way for a while.

I was willing myself to run after the ball. To this day I don't know how I kept going. At about ten minutes left in the game I decided I couldn't go on anymore. The years of hanging out with freaks and artist was starting to take a toll on me. I had a great game so far. I knew it. It was time to get thrown out. I save face. I don't die on the field, which is what I felt like doing at that second.

I made a decision. Someone on the other team was going to get a punch in the face. I would be tossed out of the match. I would be alive later on that night.

One guy on Manhattan was having a good game too. I decided he would be the guy to get the punch in the face. He would fight back. I'll let him get a couple of shots in on me. The ref would see us punching each other and we would get tossed out of the game. That was the plan.

It took about a minute until I was in hands reach of my marked man. The ball was loose. I picked it up. I started running. My marked man and three of his teammate hit me with their shoulders. I wasn't going down. I turned my back in the maul waiting for my team. They mauled around. Alejandro grabbed the ball. He flashed it out to the backs. My marked man was still on me. Here was my chance.

"Hey, what the fuck! Fuck you! You fucking jerkoff! You grabbed my balls," I yelled.

I gave this poor innocent guy, who didn't grab my balls, a direct punch to the side of the jaw. A perfect connection.

He started swinging back at me. He was punching like a wild man. I let him hit me. I was too tired to fight back. The play stopped. The whistle blew. Three Manhattan guys joined in wailing on me. I had five seconds to catch my breath while they were pummeling me. I started punching back making a scene. My Village Lions guys jumped in. There was eight guys fighting now. We were swinging fists in the middle of the field. The ref ran over to break it up. Alejandro jumped in grabbing me. He pulled me out of the melee. He began screaming at me.

"What the fuck are you doing? We need you man! Don't get thrown out! You're doing great. If you get thrown out! We will lose! We won't win without you!"

Alejandro's accent went away for the moment. I heard him loud and clear. The other Village Lions were nodding in agreement with Alejandro. They were also saying they needed me in the game.

I saw the genuineness in Alejandro's eyes as he yelled at me. I met this guy two hours before. Now we were bonded through this Rugby game. My mind wanted to keep going for Alejandro. My body said, "I'm done."

The ref ran over. He got right in my face. He started screaming, "Oh! No! You aren't gonna have it that way! You are finishing this game! I know you want to get thrown out. That punch was blatant! I'm not throwing you out. That was bull-shit! Play on!"

My plan didn't work. I gave some innocent guy a nice punch to the jaw and I didn't get thrown out of the game. I wasn't on the side lines drinking from the safety of the enormous cooler. I was still in the game. A game where I was now a marked man.

I did realize at that moment Alejandro and The Village Lions were counting on me. I never met any of these guys before. I only knew the names of four guys on the field. Alejandro, Chris Ratay, and two other guys who introduced themselves earlier on Bleecker Street. We were now all one on that field against a common enemy. My body suddenly woke up.

Play resumed. I had a new zest knowing my team was counting on me. I began tackling guys harder. The guy I just punched in the face was running with the ball. I nailed him like a savage, sticking my shoulder into his ribs. The ball came loose. I grabbed the rolling ball off the ground. My team mauled around me like they had done at least twenty times so far this game. Alejandro grabbed the ball from me. He flashed it out to our backs. The ball ended up in the hands of a bright red haired back. That back would later become my band member for years and we would have many adventures together. His name was Peter Cavanagh. He was a fast Benny Hill type runner. Peter juked a few moves and ran forty yards for a score.

We were up by one score with about five minutes left in the game. I went into defensive mode.

I thought, 'Do not let anybody get past me. The game is almost over. Do not die on these guys. We have to hold them off'.

Manhattan had three or four good pushes for goal. They weren't going to go down easy. The Village Lions tightened up. I had at least four tackles in the last five minutes. The Ref finally blew the whistle. The game was over. Exhausted, I fell to the ground. I laid there for a few seconds. Alejandro came over to me. He was yelling at me in a nice way, "Come on get up. We have to shake Manhattan's hands."

I noticed I could now understand everything Alejandro said through his thick Argentinian accent. He put his hand out to help me up. I stood up like a punch-drunk boxer.

"That was a great game you had. Where did you play before?" Alejandro asked.

"Seton Hall University," I breathed out the words, almost inaudible.

I shook the other team's hand. I was hoping the guy I punched in the jaw wasn't going to start up. I was mushed peas. If he wanted vengeance for the cheap shot I gave him. I was in for it. I saw him. I shook his hand. All was forgiven. One thing I forgot about Rugby, "What happens on the Rugby field - Stays on the Rugby field."

I walked over to our sideline very slow. I felt a great sense of relief. I was alive. The A-team gathered around patting me on the back. Terry the French A-team captain walked up to me, "Next week you play with us on the A-team. We are playing The Boston Irish."

I wanted to be happy about it, but I wasn't at all. I was too tired. I didn't want to play another Rugby game ever again.

Alan walked over to me. He looked me up and down before he spoke, "Seton Hall Rugby, huh! We got Boston Irish next Saturday. Thursday you can start at The Red Lion at 8pm. I need a bouncer for the back door. It's your permanent shift. If you want it?"

"Yes, I do. Thank you."

My life on Bleecker Street had begun.

Jersey City Pool Stick Brawl - War With Iraq 1991

CHAPTER 7
JERSEY CITY POOL STICK BRAWL
BUSH 41 ANNOUNCES WAR
IN KUWAIT AGAINST IRAQ:
JANUARY 16, 1991

In 1991, New York City and its immediate surrounding areas were turbulent. Danger lurked in the backstreets of the wrong neighborhoods on a constant pulse. As the crow flies Barrett's bar on the border of Bayonne and Jersey City stood a few miles from the Statue of Liberty and the Twin Towers. Barrett's bar was an Irish bar in a rough neighborhood. It was a blue collar haven run by a no nonsense man. I lived two blocks away. I was a regular.

A big part of Barrett's business was takeout package goods from people living in the projects across the street. The other part of Barret's business was the hardcore regulars that would sit for a daily drinking session. The beer was always cold and the drinks were always honest.

Most mornings Barrett's Bar was filled with night shift people starting from 6am in the morning. In the evening the crowd at Barrett's was your local boozers. Most of the local factory and dock workers would cash their paychecks at Barrets and stay for a few drinks on payday. Barrett's was as old school as old school could get.

On January 16, 1991 I was in Barrett's Bar with a friend. It was evening time. We had been drinking for about two hours when a break in programming burst on the TV. It was a special announcement from President H.W. Bush (Bush I). A drunk at the end of the bar yelled at the bartender to turn up the volume on the silent TV.

The jukebox hadn't been played for about an hour. Most times I'd have money in it to hear songs while we drank. But my friend and I were lost in a conversation about some angry young man nonsensical lyrical bullshit I had just written.

When the President interrupted the bar was quiet. The only thing heard at the time were other nonsensical bullshit conversation, the sound of pool balls clanking every shot, and the ring of the cash register. Twelve other people were in the bar ranging from early twenties to late seventies years of age.

Seeing the President looking worried in a TV interruption had everyone hushing each other.

"Air strikes have begun...," President Bush said.

The eeriest tone overtook the room. We all realized the nation was at war. The country hadn't been at war since Vietnam, a decade and a half earlier. There were a few Vietnam Veterans drinking in the bar watching alongside me.

An old timer pointed at the TV laughing. He was five seats away. I saw him every session I had in Barrett's. I never talked to him because he was very gruff. He fought in World

War II. I always heard him drunk mumbling about war. He didn't like me. Than again, he didn't like anybody. I always felt sorry for him. His only friend was a short draft beer and a neat bourbon. He would look down at the bar as if it were some kind of movie screen. He wasn't crazy. I've seen him have conversations with other old timers. I couldn't help but hear his war stories. He'd laugh while telling them. Right now this Old Timer was laughing at the President.

When Bush was done with his announcement that America was going to war with Iraq, all in Barrett's were silent. Except the laughing Old Timer. The bartender stared at the TV. Everybody in Barrett's bar was in their own mind. A regular in his thirties walked toward the front of the bar where the jukebox stood. He put his hand on the top of it. The laughing Old Timer ran out of breath. He coughed for a few seconds before he joined the eerie silence.

The jukebox was an old one - The kind that played 45 vinyl records. The kind that made loud sounds when a record was being setup to play. The guy put a quarter in the jukebox and hit the search button. The sounds echoed throughout the bar like thunder.

At the other end of the bar was another thirtyish regular. I had seen him laughing and talking with the other thirtyish guy about to play the jukebox many times. They knew each other. I thought they were friends.

In Barrett's, you never talked to anybody unless they talked to you. I never had a conversation with either of these guys, although I've seen them many times. They were like wallpaper in there.

Pounding his mug on the hardwood, the thirtyish guy at the end of the bar began to yell, "What The fuck! You gonna play the jukebox right now! We're going to war! This is no time to play fucking songs!"

"Fuck you! I'll play songs whenever I fucking want," the

jukebox player screamed back. "This is still America! If I want to hear a fucking song! I'm gonna play a fucking song! Fuck you!" He turned back and pressed numbers on the juke box.

Nothing was your business in Barrett's. We all watched, not giving a fuck, not getting involved. The jukebox mechanism made another clicking sound. Hearing that sound sent the guy at the other end of the bar into a rage. He let go of his mug. His face filled with hate. He slammed both palms on the bar then, in a fit of rage, rushed toward the jukebox player.

Hearing the loud palm splat against the bar, the jukebox player turned seeing the other guy charging him. Instinct took over the jukebox player. He grabbed one of the three pool sticks hanging on the wall right next to him. He charged back at the other guy.

In a full sprint the other guy sees the jukebox guy grab a pool stick off the wall. Without missing a step. He grabs a pool stick laying on the table in between them. They meet stick swinging in the middle of the bar.

They both screamed, "Mother Fucker!" as they whipped each other for their first shots.

The jukebox made another clicking sound. One more click and the song will play.

On their second swings both pool sticks broke in half. Large shards flew everywhere. I had to duck the thick handle from the jukebox players stick. It steamed at my head an inch from my left eyeball before sailing into the top shelf whiskey behind the bar. Nothing broke. The frayed stick fell at the foot of the bartender. The bartender didn't care. He watched the fight like the rest of us.

With both pool sticks decimated the fighters began throwing violent punches. They kneed, elbowed, and kicked each other. The jukebox playing guy was beginning to lose. We all watched in silence, still not caring.

The last clicking sound of the jukebox echoed through

Barrett's bar between the snarls, the punches, and the grunts. The fighters wrestled each other on top of the pool table. They rolled around choking each other. The eleven ball got knocked into the side pocket. The song blasted thru the air.

"God Bless America Land that I love. Stand beside her and guide her..."

Ethel Merman's finest rendition of one of America's most patriotic songs blasted loud.

I kept watching the fight prepared to duck flying objects. The jukebox guy was now bent backwards on the pool table. The other guy was standing over him wailing punches. The juke box guy wailed back.

The other Guy hears the song is "God Bless America". He immediately stops punching. The juke box guy still in fight mode connects a left right combination.

The other guy jumps off the jukebox guy. He puts his hands up. He speaks hurried and apologetic, "I'm sorry! I'm sorry. I didn't know you were playing that song."

"You didn't give me a chance to tell you! You stupid fuck!", the jukebox guy gasped. He rose from being bent backward over the pool table.

"I'm sorry, man. Can I buy you a shot," the other guy asked, dusting shards of broken pool stick off his former enemy's shoulders.

"Ok," the juke box guy answered back, out of breath.

Arms around each other the two men walked to the bar. Fresh shards of pool stick glistened in their hair like thick dandruff. The bartender poured two shots of some nasty house whiskey. They clanged shot glasses and downed the shots. Arm in arm they began to sing to the jukebox.

"God bless America land that I love..."

My friend and I turned to each other. We began to sing along. Everybody in the bar except the WWII Old Timer sang. Even the bartender sang.

Stabbing In Front Of Bitter End 1991

CHAPTER 9
STABBING IN FRONT OF THE BITTER END
BLEECKER STREET 1991

When the sun went down your guard went up in 1991 New York City. Crack was a plague that made good people bad. It was easy to buy weed, coke, crack, heroin, angel dust, or whatever you wanted on the street.

In Greenwich Village, the Bleecker Street and Washington Square Park areas were crazy. Jamaican gangs worked selling weed. The gangs were not the thug type that randomly bought fear, mayhem, and violence for the sake of fear, mayhem, and violence. They were very chill until they were messed with.

Most of the time the Jamaican gangs stayed to themselves in Washington Square Park. A few times a night they would venture out from the park to troll the seven block area of west 3rd, west 4th, MacDougal, Sullivan, Thompson, LaGuardia, and Bleecker Streets. They would backhand nickel and dime bags of weed to 'Out Of Towners' looking to get high.

The Jamaican weed whackers were never looking for trouble. They had their own code and corners of the park. You could hear their loud whispers in the streets, "Weed. Smoke. Weed. Good smoke. Ganga."

The cops left them alone as long as they stayed non-aggressive to the drunks that wandered the streets. The cops weren't worried about guys selling small bags of spiced down marijuana.

In 1991 the cops were worried about the crack heads robbing and stabbing people. They were worried about the gangs of young uptown Spanish gangsters with their initiation rituals of beatings and murder.

Most of the Jamaican dealers that got busted were back on the street within hours, because it wasn't illegal to sell oregano on the street. The judges didn't care about the weed whackers. They were worried about the crack slingers.

The bands playing on Bleecker Street in 1991 were good. Blues Traveler, Joan Osborne, Spin Doctors, were a little while off the block and into the mainstream of the international music scene. Players from David Letterman's band, Joan Jett's band, Billy Squire's band, Billy Joel's band, and many other mainstream bands, on any given night, could be seen spontaneously performing in the clubs on the Bleecker Street strip: The Bitter End, The Rock N' Roll Cafe, Terra Blues, Mondo Carne, Mondo Perso, The Back Fence, Kenny's Castaways, or The Red Lion Pub.

It wasn't odd to see Keith Richards, Bob Dylan, or movie stars walking around if they were in town playing a venue, or filming a movie in the city. When in town Pete Townshend of *The Who* would stop by the Red Lion to watch his brother Simon perform. Simon Townshend was a regular performer at The Red Lion.

There were always very talented people drinking in the bars of Bleecker Street. It was a great and magical time. If a famous musician or actor wanted weed, "They'd know someone, who knew someone."

The musicians, bartenders, bouncers, waitresses, and Village locals all knew not to buy weed from the Jamaican street guys. They went to the "Go To" weed people that were never on the corners. These "Go To" guys would come to them.

Every night was busy on Bleecker Street in 1991. People came from all over the world to experience the music. This night I was working the front door at the Red Lion Pub on the corner of Bleecker and Thompson Streets. It was a Thursday. The street was loud. The weather was hot.

I heard a commotion coming from the front of The Bitter End, seventy feet to my left. I looked toward the noise. I witnessed a guy stab another guy in the chest area. He started running towards me.

I never saw this guy before. He had mid-length dreads. He was flying down the sidewalk about to run past me. My instinct took over. This guy just stabbed someone. I couldn't let him go past. I lifted my elbow and slammed it into his face. He hit the ground almost unconscious.

I heard more commotion. I looked up. The entire Jamaican Village weed gang was running my way. The Jamaicans had knives and clubs out. They were looking to kill. The guy who had been stabbed was running in the middle of the wolf pack. He was holding his shoulder. I recognized him from the street. His back was to me when he was stabbed. I didn't see his face. I realized the guy I just nailed stabbed one of the local Jamaican weed whackers. Now they were coming to murder him.

I bent down picking the woozy man up. With the strength of a Lion and a prayer to God, I shook him. He came around. This all happened in a blink. I started pulling him away from the oncoming knife and stick wielding mob. I screamed for him to run. A Miracle hit. He snapped back to reality bolting in a full sprint toward The Back Fence.

A cop was across the street. I knew him. I saw him almost every night. He was a good cop. Not aggressive but he could kick ass. The cop ran toward the action.

The Jamaican gang was right on the stabbers heels. They were almost on him when in a panic the stabber rushed inside the Back Fence sixty feet to my right. He was met by the bouncer named Big Sal.

Big Sal had no idea what happened. He followed bouncer protocol; **RULE # 03:16 Never let a person sprint into your club at full speed.**

Big Sal pushed the stabber out the door. It looked like the stabber bounced off a wall because he did. A wall named Big Sal.

The stabber sling-shotted out the door into the Jamaican gang's hands. They started beating him with clubs.

The cop caught up to the action. He dove right in. The cop threw the stabber into a small pocket between the corner of the front door and the outside of the Back Fence. The cop shielded the stabber from the pissed off mob.

I saw the cop helping the guy. I couldn't watch him take it alone. I ran over. I covered the cop with my body. The cop covered the stabber. Big Sal got involved. He covered me.

Big Sal and the cop had no idea the guy we were protecting stabbed someone. Knives were flying over my shoulders.

It was hard for the Jamaicans to get around Big Sal. Clubs were swinging all around my body. They were trying to kill this guy.

I realized they weren't going to stab me, Sal, or the cop because they easily could have. The cop called for backup on his radio between forearm blocks of swinging knifes and clubs. There were too many people on the street for the cop to start shooting. Innocent bystanders would have been definitely hit.

It didn't take long before twenty cops were on the scene from out of nowhere. NYPD gathers quick. The Jamaicans scattered. Two or three of them were grabbed by the cops.

A tourist woman, who watched the entire episode, approached the cops. She told them in a German accent that the guy we were protecting stabbed someone. She pointed to me. She told them I smacked the stabber in the face.

A Sergeant came over to me nonchalant. He knew me. He pointed to the stabber.

"Did you see that guy stab someone?" He asked.

"Nope. I didn't see anything," I replied, deadpan.

"He hit him in the face!" The German woman screamed. She was frantic pointing at me, "I saw him knock the man down!"

"Did you punch that guy in the face?" The Sergeant asked.

"Nope. I saw your guy in trouble and I went to help him. That's all I did."

"Good enough for me. Thanks for helping," the Sergeant said stern. He turned and walked away.

The German woman's face bunched up. Still pointing at me, she screamed, "I saw him hit the man! He knocked him down!"

I was in the dog pile when the Sergeant showed up on scene. He saw that. He knew I was helping his guy.

I wasn't going to rat on the stabber. It was gang business, none of mine. After all, I almost killed him with my atomic elbow to the face.

When the smoke cleared, the cop I helped came to me at the front door of the Red Lion, "Thanks for helping me.

There were a lot of guys. I think they would have killed him if you and Big Sal didn't jump in."

"No problem. I couldn't watch you be out numbered. Those guys meant business," I said.

I never told the cop I saw the guy we were protecting stab another man.

Those particular members from that Jamaican gang were never seen again in the neighborhood. I found out they relocated uptown out of the 6th precinct. They were too hot to be walking around Greenwich Village. The guy who was stabbed was taken to Saint Vincent's Hospital with a wound to his shoulder.

I later found out the story was the stabber was infringing on the turf of the established Village weed whackers. An established weed whacker told him to back off. That's when he got stabbed.

If I would've been able to tell it was a Jamaican turf war, I would've never elbowed the stabber. I would've let him run by like it was nothing. All I saw was a person stab another person and take off. I don't want that type of maniac running around Bleecker Street. One of my friends, or I, could be the next victim of their knife.

The rest of the night was uneventful compared to that horrifying minute. Just a few minor skirmishes between drunks.

Peter May Smakes My life Again 1991

CHAPTER 10

LIFE GETS SMACKED IN ANOTHER DIRECTION 1991

Peter May's Speech

One night I was telling a story while bouncing in front of The Red Lion on Bleecker Street. Peter May the legendary Village musician had just finished a show. He came out front to get some air. He started listening to me.

After a few minutes he told me, "You should be on stage."

A year later I was bartending at the Lion's Den on Sullivan Street. Peter May was playing with his band Mayhem. He screamed on the mic, "Hey Kev! Get up here. Give us a song!"

"Fuck it! Why not!?" I replied.

I slammed a double shot of whiskey then headed on stage. The monster was spawned. I ad-libbed a ten minute blues song. When finished I received a three quarter standing ovation. The music career had begun.

After the show Peter May told me to come and sing with Mayhem anytime I wanted. I did.

After a few guest spots at Peter May and Mayhem shows I decided I was going to start writing songs.

Peter May sat me down one night after the fourth or fifth gig, "You better watch yourself. You are starting to like being on stage. Your life is going to change if you keep going. You were doing fine without music but now you got the bug. It can be, not good. I don't want to be responsible for getting you into this way of life. It's not easy."

I replied, "I'm a big boy Dude. I can look after myself. Beside I love it."

"You do. That's why I'm thinking of stopping it now before it is too late for you and your life is ruined by Rock N' Roll. It's taken many a good person over the years."

"When is the next show Dude?" I replied.

Two years later Peter May and I were packing clubs in New York City and up and down the East Coast with our new band *The 4th floor*. Soon a record deal, then opening slots for Alice Cooper, The Scorpions, and a tour with New York City legends KISS in 1996.

They say you can dissect a life to two or three instances where everything changes your direction and fate. For two of my three instances Peter May was involved. The first was introducing me to Alan at The Red Lion and the second was bringing me on stage that night at The Lion's Den.

I never regretted selling my soul to Rock N' Roll. As the years went by I understood why Peter May gave me the speech. A life in music is not all glitz and glam.

I have given the same speech Peter May gave to me to other young Rockers. I should maybe call it a warning, not a speech.

The early 90's was a magical time for music. I was all in with 'No Regrets'.

11

Fleet Week Bleecker Street 1991

CHAPTER 11

FLEET WEEK BLEECKER STREET 1991

There are no empty sounds in New York City during Fleet Week. The streets are loud with Military people from all over the world. The United States Navy and Marines in full uniform are the majority of the foot traffic on Bleecker Street. These United States servicemen and women hail from all over the country. It is usually the first and only time many of them will ever be in New York City.

The first war in the Persian Gulf ended a short time before the start of Fleet Week 1991. The air was filled with the spirit of liberators. Kuwait was free because of many whom roamed New York City this week.

I was always lax with checking uniformed military personnel ID's. I never looked at them. Uniformed Military people would pull out their ID's. I would wave them in. I didn't care what age they were. I would take the heat if I got caught. I figured, 'If you could die for me and my family I'm letting you in to drink. I don't care how old you are.' The age to drink was twenty one.

The Tuesday of Fleet week 1991 I was working the front door at the Red Lion Pub on the corner of Bleecker and Thompson Streets. There was no sign of trouble until two sailors rushed out to me from inside the pub. They were red-faced and worried.

"There are two imposter Marines in the bar. They're about to get their asses kicked," the sailors said together.

"Imposters?" I asked.

"They're fake Marines trying to get girls. I don't want my friends going to jail for murder. They're pretty drunk. You're the only one who can stop it."

"Let's go!" I said.

I followed the Sailors inside. They were in a hurry. In the back of the Red Lion was a dart board at the time. The sailors led me there. A pack of about ten Navy men had two Marines pinned in a corner. I pushed my way through. The Navy guys were about to pounce. The bar would've been ransacked. Just in time I jumped between the Marines and the Navy guys.

"Hey! Hey! Not here fellas. Outside on the street. Not in here," I said.

They all recognized me as the bouncer. I was very friendly and welcoming to them when they came in.

"Fuck these guys! These guys ain't Marines! They don't even know where their stationed. They don't know anything about the Marines at all. Fucking imposters! I'm gonna fuck them up!" A giant sailor yelled.

I got in front of the giant sailor with my hands up open palmed, "Not here man."

I turned to the Marines, "You guys Marines?"

"Yeah," they said.

The way they answered, the tone in their voice, I could tell they weren't Marines. I wanted to kick their asses. Real active uniformed Marines would never say the word "Yeah". And most importantly, real active Marines would never let anybody surround them, especially sailors. Real Marines would've been swinging like wild men. The Red Lion would have been in shambles. Black eyes and blood would have been everywhere. The Navy guys swarmed closer.

"Not here Navy! Outside! Step back! I want all you Navy men to step off! Let's Go! Get to the right. You can take care of this problem out on the street. I'm going to ask these guys to leave and you men are going to respect this house. Step to the right, Navy!"

All but three of the Navy men listened to me. I motioned for the fake Marines to leave. They didn't move. I saw in the three non-moving sailors clenched jaws and fire-filled eyes they were going to throw punches. This was one hundred percent. I've seen that look hundreds of times. These fake Marines were low lives. I wanted to smack the shit out of them myself.

In a situation like this I can't show any fear whether I am afraid or not. To tell the truth I was scared, because I knew if these Navy guys could just do whatever they wanted in this situation. Murder these fake bastards or even murder me. I gave a tough unafraid stare.

"I'm going to ask that you three men, out of respect for this business, to move to the right. You can handle what you have to out on the street."

The three Navy men stared me down. The way they looked at me I thought, 'Holy shit! They're going to come after me.'

I took a step backwards toward the fake Marines. My back was almost on them. I faced down the last three Navy men. I looked each one direct in the eyes with a slight head turn.

"You can handle this matter outside," I said.

"Oh! We're gonna handle this matter," the biggest and angriest Navy man said.

He nodded to the other two Navy guys. All three stepped to the right.

Ten pissed off Navy Men were now to my right. Two fake Marines were to my left. I was the barrier in between the warring parties. I pointed for the fake Marines to head toward the front door thirty feet away.

The fake Marines started walking. I got behind them. Thank God the area that led to the front door was only four feet wide. Nobody could get around me. I let the fakes walk a few feet before I followed. I wanted some distance between them and the Navy Men.

The Navy Men formed a line three at a side inches behind me. I enlarged myself by widening my walk so no Navy guy would sneak around me. They followed on top of my back. I could feel the heat of their breath on my neck.

I knew once we got to the street it was going to be ugly. I didn't care. I wanted the real Navy guys to kick the shit out of the fake Marines. My job was to keep The Red Lion Pub from getting trashed. I couldn't let my emotions get involved.

Three feet from the front door the fake Marines made a break for it. They dashed. They flung the door out open knocking to the side two uninvolved Navy Men entering the club. The involved Navy Men put it into high gear. They ran over me. Bulldozing me to the street. They trampled the two uninvolved Navy Men on their way out the door.

I heard one of the uninvolved Navy Men say, "What the fuck is going on in this place. Let's go somewhere else."

The fake Marines ran for their lives toward The Back Fence and 6th avenue. The ten Navy guys chased after them.

Cops are everywhere during Fleet Weeks. NYPD was right out front of the Red Lion. The cops saw the ten Navy Men sprinting out the door and me twirling around like a leaf in the wind.

The cops yelled, "Hey! Whoa! Stop right there! What's the rush?"

The real Navy Men stopped. The fake Marines kept hauling ass down Bleecker Street.

"What's going on fellas?" The cop said.

"Those guys that just ran past you were fake Marines. It's illegal to impersonate United States Military personnel. We were going to catch them and bring them to you," the angriest giant Navy man said.

"You were going to catch them and bring them to us?" The cop sarcastically spoke. He smiled, "Well, thanks for the help but we don't need it."

The cops came over to me. I knew them. The Navy guys followed the cops. They all surrounded me.

"What's up, Kev?" The cop asked.

"These guys are right. They weren't real Marines. They were bogus dicks hitting on chicks."

"How could you tell?"

"You could tell. They were pussies. Marines aren't pussies."

"Did you see their ID's? Were they fake?"

I couldn't tell them, even though they knew, I didn't check their ID's. They knew I was going through the motions and waving everyone in Military uniform inside. They were right outside The Red Lion all night. It was an unwritten rule. I came up quick with an answer to save face for me and the cops who were rooting for me to save face.

"They must've gotten in before I came on. I don't know what their IDs said."

"Ok. Good enough for me. They're long gone now," the cop responded.

The cop turned to the Navy guys, "Listen! If you have a

problem while you're here. Come get one of us. We'll deal with it. You guys don't need to be running around the streets like lunatics. Ok?"

"Yes sir!" All the Navy guys answered at once.

"Now go have a good time," the cop said.

The Navy Men headed back into The Red Lion. I opened the door letting them back inside like they were old friends of the bar. The rest of the night went smooth.

The next day I was back at The Red Lion at 8pm. The white United States Navy uniforms blanketed Bleecker Street like a snow covered mountain top. Thousands of sailors with huge smiles walked around looking for the best deals to drink. In 1991, Bleecker Street - from LaGuardia to 7th Avenue - on both sides of the street - was one bar or club next to another for the entire just over a half mile. Music filled the air.

Most of the Navy men out this day were from the USS Wisconsin. The USS Wisconsin was a major player for America in the first Persian Gulf War.

Months earlier these guys were launching missiles at the Iraqi army. Now these Navy personal were walking the streets of New York City. Every one of them that came to my door I let in. We did have to go through the motions of pulling out ID's. But I never looked.

Bleecker Street was extra packed. The Red Lion always had music from 7pm until 4am every night. They paid their musicians well so the acts were always top-notch. I noticed most of the personnel from the USS Wisconsin in The Red Lion were older Navy men. When I say older, I mean twenty-five to thirty years old. They were young officers, older than most of the eighteen and nineteen year old Navy guys running around plastered in the street. This Fleet Week night our crowd was regular New Yorkers, tourists, and The USS Wisconsin Officers.

The underage Navy guys that came in would see officers

and leave immediately. If they walked to the left they would see a giant chalkboard sign, "Dollar Drafts and No Cover Charge for anyone in Military uniform! Thank you for your service! Love, The Rock N' Roll Café!"

The Rock N' Roll Café was a great place. It was right next door a few feet from my post. My friend Jimi was the door guy out front. The staff of The Rock N' Roll Café hung out at the Red Lion most nights after they closed. The Red Lion closed at 4am every night. The Rock N' Roll Café would only close at 4am on Friday and Saturday nights. The rest of the week they closed between 1am and 2am after their band finished for the night. The staff would then come next door to have a drink with us. Our two staffs knew each other well. We all got along and were pretty good bar friends.

My night was going smooth. The Rock N' Roll Café was wall-to-wall white with Navy uniforms. It was a zoo. So many Navy guys were inside they were pinned up against the front windows. They were all having fun.

About 10 O'clock my six-foot-five English Rugby player teammate and waiter came up to me. He was in a panic.

"I had a walk out. Fuck!"

"Are you sure they aren't in the bathroom?"

"No, I saw them leave. I was in the back of the bar. I went to the table. No money for the check. They went to the left. I think they went into The Rock N' Roll Café."

"Were they Navy guys?"

"No. Two guys in t-shirts and jeans."

I figured if the walk outs were dressed in t-shirts and jeans in the Rock n' Roll Café they'd be easy to spot. They'd stick out like sore thumbs in the sea of Navy white. I also knew when someone walks out on a check they get as far away as possible. I doubted they were in the Rock N' Roll Café five feet away next door.

"Let's go," I said.

We took the five foot walk to the front door of The Rock N' Roll cafe.

"What's up?" Jimi at the door asked.

"Limey has a walk out. He thinks they're in here. We're gonna check it out. You see two guys in jeans and t-shirts come inside in the last few minutes?"

"No. Maybe. Mostly Navy guys in there. I was in the can for the last few minutes anyway. Steve was here. He's in the back. Go check it out."

We walked inside. It was a blinding sea of white. Drunk Navy guys were hanging onto each other. They were all laughing and screaming - having a ball. I was jealous. We went to the back. Nobody in jeans and t-shirts. We went to the side of the stage. The band was there. I knew the band. There were two guys I didn't know in jeans and t-shirts talking to them. I pointed, "Is that them?"

The Englishman looked, "No."

Those guys must have been friends with the band. They were also the only people in the bar beside the band and staff that weren't in Navy whites.

We circled around the entire bar. The Englishmen was looking around like a periscope. He was in distress. He knew the walkout was going to come out of his own pocket.

"How much was the check for?" I asked.

"Twenty two dollars. I'm going to go broke tonight. I can't afford twenty two dollars. I got the worst section. I'm gonna make twenty two dollars all day after this," the Englishmen pouted.

I didn't say anything.

The Rock-n-Roll Café waitress was walking by with a tray of beers. I knew her. She would stop by The Red Lion with The Rock N' Roll Cafe' bartenders, bouncers, and the owner Steve after their weekday shifts. She'd have a drink and we'd all chit chat about the night for a little bit. She never stayed long. She saw me looking around with the Rugby player. She acknowledged me with a nod and a smile. I was nodding back when a drunken Navy guy, about 18 years old, punched her in the face through the tray of drinks. He connected right in her grill. All I heard was a deep thud and the splash of beers flying everywhere.

I had no time for thinking. I reacted. I punched the Navy kid in the face automatic. I flipped him around, put him in a full nelson, and headed for the door with the young ass clown squirming in my clutch. This all happened in less than two seconds. The waitress followed clawing at the guy's face. This young Navy kid got messed up pretty quick.

One bad thing about acting on instinct is forgetting your whereabouts. I was surrounded by three hundred under-age-drunk Navy guys that were just back from a war. I didn't get far, maybe ten feet, before a hail storm of punches rained down on me. I soon realized why my country has the toughest Military. I felt a barrage of probably twenty punches all over my head. Eight of the closest Navy guys were teeing off on me.

The guy who punched the waitress was half my size. I let go of my full nelson. I wrapped him in a bear hug. I had his arms immobilized. He became my human shield from the relentless punches my American Navy was throwing at me. I never felt so alone in my life.

None of the Navy guys attacking me saw their man punch a woman in the face through a tray of beers. They saw a civilian grabbing a Navy guy. If they saw what their guy did they would be attacking him. But they didn't and I was now getting pummeled.

I looked for my six-foot-five Englishman waiter teammate. I figured he would be easy to spot in the sea of white. He was nowhere to be seen. Not that he could have done anything against this swarm.

I decided my holding the young Navy guy as a human

shield wasn't working. I was taking too many shots from behind. Navy guys were falling all over each other to get at me. It was time to take advantage that.

I threw the woman-punching ass on the floor at the feet of the guys attacking me from the front. Three guys went down like bowling pins. I started to swing at anything in white. I connected face shots three out of the first four punches I threw. It was hard to miss there were so many of them. They were tripping over each other trying to get at me. I didn't have to do much for them to fall they were doing it to themselves. They were everywhere.

I was taking hard pot shots to the back of my head. There were seventy five Navy guys in the way of the front door to get outside and they were all coming at me. I needed to retreat to a wall to cover my backside.

I ran high stepping to make sure no one grabbed my legs. If I hit the deck it would be over for me. Boot stomps to the face and kidneys would put me in the hospital, or morgue. I was determined to go to neither.

I knew if I didn't get something behind me I was going be knocked out. I was getting smacked behind my ears and in my kidneys.

I swung my way to the Pac Man machine in the corner of the bar. I played this Pac Man machine many times with Steve Principi the owner of the Rock N' Roll Café. At this second it shielded my back from a beating. I never imagined it would be a tool for saving my life.

Three sailors were grabbing me by the shirt. They were trying to pull me to the floor. At that instant I saw a flash of blue across my eyes and then bam, they were off me. Someone knocked them away. I looked over to see who it was. It was one of the blue jean t-shirt wearing guys that was talking to the band. I didn't know this guy at all but he just saved my ass. I owed him. He knocked three guys off me.

The Blue Jean guy popped up by my side. He started throwing punches. I nodded to him. He nodded back. We swung fists at the Navy. This guy was my guardian Angel Savior at that second.

It looked like a black and white World War II movie in The Rock N' Roll Café this night of Fleet Week in 1991. Two civilians fighting drunk sailors. The sailors who couldn't get near to smack us, began to smack each other. Total pandemonium was awry. There must've been close to three hundred guys in Navy whites, two hundred and ninety eight of them were throwing punches at anyone close.

It was a never-ending forever. It was probably twenty seconds of nonstop swinging for me and the Blue Jean guy. Thank God for the comfort of the Pac Man machine as our back guard.

Sailors were falling over each other to get a piece of us. Many of them had no idea why they were attacking us but they kept on coming. I looked toward the front door thinking we got to get out of here. This isn't going to stop. There are too many of them.

A bar fight usually lasts eight to fifteen seconds tops. This one was going on for the longest minute of my life. I was exhausted. Adrenaline and a fear of death kept me swinging. Thank God I was in shape from being on the Red Lion Rugby team.

I saw the front door swing open. It was my buddy Jimi. He had twenty cops with him. NYPD was here. "Thank the Lord!" One thing about NYPD is they gather quick. I will always say that.

Billy clubs in hands twenty cops charged in the door. Jimi told the two beat cops outside on Bleecker Street about the brawl. The beat cops gave one radio call. Within a minute twenty cops were in formation outside The Rock N' Roll café.

The cops were in a marching line. They plowed in the

door. They asked no questions. They started pushing the brawl-ing Navy guys against the wall. The Navy guys were young and drunk, but they weren't stupid. They knew not to fight back against a uniformed police officer.

The cops made their way back to me and the blue jean guy. I knew most of the cops from the block. The two from the night before with the imposter Marines were there. Another cop I knew was a guy I talked to almost every night on his beat. He was from Staten Island. He was rough and nice at the same time. A perfect combination for a New York City cop. He asked me, "What happened Kev?"

Normally I would say, "It was a misunderstanding. I just want everybody to leave."

I never want people to go to jail over drunken stuff. But this young Navy guy punched a woman in the face out in the open. He wasn't right in the head.

"A Navy guy punched the waitress in the face. I grabbed him. Then the entire Navy grabbed me."

"Which one threw the punch at the waitress?" The cop yelled.

The cop knew the waitress too. We all knew each other on the block. The cop was pissed. I scanned the crowd of hun-dreds of bloody Navy guys standing in order with their hands at their sides. I spotted the worm-woman-puncher hiding be-hind some bigger guys. I got him good. He was bleeding from the side of his eye socket. The waitress got in some nice deep scratches too. I walked over to him.

"This prick right here!" I pointed him out in disgust. "You fucking piece of shit! You're a disgrace to that uniform for punching a woman."

He must've been about eighteen years old. He looked like he could've been in High School. The kid had a glaring gri-mace on his face. He reminded me of the child Damien at the end of the 'Omen" movie. He had no remorse. He was chuckling. A few older navy guys maybe twenty-one or twenty-two stepped up. One of them spoke to the cop.

"Look he fucked up. Let us handle him. We'll straighten him out back at the ship," the Navy guy said.

The woman-punching Navy kid grinned like the devil.

The cop shook his head, "No way. We'll handle this guy. I was in the Navy."

The Navy guys stepped back. The cop spoke to me, "Who else Kev?"

My head was lumped. I was bleeding. There were at least thirty guys standing there with bloody knuckles from punching me.

"Nobody else. Everybody else is good."

The Navy guys were shocked I didn't point any of them out. I didn't want anybody to get into trouble for this one jerkoff.

The cops took the kid away. I followed them out the door on their tail. I didn't want to be left alone in The Rock N' Roll Café with the rest of those Navy guys. I walked back to the Red Lion. I saw the blue jean guy standing out front.

"Thank you for helping me," I said.

"I couldn't stand there and watch all those guys kick the shit out of you. I figured civilians have to stick together," the blue jean guy laughed.

I found out he was a Carpenter from Bay Ridge, Brooklyn. This stranger saved my ass by the Pac Man machine. I was probably going to the floor if he didn't get those three guys off me. I never saw him ever again. But, I will never forget him.

Jimi walked up, "You ok?"

"Yeah. I need a new shirt though."

My shirt was ripped and covered in blood. I looked like I was in a ship wreck. I walked into the Red Lion. The bartender John Cavanagh had no idea what I had just went through.

"What happened to you?" He asked.

"Don't worry about it. I'm alive. I need a shirt."

John gave me a shirt from behind the bar. The ones we sell to tourist. I looked around for the Englishman. I wanted to know where he went. I didn't see him. I went back to my post out front of the Red Lion. A minute went by. Out from The Rock N' Roll Café the six-foot-five Englishman staggered. He looked ten times worse than I did. I realized he didn't run.

"You ok?" I asked.

"Not really. When they jumped on you. I jumped on one of them. Then I got swarmed. One got my leg. I was whipped to the floor. Then it was a stomp party."

I now knew the Englishman didn't abandon me. He got his ass kicked. I was happy. Not that he got his ass kicked but that he didn't abandon me. He was a good guy. I couldn't see him when I looked for him in the fight because he was on the floor. Not only did he get his ass kicked. He was out twenty two bucks.

The Rock N' Roll Café threw everyone out of the club. They removed the dollar draft for everyone in Military uniform sign. They started the night over. They put on a $5 cover charge. The Rock N' Roll café had a peaceful rest of the night.

Some of the Navy Guys in the brawl were out on Bleecker Street. They noticed me. I saw them coming. I thought, 'Here we go again.'

I put my dukes up ready to brawl. They raised their hands open palmed in a show of peace. They apologized to me, explaining they didn't know the kid punched the waitress in the face. They told me they were embarrassed about what he did. They said they knew who the kid was. They also said he was going to get "it" when he got back to the ship after the cops were through with him.

"Don't worry about it," I said. "I'm just glad you guys are back safe from the Gulf."

12

The Hypnotist 1992

CHAPTER 12

THE HYPNOTIST 1991

It was about 7pm on a normal weekday. I was getting on the subway for Bleecker Street to work the door at the Red Lion Pub. I had just got back from the gym and was in a total sober state of mind. I found a seat and looked around. All seemed ok. The doors shut. The train pulled away.

I began to lucid dream about lyrics I was working on while staring at the floor. A minute passed until the next stop. I snapped back to reality to watch for maniacs boarding. A few hip hoppers acting tough got on. They played a boom box of angry music. The beat was good. They drifted to the other side of the train.

I looked around the car at the other riders. An overweight woman in a fur Russian hat sat oblivious to my right. Straight ahead sat on old man. I saw him when I first came on the train. He had to be at least 80 years old. He was staring at me. He wore big telescopic black rimmed glasses on his sagged face. The magnification of the lenses made his blue eyes look like two giant Cool Whip lids. I stared back the socially accept-able half second. I looked away.

Old people and babies always gave me long stares on the subway. I never reacted when they did because they were old, or they were babies. I had a four inch goatee and a purple Mo-hawk. I did not look ordinary. I understood the stares.

I gazed about the train mundane. I found my eyes drawn back to the Old Man. He was still staring at me. His big blue eyes seemed to spin like psychedelic kaleidoscopes behind his huge coke bottle glasses. In his hands was an extra-large book. It looked like something a wizard from the movies would have. It was the biggest book I ever saw. It had to be two feet high and a foot and a half wide. The cover was tilted down. I couldn't read it.

I looked back up toward the Old Man's direction. He was still staring at me. Again, I gave the socially acceptable half second look.

I bought my gaze to the reflection of the window across from me to sneak a further look at the Old Man. On New York City and Path subways you can indiscreetly watch the person in front of you by looking in the window behind them. I call it the barber shop mirror effect. Two reflections facing each other going on for infinity. I could see him still staring at me in the reflection.

The train began to move again. The start up jolt hit the car. The Old Man slightly shifted off balance. The giant book's cover tilted toward me. I took my eyes off the reflection and zoomed my sight to the book for that split second. I read the ti-tle, "*The Art of Hypnotism*".

I looked direct to the worn face of the Old Man. He was still staring at me.

'Is this old guy trying to hypnotize me?' I thought.

I looked at the giant book to see if I could read any words. I couldn't make out anything.

I looked back at the Old Man. His eyes bulged. I became overcome with a tingling in my brain. I felt something emanate from the deep recesses of my mind. It felt like an itch inside my skull on the other side of my head bone.

I looked back at the Old Man. His glare squinted in concentration. He looked way deep beyond the interior of my eyes. I felt his will. Vivid images entered my thoughts. I could suddenly see myself in my own mind's eye through his sight. There I was sitting on the train across from this Old Man's perspective. I saw myself, my whole body, as if I was watching a monitor of him filming me.

I thought, 'This can't be happening. This Old Guy is in my thoughts'.

A pressure in the front of my head started to throb. Was he really attempting to violate my mind? Was this throb in my imagination? I didn't know what to do. I never had anyone, that didn't want to bang me, or fight me, stare at me this long. I needed to act. There was no way I was going to be hypnotized on my way to work.

I needed to get an offense going. I began to stare deadpan back at the Old Man. I sat up straight in my seat. I leaned in toward the staring kaleidoscope eyed Old Man. I began squinting an angry gaze back at him. He now knew I was on to him.

His bulging blue eyes seemed to spin more frantic. I felt him inside of my mind. It wasn't my imagination. I was having telepathic communications with an Old Man mind stealer.

I began to think of the most absurd pure true thoughts to scare the Old Man out of my mind. I imagined in vivid focus a spear crashing through his head. I imagined hordes of cannibals rejoicing at the sight of pieces of this Old Man's brain spilling onto the dusty ground.

The Old Man's eyes welled with anger. The next stop arrived. Our stare down didn't break. People scurried in front of us leaving and finding seats. We never unlocked our fastened glares.

His eyes grew larger. My mind was being invaded. I stared back unafraid. He looked annoyed feeling my fight.

I visualized myself laughing as I swung a ball-peen hammer toward his face breaking his nose. He kept on staring. I kept on staring back. My thoughts filled with hate, violence, and rage. The Old Man was not backing down with his stare.

Five stops passed. People walked in front of our stare down at every stop. Our eyes never unlatched. I wouldn't let my uneasiness get the better of me. His whirling blue-cool-whip-lid eyes tempted me to get off a stop early. But I stood my ground.

"I don't need this crap," I said in my mind.

The Old Man gave a slight head turn like he heard my thought.

This night I was bouncing at the Red Lion. I had to be ready for anything. I didn't need a telepathic mind battle on my way there. Each day my train ride was my sanctuary. My place of peace. I refused to give in and let this Old Man take that away. I was staying up to my stop.

A few minutes past. The stare down never unlocked. My station arrived. I stood up never breaking my eye grip with the Old Man. I walked past him. His overexposed mad scientist gawk followed me. I stepped onto the platform never taking my sight off his.

I threw one finale thought at the Old Man mind stealer, "Go fuck yourself! You piece of old shit! I ain't gonna be hypnotized by you! Fuck Face!"

He looked more angry and determined. Our intense lock magnified. Our stares strained. I stood outside the train wrestling myself from rushing back inside. The doors slid shut.

Through the dirty windows our stare down continued. The train began to move. I jogged alongside until running up to a full sprint when it got faster. The Old Man turned his body and head never unleashing his eyes from mine. He then stood up on the moving train holding onto nothing. His arms eerily hung at his side as he balanced himself like a surfer on the speeding train. He kept his stare on me for as long as he could. He leaned over to burn every last millisecond of hypnotism on me until the train was out of sight and into the tunnel.

We never unlocked our stare.

I stood at the end of the platform. I heard the train's clanging getting softer the further away it got. I shook my head. People were staring at me after seeing me running on the platform. They were moving away from me as far as they could. I didn't care. I noticed a cold sweat seeping through my shirt. A chill hit me. I walked up the stairs toward the street. A cold breeze greeted me. There were no fights at work that night. The old man was on my mind for most of it.

Halloween Nixon vs Space Robot Fight 1992

CHAPTER 13

HALLOWEEN BLEECKER STREET 1992

Richard Nixon vs. Space Robots

Every October 31st the biggest Halloween Parade in the world runs through the heart of Greenwich Village, New York City. Witches, puppets, ghouls, gargoyles, monsters, movie stars, medieval knights, Jesuses, Apostles, cavemen, and anything you can think of are all in attendance.

The parade starts in Soho at Spring Street. Over sixty thousand people dressed in every imaginable costume merrily prance up 6th avenue past Bleecker Street to 16th street. The parade attracts over two million spectators each year. It's a great day for all.

I love Halloween in Greenwich Village. Everyone is happy. Halloween 1992 was a crisp mild cool night. There was no sign of horrible weather. The subways and buses were filled with costumed revelers heading to The Village.

I had my work cut out for me this night. I was working the back door at The Red Lion Pub on the corner of Bleecker and Thompson Streets. I had to be on the clock four hours earlier than my normal 8pm shift. I arrived at the Pub fifteen minutes early. I ate three Gray Papaya hot dogs at 8th street and 6th avenue before I headed to The Red Lion. My belly was full. I was ready for anything.

The streets were already packed at 4pm. I always got a kick out of people when they took on the personalities of their costumes. Guys dressed as superheroes in their minds had special powers for the night. Girls, normally reserved in their lives, acted like total whores dressed as clappers, or sexy cats, or strippers, or naughty nurses.

Guys dressed as women had glee in their eyes because they really loved to put on woman's clothing. Girls dressed as army men, or cops, were amped up as they acted out their machismo fantasies. A Halloween public prance can be liberating for a closeted cross-dresser. It was always fun to watch people's happiness on Halloween.

A doorman's job on Bleecker Street is to not let assholes and underage people into the Pub. I'd have to ask people to remove their masks when they'd show their ID's. It's a pain in the ass but it has to be done. Mobs of teenage kids with masks try to gain entry into bars. They aren't a welcomed group. Drunk New York and New Jersey teenagers can ruin everything.

Halloween 1992 was a Saturday. That meant nobody was going home for work in the morning. A Saturday Halloween meant extra robberies, sexual assaults, regular assaults, and fights. Unruly behavior was going to be rampant. It's nothing for a guy to put on a Dracula outfit and stick someone up.

"What did the perpetrator look like, sir?" A cop would ask.

"Dracula! It was Dracula who mugged me," the penniless victim would cry.

Thousands of Draculas walk around on Halloween. Most are law abiding people looking to have a good time. If you want to commit a crime on Halloween in New York City dress as either Dracula, or Frankenstein. There are thousands of them roaming the streets.

"Who did you say grabbed your crotch, miss?"

"Frankenstein grabbed my crotch! He stuck his hand down my pants. He had green bolts sticking out of his neck. He was hideous!"

People in disguises masquerading around drunk is a concoction for trouble.

Just after 9pm the parade crowd began fanning out into the city. Bleecker Street was closed off to traffic. Costumed people walked around looking for a place to party. They staggered around in a menagerie for the ages.

Most people were drunk on sneak bottles of whiskey, black berry brandy, and vodka. A sneak bottle is a pint bottle of hard booze hidden in a pocket. It's perfect during a parade. Take a swig every once in a while and before you know it, you're bombed. After the parade there are thousands of empty pint bottles strewn in the gutter along 6th Avenue.

At 10pm the night was running smooth for me. The Red Lion had a great crowd. Everybody was having fun and of age. Out on Bleecker Street was a different story. Guys dressed as Knights of the Round Table ran around agitating people. They chased a group dressed as Benedictine Monks. Three guys on stilts walked over people's heads. A guy dressed like a dog crawled on his hands and feet. He lifted his leg on a fire hydrant. He howled at the moon. Another lady dressed as a drum majorette twirled a baton like she should be in the Circus.

I was enjoying the cavalcade from my post until I heard a pissed-off drunk screaming. I looked to the middle of the intersection of Bleecker and Thompson Streets about twenty feet away. There I saw a guy in a suit wearing a Richard Nixon mask. He was in a rage. I had seen him earlier walk by giving people the double peace sign. Now he was yelling at another reveler dressed as a space robot. No more peace signs for Nixon.

The space robot costume was homemade. It was a cardboard box made into a robot body with a plastic beach pail as a helmet. Both were painted white. The beach pail helmet was modified with a dark tinted visor cut in for an eye piece.

"Hey! Watch where you're going! You dumb robot fuck!" Nixon yelled.

I heard the robot's muffled voice yell back, "Lighten up Nixon!"

I noticed the space robot having a hard time walking inside the card board box. I assumed the space robot bumped into the ex-President.

"Your costume sucks! What did you make it in your Mom's basement?" Nixon slurred.

"You're real original with a store-bought mask. Fuck you!" The space robot answered. Again muffled through the plastic bucket.

"Oh, Yeah! Fuck You!" Nixon screamed as he pushed the space robot.

The space robot twirled around 360 degrees unable to move its arms. Nixon saw this and pounced. He started throwing punches at the space robot. The sound of a hollow cardboard box being punched echoed on Bleecker Street. A crowd quickly gathered to watch the fight.

The space robot had two friends dressed with the same exact costume. Nixon did not see them. They were fifteen feet away. They heard the commotion. With no hesitation the space robot reinforcements steamed toward Nixon from behind. He didn't notice them charging.

Stuck in their card board boxes, unable to swing punches, the two new space robots chose a strategy of running straight into Nixon. They blindsided him knocking him backwards.

Nixon stood startled for a split second. He was now out numbered. He put up his dukes and squared off at the three space robots. He started swinging wild punches.

Stuck in their cardboard boxes the space robots fought like three alligator armed guys. They had no mobility. They chose to bang into Nixon using their shoulders as weapons. More people gathered cheering the Halloween brawl.

Unbeknownst to the space robots Nixon wasn't alone either. Two guys, one with a Ronald Reagan mask and the other with a Jimmy Carter mask, came rushing in from across Bleecker Street to help Nixon. They were chatting up a couple babes dressed like cow girls by the pay phone near the Back Fence bar. When they saw Nixon in trouble they sped toward the fight. They greeted the space robots with swinging fists.

The Jimmy Carter Mask had the biggest toothed grin. The teeth took up half the mask. Carter and Reagan both wore suits. Nixon, Reagan, and Carter had the advantage over the arm restricted Space robots. But the shots the presidents were getting in weren't hurting the cardboard box protected robots.

The punches were raining down hard. The space robots were frantically trying to wriggle out of their costumes. Seeing this Nixon, Reagan, and Carter kept on the pressure with a constant hammering.

A good ten seconds of fighting went past. The crowd grew huge to a couple hundred people. There were five or six Draculas, four or five Frankensteins, a guy in a dress, a genie, two Abe Lincolns, one Betsy Ross, a guy dressed as an ape, two tooth fairies, a lumber jack, a Leprechaun, Godzilla, and at least ten zombies cheering on the fighters.

The original fighting space robot was off balance for a split second. Nixon took advantage shoving it to the ground.

The space robot's helmet flew off when it hit the pavement. A long mane of thick red hair was exposed.

Like at blocked shot at a hockey game the crowd went, "OH!"

It was a girl. Nixon had been beating up a girl. She was on the ground rolling around. She noticed she could escape her cardboard box if she slid out the bottom. She wriggled to freedom then jumped up. She started chucking freehanded haymakers at Nixon.

The other two space robots saw her escape the costume by being knocked to the ground. They threw themselves onto the street. They wriggled from their boxes and threw their helmets aside. They weren't girls. They were pissed-off guys that looked like athletes.

"You want to punch my girlfriend," the bigger one screamed.

The boyfriend went after Nixon. He started beating the living hell out of him.

The other space robot guy looked like he could have been the boyfriend's younger brother. He went after Reagan.

The redheaded girl ganged up on Nixon. She got in scratches and kicks. Jimmy Carter tried in vain to get the boyfriend off of Nixon. He was punched in the nose by the enraged beau. Carter fell to the street woozy. The brother space robot and Reagan had an even fight to the side.

Nixon was taking a real major beating. It wasn't funny anymore. The space robot couple were going to kill him. Nixon deserved a beating. He didn't deserve to die. I thought about going over to break it up. Nobody was doing anything to stop it. These space robots were going to take Nixon's life.

The street was packed wall to wall. I knew if I went to go break up the fight twenty unchecked drunks of all ages would run through my back door. Our night would turn sour.

Nixon was now unconscious. The space robot couple

still punched his limp body. The fight-watching crowd went from laughing at a funny brawl to scared silence witnessing a possible murder.

I couldn't sit by and watch the death of another human being. I decided to go break it up. I looked to the sky, "Please God let no one run thru my door".

I took a step toward the fight.

At that instant the ape, the Leprechaun, and the dude in the dress jumped on the back of the swinging boyfriend. Two Draculas and a guy dressed as King Henry the 8th also jumped in. They tried to subdue and calm the angry space robot. Telling him, "Enough! Enough! You got him! Enough...."

I took the step back to my post. King Henry The 8th was a big guy. Maybe six-foot-four 350 pounds. He got in front of the boyfriend blocking him from Nixon. The boyfriend tried to get around the mid-evil tyrant for another go at the unconscious Nixon. He was pulled back by the Leprechaun, the dude in the dress, and a new guy dressed as The Mummy. King Henry the 8th grabbed the boyfriend in a bear hug. The boyfriend couldn't move. He snapped back to some sort of humanity.

"I'm ok! I'll stop! I'll stop," the boyfriend huffed realizing he couldn't escape the clutches of King Henry The 8th.

King Henry the 8th spoke, "I'm gonna let you go. It's over. You won. It's over. Ok..."

"I'll stop. I'll stop. I promise," the boyfriend said coming out of his frenzy.

King Henry released the boyfriend. The red headed girlfriend was standing right there. The boyfriend put his arm around her. The brother came over and joined the hug. They walked off.

Carter and Reagan knelt down by Nixon. He was coming back to consciousness. They pulled his mask off. There was blood everywhere. His nose was broken. They dragged him over to the street light by The Penny Arcade sign of the Village Gate. They propped him up. The space robots, the ape, the Leprechaun, the Draculas, the guy in the dress, the Mummy, and King Henry the 8th all melted into the night.

The street was wall-to-wall people. Reagan ran to the pay phone by the Back Fence to call an ambulance. Less than a minute before he was at that pay phone talking to cowgirls. Now he's at the payphone talking to 911. Nixon sat against the street lamp with Carter looking over him. He was bleeding hard.

I heard the ambulance's sirens a few seconds after Reagan hung up the phone. Two foot cops showed up a minute later. They did what they could to help Nixon.

Because of the amount of people in the street it took the ambulance ten minutes to get there. I heard many revelers walking by comment, "Hey that guy sitting against the light pole has the best makeup job I've seen so far today."

Halloween 1992. Bleecker and Thompson Streets, Greenwich Village, New York City.

The 4th Floor Band Assembles 1992

CHAPTER 14

THE 4th FLOOR BAND ASSEMBLES 1992

My life was one hundred percent that of an artist in 1992. I was constantly writing. If I wasn't writing I was making short films with Wayno Draino and The New Underground. If I wasn't doing either of those I was making music and videos with *The 4th Floor*.

I worked as a bouncer at The Red Lion four nights a week. I loved every instant of my time. Peter May was someone I saw every day.

Peter May, a classic 'band-guy-go-getter', prepared every show like he was on mission. Over the year of 1992 Peter May assembled a group of guys that became *The 4th Floor* band. I was a very proud member.

Kenny Kramme was the drummer. He was the nicest-mellowest guy and a great drummer. Peter May drafted Kenny into *The 4th Floor* band after seeing him at an open mic at The Red Lion.

A little while after Kenny was in the band he told Peter May about a guitarist buddy he grew up with named Marcello Capparelli. Marcello was a knock out player with a big bushy head of hair. Kenny bought him down to Bleecker Street. Peter May asked Marcello to join the band after he saw him play at another open mic at The Red Lion.

The bass player in the beginning was a guy named Kevin "Bones" Williams. He was a fabulous player who was the bassist of Peter May's band Mayhem. Bones was another great guy. He suffered from back problems. One night he couldn't make it on The Red Lion stage with us. An Australian guy *'on a walk about'* named Lee Matheson was a waiter at the Red Lion that night. We knew he played bass. We saw him play at The Red Lion open mic a few weeks before. We asked him to put his apron down and get one stage. He did and he was great. Lee was one of the wildest human being I ever met. His energy was great. After a while Bones's back took him out of the game and Lee became the permanent bass player.

It was the early 90's. It wasn't odd for a band to have two or three mc's ala *The Beasty Boys and Run DMC.* We were a rock band but we had three guys out front in *The 4th Floor.* I was one. My longtime childhood friend Captain Al Batenko was another. I was hanging out with Al my whole life. He was a guy who liked to write and make stuff like myself. We always did projects together.

The third singer was Peter Cavanagh. He was the main singer. I loved writing stuff for him. He was very talented. Peter Cav was a Red Headed Irishman who played on The Red Lion Rugby team with me. I always saw him in a good mood while he was out and about on Bleecker Street. He was always laughing. I liked his energy allot. I saw him sing a song one night at The Red Lion. He was full of charisma and was fearless.

One day Peter Cav was walking into The Red Lion while I was out front bouncing. The voice in my head told me to ask him to be in *The 4th Floor* project. I did just that. He said, "Yes." It was on!

That was the main line up that ran for a few years. Kenny drums, Marcello lead guitar, Peter May rhythm guitar, Lee bass, Peter Cav, Captain Al, and myself vocals.

One of our first huge shows was a Christmas show we did at The Lion's Den on Sullivan street 1993. It was a multimedia experience. We were scheduled to perform our live band show and have a viewing of our ' *The 4th Floor Christmas movie*'.

During the few month before Christmas 1993, Captain Al and I wrote and produced a half hour Christmas Movie starring Peter Cavanagh, Myself, Captain Al, Alejandro from Rugby, Roadhog from New Underground, Canadian Dan Newman, Peter May, and comic Patrick P.J. Landers. Most of the members of The 4th Floor and various real life characters from Bleecker Street were in it also; Mike Tait, Fia, Brian "Bubba" Overstreet, Narcosis Dan, Has, Albino Steve, Comic Irene Bremis, and Greg "The Monster" Patchen. We called it '*The 4th Floor Christmas Show*'.

It is a feel good movie with the theme, "We're All Good People Except The Jerkoffs".

The concert and viewing at The Lion's Den attracted a few hundred people. We played the half hour movie. Then *The 4th Floor* band performed live. Kevin "Bones' Williams was the bass player that show.

It was a great time in my life. Every night I was either working The Clubs of Bleecker Street or writing with *The 4th Floor* or *The New Underground*. I was having a ball.

Google "Peter May 4th Floor Christmas Show" on youtube to watch Christmas Show.

Clockwork Cousin Beat Down (Timeless)

CHAPTER 15

CLOCKWORK COUSIN BEATDOWN (timeless)

During the 1990's The Lion's Den on Sullivan Street in Greenwich Village, New York City was a crazy place to be. The Lion's Den was owned by Alan Whelan the man who also owned The Red Lion. I would work both bars but was spending more and more shifts at The Lion's Den. It was around the corner from The Red Lion.

I was the night manager on the day of this story. Our doors opened to the public at 7pm. A band from New Jersey was starting the show off at 8pm. They were in front of the club when I arrived at 6pm to set up the bar. I told them to wait outside while I went in to turn off the alarms. That took about two minutes.

Alejandro the bartender (the same Alejandro from the rugby story) and Bryan the soundman were standing with the Jersey band when I went back to let them in.

Alejandro gave me a fist bump. He went to the ice machine to get ready for the night. Bryan began to help the band. I locked the door behind everyone.

At about 6:45pm I noticed a group of eight guys gathered outside the locked door. They were pulling on the handle trying to get inside. The official time for the bar to open was 7pm. I let people in early if we were ready to serve booze. Alejandro gave me a thumbs up. The registers and the bar were ready to go.

I unlocked the door. I let them inside the vestibule. I told them there was a five dollar cover charge. They started to argue with each other over who was going to pay. I knew they had to be related.

"You guys related?" I asked.

"Yeah, we're all cousins and brothers."

"Nice," I said.

The door guy's job was to ask, "What band are you here to see?"

He'd than mark down a money credit for that band. I assumed they were there to see the band going on at 8pm, since they were here so early.

"You guys from Jersey to see the 8pm opener?" I asked.

From the back of the pack a short guy answered like a proud father, "No! We're from Long Island. We're here to see the band that goes on at eleven. Our cousin is the singer. He's great! We're all cousins and brothers."

My mind went into high alert on the spot. Eight male cousins coming into a bar four hours before their family member goes on stage was trouble.

"Is it a guy's night out? No wives or sisters coming tonight?" I asked.

One woman can quell a mob of beasts. That's why I asked.

"No! Fuck that! Big Boys night out!" The same short family member said.

"Fuck!" I said to myself. "These guys are never gonna make it. This is a recipe for disaster."

I scanned them. They pushed each other to pay. My keen years of barroom powers zoned in on the littlest cousin. The one who spoke proud his cousin was the singer of the eleven o'clock band and that it's a Big Boy's night out. I knew he was going to be a problem.

I surmised an educated guess that around nine o'clock, in little over two hours, there would be trouble. I would bet the house on fists from the little guy. He looked like he had a few drinks in him already. They all did.

This wasn't my first show with packs of drunken relatives. About sixty five percent of the time it ends ugly. By the looks of these guys I knew they were going to be in the sixty five percent ugliness category.

The oldest, biggest cousin, pushed everyone aside. He paid for everyone.

"Listen, I don't have the hand stamp right now. My door guy will be here in a little bit. He's gonna stamp your hand when he gets here. You guys will be able to go in and out of the club when you want. But for now come on in!"

"Ok. That's cool," they all said nodding in agreement.

I could've stamped them. The stamp was in my pocket. I didn't for a reason.

Big Rob, my six-foot-four bouncer, didn't start until 7pm. He usually walked in eating some sort of street vender crap three minutes before his shift began. His last bite was always at 6:59 and 53 seconds. Big Rob was a sweetheart of a guy who could kick major ass. He was big, and black, and very smart. He was also my friend.

Like clockwork, (We'll be using that saying a few times in this story) Big Rob walked in eating an almost finished gyro at 6:57pm. His last bite was finished at exactly 7pm. He was exactly where he needed to be.

I had respect for people's own time and business time. I walked over to Big Rob. He was officially on The Lion's Den clock now.

"We have a group of cousins and brothers in here from Long Island to see the eleven o'clock band," I said looking Big Rob direct in the eye.

"Already? Oh shit! Those guys there I guess," Big Rob said concerned pointing to the only guys drinking at the bar.

"They paid," I handed the money to Big Rob. "I didn't stamp them. You need to do that."

Big Rob didn't ask questions. I handed him the stamp. We worked together for years at this point. He knew why he had to stamp them.

Big Rob walked in the club to size them up. He walked inches from the cousins. They all noticed him. He walked over to Alejandro gave him a high five over the bar. He then walked to the garbage can at the side of the bar. He threw his gyro wrapper in the can. He walked up to the chatting pack of cousins.

"Hey guys. How you doing?" Big Rob said very nice. He smiled in a very welcome manner.

"Good," they all answered looking at Big Rob with suspicious eyes.

Big Rob pulled out the rubber ink stamp.

"I got to give you guys a stamp. In case you want to go in and out."

They all dropped their guard, "Ok. Cool. Thanks, Man."

The shortest cousin spoke to Big Rob filled with pride, "Our cousin is the singer of the eleven o'clock band. He's an awesome singer."

"That's great. I heard a lot about them. I can't wait to

see their show," Big Rob said while stamping the backs of their hands.

The reason I didn't give the cousins a stamp was I wanted them to see and interact with Big Rob. Maybe get to know him. Big Rob could show he was friendly. I also wanted them to see that I wasn't alone and Big Rob was a monster.

"Ok fellas, have fun! I'll be at the door if you need me," Big Rob said.

Back at the door Big Rob shook his head, "Damn the eleven o'clock band. Fuck! They're gonna be out of their minds by nine o'clock. They're drunk already. The forecast calls for fists. It's going to be that little one that acts the ass!"

"I know. I'm going to make the rounds and tell the boys on Bleecker Street to be ready. Pete and Jerry are at Kenny's Castaways, Louis and Alfonso are at The Back Fence. Kelly is at The Bitter End. Drew is at The Red Lion."

"Who's our flyer guy tonight?" Big Rob asked.

"Monk."

"What about porter?"

"Kahn."

"Second bartender?"

"Joanna... Alejandro, you can see, is behind the stick right now. Monk comes in at 7:30. I'll have him stand on Sullivan and Bleecker handing out flyers. I can signal him from here. He can signal the Bleecker Street boys."

A direct line of sight from the Lion's Den in the middle of the block on Sullivan Street to its cross street Bleecker Street was a big help. My flyer guy Monk would be stationed there. Monk was all about justice and calling in the troops.

The plan was I would signal Monk with my flash light. Three or more flashes was the universal bouncer's sign for trouble. Monk would then signal the door guys on Bleecker Street, some of the toughest guys walking the city.

In the 1990's all bouncers in the Bleecker, Thompson,

and Sullivan Street area of Greenwich Village communicated by flashlight flashes.

One flash is, "You ok?"

One flash back is, "Yep."

Two flashes is, "I got to use the bathroom. Watch the door."

Three or more flashes is, "Trouble."

I told Big Rob, "I'll be back in a few minutes. I'm going to see if anyone is around on Bleecker."

Most of the Bleecker Street bouncers started their shifts at eight o'clock. Some of them got to work early to eat a decent dinner at the bar. Unlike Big Rob who showed up exactly on time every day gobbling some street slop.

The Bleecker Street guys at The Red Lion and Kenny's Castaways worked from 8pm until 4:30am. The Lion's Den, The Back Fence, The Rock n' Roll Café, and The Bitter End bouncers worked from 7pm until the last band ended between Midnight and 2am.

I needed to alert my friends I was going to have a problem. People never realized when visiting Bleecker Street in the 80's and 90's that the bouncers out front of each club all looked after each other. If we had too, we would swarm together on a club that was having an out of control group. And, we always won.

When a pack of four or more male cousins went out together it was the same story. After four beers, like clockwork, one cousin would exclaim, "Shots"! All the cousins like Vikings would agree. A half hour would go by when one cousin would decide it was a good idea to either: A). Jump on the stage. Or B). Jump on the bar.

The jumping cousin would feel that his drunken family could take on the world. The Jumping cousin would refuse to come down. Which would send the very tough New York City bouncer over to coax him off the bar. Having seen the cousins' gone rouge syndrome hundreds of times - an experienced bouncer, in the nicest way - would politely ask, "Come on buddy. Come on down."

If the bouncer asked in a mean or tough way it would be a 100 percent fight with a group of cousins. If you ask nice you might have a 50/50 chance of no fight. That is why you ask nice.

When the bouncer would put his hand out to help the drunk cousin down. The nice move might cause the cousin to think the bouncer was soft. The cousin might think he can take the bouncer. The cousin might refuse to get down.

"Fuck that! I'm with my family! We always dance on the tables at our reunions!"

When that would happen the bouncer would have to show his teeth a little.

"This isn't your family table, brother."

Seeing the bouncer getting a little tough most often causes all the cousin's to gather around screaming, "That's my cousin! That's my family!"

When that would happen, like clockwork, the club's troops would assemble unknowing behind the 'ballsing up' drunk cousins. The coat check girl, the flyer guy, the bartender, the porter, the bouncer from next door - who alerted every bouncer in the area - a cousin's gone rogue situation was happening.

The cousins screaming at the bouncer would last for about three minutes before all the troops would have assembled. At about that time the cousins would think the bouncer is a pussy because he hadn't done anything yet, but get yelled at. They would think they outnumbered him and shout, "We're the toughest family in the world! Let's fuck him up."

It is at that second one of the cousins would think, 'I'm going to punch this bouncer in the face'. He would get ready for the punch.

By that time there would be ten to fifteen club people standing behind the unknowing screaming cousins.

After the bouncer sees all his reinforcements. He would reach up and touch the refusing cousin trying to coax him to come down.

Then Bam!

It would be automatic. A cousin would throw a punch. Then all the cousins would move to pounce.

Then Bam! Again!

All the club people would move to pounce.

Before they knew it all the cousins would be out on the street screaming, "Don't touch my cousin! That's my family!"

At that point the beat cops, who are never more than a hundred yards away, would hear the commotion. They'd run over telling the cousins to pipe down. Like clockwork, a bloody cousin would get in a cop's face chest bumping him while screaming, "He touched my cousin!"

The cop would proceed to flip the cousin around to cuff him. Which would incite the other cousins to jump on the cop yelling, "Don't touch him. That's my cousin. That's my family!"

The act of touching a cop would incite the four new cops, who just showed up, to start pushing the cousins up against parked cars with their Billy clubs.

Touching a New York City cop, or any cop, is a big "No No". In the 1990's the cops in Greenwich Village, New York City traveled in packs.

The next day the cousins would wake up in jail feeling the aches of their family beating. The cousins would make a pact to never talk about getting their asses kicked and their arrest at any future wedding, reunion, or funeral for as long as they lived.

I was hoping for none of that to happen but knew those odds were small.

Like Clockwork on this night at 9:10pm the short

cousin jumped on the bar. Big Rob and I gave each other the nod.

Big Rob did a lackadaisical walk into the bar for the three minute stall. I went out the front door. I flashed three flashes to Monk on the corner of Bleecker and Sullivan Streets. Monk flashed the repeated flicker down Bleecker.

Like clockwork, Monk and five bouncers were at The Lion's Den within a minute and a half. Like clockwork, the drunk cousins got mouthier with Big Rob for his inaction.

"That's my Cousin! That's my family! Don't fuck with us. Our cousin is in the band!"

Like clockwork, the cousins tighten around Big Rob. Like clockwork, Big Rob saw me, five Bleecker Street bouncers, Monk the flyer guy, Bryan the sound guy, a couple of Village Lion Rugby players (who just happened to be drinking at the bar this night), one of the Gypsies next door (who saw me flicker flash Monk), the porter, and a couple Bleecker Street musicians (who also happened to be drinking in The Lion's Den that night), all standing behind the drunk, enraged (unaware that they are surrounded) cousins.

"I'm going to pull him down if he doesn't come on his own," Big Rob told the cousins.

"You touch my cousin! We're gonna fuck you up! That's my family! Fuck you!"

Big Rob spoke one last time to the standing on the bar cousin, "Are you gonna come down?"

"Fuck you! My cousin is singing in the band!"

Like clockwork, Big Rob made his move for the on the bar cousin. Like clockwork, the on the floor cousins made their move for Big Rob. Like clockwork, half the village made a move for the cousins who didn't know what hit them. Like clockwork, in less than ten seconds, all the cousins were outside the bar on Sullivan Street screaming.

Like clockwork, the cops heard the commotion and

came over. Like clockwork, the short cousin, who was ripped off the bar, swung on a cop. Like clockwork, four cops started billy clubbing and handcuffing the short cousin. Like clock-work, all the cousins jumped on the cop. Like clockwork, the other cops started Billy-clubbing and handcuffing cousins up against parked cars. Like clockwork, the cousins were thrown in the back of cop cars. Like clockwork, the cousins were taken away crying and screaming, "That's my family! My cousin is in the band! Boo-who."

Like clockwork, I thanked everybody. Like clockwork, everybody went back to their jobs, bar stools, fortune telling, drinking, and the rest of their night. It was now 9:17pm. Peace, once again, held reign at The Lion's Den.

At 9:28pm the eleven o'clock band came to the door. There were four of them. They introduced themselves. I was standing with Big Rob. The one guy not carrying an instrument came up to Big Rob.

"Hey man! I'm Vito. I'm the singer for the eleven o'clock band."

"What's up Vito," Big Rob said as he shook his hand, "You guys can go backstage and put your gear back there."

Vito and the band went inside. Five minutes later Vito came to the front door. I was still standing with Big Rob.

"My cousins and family were supposed to be here. Did you see a group of about eight guys come in to see us?"

Like clockwork, Big Rob and I shrugged our shoulders answering at the same exact time, "No, we didn't see anybody like that."

Lee Defys Gravity 1995

CHAPTER 16

LEE DEFYS GRAVITY 1995

"Don't be a Killjoy. Be a Joyboy"

In 1994 and '95 my band *The 4th Floor* was bringing crowds to every place we went. I had moved from Jersey City into an Apartment right above the Red Lion on Bleecker Street. Most of the band lived in that building by now. It was great.

We were doing so well that Bass Ale was sponsoring us. One weekend in the summer we had a Saturday bus trip to The Tipperary Inn in Montauk Long Island. Bass Ale chartered a bus for a bunch of fans and the band. We were hired to do a one night two sets show.

I was sitting toward the front of the bus trying to take it easy before the show. We were driving sixty miles an hour on the Long Island Expressway. I was leaning my head on the window with my eyes closed. Bryan the sound man was next to me. The normal hooting and hollering was going on in the bus. I was immune to it until I heard Lee's Australian screaming voice

129

coming from outside the bus, "Yeah! Fuck yeah mate! Go faster you fuck!"

My eyes shut I thought, 'That's not right. The screams should be coming from inside the bus. Am I dreaming?'

I opened my eyes and turned to look toward the screams outside. To my complete amazement there was our bass player Australian Lee, a true madman, hanging out the window a few rows back. He was wearing a big happy grin and screaming like a hillbilly, "Yee-Haw!"

Lee wasn't just sticking his head out the window the way a normal person would on a bus going sixty. No, this true down under lunatic couldn't do it that way. He had to push the limits. Lee's entire body, up to the top of his boots, were out the window. He was defying physics somehow. He was totally out stretched parallel to the highway. I was in disbelief at this impossible feat.

Lee was over six feet tall. Five-feet-eight-inches of his entire person was outside the speeding bus's window at a perfect right angle.

I loved Lee a lot. He looked like a young Robert Plant from Led Zeppelin. He was tall and thin. He always wore hip hugger bell bottom pants with some kind of cool weird shirt that enhanced his long lion's mane of blond hair. Lee had a heavy Crocodile Dundee Australian accent.

Whenever we were together Lee and I had major laughs. He was a great bass player. I always said when Lee joined the band he was the straw that broke the camel's back. His style and stage presence sent us on our way. Lee was the last cog in *The 4th Floor* machine. Lee was also one of the wildest guys I ever met. And I met allot of wild guys over the years.

I stood up. I was scared for Lee to fall to an almost certain death. I opened my window and stuck my head outside. I started yelling, "What the fuck Lee! Get back inside the bus! You sick bastard! You're gonna get killed!"

Lee's "Yee–haws" and laughs became wilder. He told me to "Fuck Off!"

We started arguing. My head was outside the speeding bus: while Lee's almost entire body was outside the speeding bus.

He was screaming, "Go faster! Go faster! Shut the fuck up Kev!"

Lee was defying human physics. How was he doing this feat? Was he holding on by his toes? Did he have hooks on his shoes? Was he part Orangutan? I was perplexed and pissed off. I screamed louder, "Fuck me! Fuck You! Get back inside!"

The 4th Floor band had a friend name Marcus. He was a great guy but he was also a wild man. He came to most of our shows. He was from Wales in The United Kingdom. I played Rugby with Marcus on the Village Lions. He was very tough and strong as an Ox. Marcus and Lee always paled around together which was always one hundred percent trouble.

I pulled my head back in the bus. I looked back to see how 98% of Lee's body could be out the window. I wasn't surprised at all to see Marcus holding Lee's ankles with his giant hands. It looked like Marcus was working a horse plow from the 1800's. It looked like he was using Lee's ankles for the plow handles. Marcus was laughing out of control.

I ran over yelling, "Marcus pull him in! He's gonna get killed!"

"Fuck off Kev! Lee wants to fly! So let him fly! Don't be a bore!" Marcus replied giggling like a Hyena.

I grabbed Lee's legs. I started yanking him in. Marcus decided it would be funny to let go of Lee.

"What the fuck are doing Marcus!" I screamed louder.

I was now holding Lee by myself out the window. Everyone on the bus was laughing. Lee was "Yee-Hawing". The bus driver was screaming, pissed off, like a fiend.

I yelled for Bryan, Captain Al, and Peter Cav, the only

other guys with half a brain on the bus. Peter Cav was three seats away pointing and laughing. Bryan was double handed knee slapping, cracking up.

I looked around and thought, 'Everybody's lost their minds.'

We were driving sixty miles an hour with this guy all the way out the window and nobody cared. Everybody was roaring with laughter.

I held Lee's legs with the might of an angry silver back gorilla. I felt the bus driver slowing down softly. He knew an abrupt stop and Lee would be a goner. He eased on the speed. People in cars alongside on the Long Island Expressway had terrified looks.

Lee was roaring, "Speed up you fuck! Speed up! Why you slowing down? Don't slow down. Speed up! Speed up!"

"Pete he's slipping! He's gonna go. Help me pull him in. He's gonna go!" I yelled to Peter Cav.

Lee was fighting me from pulling him back. I began to wonder. Did Lee have a death wish? Was he trying to commit suicide by excessive celebrating?

Peter Cav joined me grabbing Lee's legs. We tried in vain to drag him inside. Marcus was laughing so hard he was almost choking.

Captain Al was asleep in the front of the bus. I yelled for him one more time. Finally he heard my plea and rushed over. He pushed in between Peter Cav and myself grabbing onto Lee's legs. With Al's Russian bear strength added we muscled Lee back inside to safety.

"What the fuck is wrong with you, Lee? You could have been killed!" I yelled.

Lee grabbed my chest with two hands pulling me an inch from his face by my shirt. He casually spoke, "Ahhh! Fuck it Kev! Just a little bit of fun mate. Don't be a Kill Joy. Be a Joy Boy!"

I said nothing, shook my head, and went back to my seat.

We got to the club early and had the place going crazy all night. It was a great gig and no one died.

17

One Door Closes Another One Opens Up 1995

CHAPTER 17

ONE DOOR CLOSES; ANOTHER ONE OPENS UP (1995)

In the beginning of 1996 things for my band were going very well. *The 4th Floor* had evolved into a downtown New York City force. The machine was rolling. We were writing songs and bringing crowds. Everyone in the band was having a blast and it showed on stage. I loved it.

I was still working at The Lion's Den Club on Sullivan Street in Greenwich Village, NYC. I would bartend, bounce, and night manage the bar. I would also work sporadic shifts at The Red Lion. Both places were owned by Alan the same guy who got me started on Bleecker Street. Things were great.

The Lion's Den was a music venue which had different promoters operate out of the club. Sunday night was reggae night with the Skadanks. Monday was metal night with Jerry

Adams presents. Tuesday was new band night. Wednesday was Brazilian Night. Thursday, Friday and Saturdays were a mix of bands promoted by Creative Entertainment.

Every once in a while we would let other outside promoters try a night at The Lion's Den. One promoter, a big auburn haired woman I'll call "Big Red", put on a show in February. She did an all right job. Brought in a few heads. Nothing to rave about.

Big Red over heard me talking about *The 4th Floor* to someone at the front door.

"Are you in *The* 4th *Floor?*" She asked.

"I am," I replied proud.

"I heard about you guys."

"Oh yeah. What'd you hear?"

"That you guys do good. That you have a crowd that follows you. Would you like to do a show for me next month at an East Side club I promote?"

"Sure!" I said.

I cut a deal and set a date with Big Red for a show the following month.

Time past to the day of Big Red's show. It was a Wednesday night. Wednesday was Brazilian night at The Lion's Den. I opened the club doors at 7pm. *The 4th Floor* show was at 10pm. The East Side club was about ten or so blocks from The Lion's Den.

Brazilian night was a great night. It was a quick hit. A Brazilian band would be on the stage at 9pm. The club would become packed with drink-pounding-gyrating Brazilians. The band would stop between 11:30pm and midnight. Everybody would then leave. We made money. The band made money. The Brazilian fans would have fun and the club is desolate within twenty minutes of the last note. Always a big money fast hit.

I left The Lion's Den at 8 o'clock to meet *The 4th Floor* guys at The Red Lion on Bleecker Street. We were going to have a few pops before the show. On my way out the door I handed the door guy Big Rob a flyer.

"You'll probably close around midnight. We'll be boozing at this club on the East Side. If you want to drink after work. We'll be there."

Big Rob grabbed the flyer, "Yeah, I probably will. I feel like drinking tonight. I'm gonna come hang."

Marcello (lead guitar), Kenny (drums), and Lee (bass) were at The Red Lion when I got there. Peter Cav (singer), Peter May (rhythm guitar), and Al (singer) arrived intermittently within a few minutes. We had a few laughs and drinks before heading off to the gig.

We arrived at the East Side club at 8:30. That left us ninety minutes to set up and get prime. Big Red was at the door when we walked in. I noticed a giant sad-sack-puss on her face. There was a man, about forty years old, behind her yapping in her ear. He looked like he was giving her shit. I could tell he was the owner. I could also tell he was a jerkoff.

"Hey, how ya doing?" I said to Big Red.

The owner leaned further into her ear. I heard him bark in a whisper, "Make sure everyone has ID's."

Not answering me and not looking in our eyes, Big Red spouted words to the floor, "I need ID's from everyone."

I thought, 'This is a new one. Getting ID'd by the person who booked you?'

I understood though. This jerkoff whispering in her ear had to tell her what to do. Just because he was the owner. I knew our crowd had to get ID'd. We did attract young people.

Aside:

At this point in my life I had been in hundreds of bars either performing, working, or drinking. I had noticed that some small bar owners buy places in order to be the boss. They don't care about being successful. They want to tell people what to do, "This is my world. These four walls are my domain. All mine. Do what I say! Regardless, if it's right or wrong. I am the boss."

You could tell a good bar owner who knows and enjoys the hospitality business. Their staff and costumers have smiles. A good vibe permeates the walls. Big Red greeted us with a five foot puss on her face and bad vibes were everywhere.

We all looked at each other. It didn't take a genius to figure out the guy behind Big Red suffered from a Napoleonic complex and was a bully. He was relishing in making Big Red uncomfortable. I could safely bet all his employees were miserable. He didn't care about creating a nice environment to have fun and make money. He was the big fish in the tinniest puddle. *The 4th Floor* didn't do well with people like that.

I complied taking my ID out. The owner stood over Big Red watching. He pulled my ID from her hands like a Nazi at a border crossing in World War II checking for French resistance members. He handed the ID back to a red-faced Big Red.

"He's good," the owner said.

At that instant I felt unwelcome. The urge to tell this guy to "fuck off" was hard to ignore, but I kept my mouth shut. He made it like he was doing us a favor having us at his club.

I knew no matter what I was going to give it my all on stage for the people that came to see us. I wasn't going to let this guy ruin my show.

Big Red was embarrassed but she didn't say or do anything. She let this guy push her around. I lost all respect for her.

"Did you guys get raided or something?" I joked to the owner while putting the ID in my wallet.

The owner stared at me in silence for two seconds. He then walked off with an angry look on his face.

I continued, "Red was that the owner? He's a dick, right?"

"He's up my ass about everything," Red replied with no eye contact, still staring at the floor.

Rhythm guitar player Peter May lived off the grid. I knew he didn't have an ID. He was also 43 years old at the time. The rest of the band was in their late 20's or early 30's.

Talking to the side of Big Red's head, as she still couldn't look me in the eye, I pointed to Peter May, "This guy is 43 years old. He sleeps on kegs underneath The Back Fence Bar. He doesn't have an ID."

Big Red stuttered in a huff, "I need everyone to have an ID."

"I'm playing here tonight! I'm 43 years old! Look at me. Do I look underage?" Peter May pleaded.

"All right. I'll let you in Peter because I know who you are. But I need to see ID from everybody else," Red said.

Peter may shook his head and went inside the club. I felt like I was being watched from the shadows behind Big Red. I looked over her shoulder. I caught a glimpse of the owner hiding in the darkness behind a curtain. He was giving us the evil eye.

I had to speak up, "I would never bring underage people in here. You know me!"

"These are the rules," Red said, never looking at anyone.

She was driving the rubber ink stamp hard into the hands of all the ID showers in *The 4th Floor.*

I bit my tongue. I knew Red was getting it from the owner lurking in the shadows. I walked into the show area. I went as far away from the front door as I could. We loaded our gear on the stage.

"What's up her ass?" Peter Cav asked, lifting an amp to the stage.

Peter Cav either worked in, or ran, New York City Irish bars since he was 14 years old. The Lion's Den was his family's business.

"I think she's getting it from the owner for some reason. I'm gonna give her a pass. I think she's a little unbalanced. She has the "far away" look in her eyes," I told Peter Cav.

The crowd started arriving around 9pm for the 10pm show. About fifty people showed up. There was a five dollar cover charge to get in. Everyone got ID'd and paid. Not a big deal.

I was on stage telling Peter Cav a funny story when a few fans approached. They motioned to talk to us. We leaned down putting our ears in their faces to hear over the Black Sabbath music blasting.

"What's with that nut job at the front door?" The fans asked.

Peter Cav and I looked over to Big Red at the same time, then we looked at each other, then we turned toward the fans speaking in unison, "What did she do?"

"She yelled at us when we came in!"

The fan began to mimic Big Red, "Get out your ID's! Its five dollars to come in here! Step to the right! I said step to the right! If you don't step to the right! You're not coming in!"

Peter Cav and I side-eyed each other a disapproving glare. Peter Cav's bright red hair turned redder as he listened too. He was pissed.

"She's a douch. Just forget it. We're going to have a good time tonight," Peter Cav consoled the fan.

The fan walked away. Peter Cav and I agreed to never do a show for Big Red, or have her do a show at The Lion's Den ever again. She was putting a total damper on the evening.

Two minutes past. Kenny the drummer stepped on

stage. He was pissed and in a rage. He shouted toward me and Peter Cav, "That lady at the door is a fuckface! I wanted to make sure my brother Walter was on the guest list. She snapped at me!"

Kenny began to mimic the frantic Big Red, "You get one person per band member on the list. Have your list ready with everybody's name on it. I'm not gonna be writing down a name for anybody who walks up to me. I don't know who you are!"

"Sorry man, I have the guest list in my pocket. I was gonna give it to them when we walked in, but I forgot because we were treated like shit when we got here."

"Is Walter on it?" Kenny asked.

"He's always on it," I replied.

"What's with her man!?" Kenny questioned.

"She put on a show at The Lion's Den a month ago. She was a gem. I think she's getting heat from the owner for some reason tonight," I said calm to Kenny.

"Heat about what? We're gonna pack this place. It's almost full right now," Kenny screamed.

I walked over to Big Red and handed her the guest list.

"Here is the guest list," I said.

She grabbed it without looking at me. I walked back on stage.

Three minutes went by before another paying crowd member came to the stage, "I hope you guys don't make a habit of playing here. The lady at the door is a fucking cunt."

"Oh no," I said. "What did she do now?"

"I asked her if the show was running on time. She flipped out. She started screaming!"

He started mimicking Big Red's frantic craziness, "Of course the show is running on time! You don't think we know what we're doing here!? You don't have to come in here you know if you think we don't know what we're doing!"

I looked toward the front door again. This time I saw

Red hand the owner a wad of bills. Rage was boiling inside me. I knew not to go anywhere near the front door. I stayed put on the stage. Peter Cav and I looked once again at each other speaking disgust with our eyes. It was almost time to play.

At 10pm the band made their way to the stage. The crowd gathered in front. It was a packed house. The club was small. Fifty people was a full venue.

I looked over at the front door. My girlfriend at the time was there. I saw her talking to Big Red. Big Red was barking at her in an aggressive manner. I saw Big Red shake her head, "No".

My girlfriend was on the guest list. I could no longer stay put. I walked off the stage to investigate.

"What's up?" I said to my girlfriend.

"Nothing. I don't have my ID. I can't come in."

My girlfriend worked in the clubs and bars of New York City. She knew everybody and was always comped where ever she went. She didn't have her ID with her. She wasn't being rude to Big Red at all. She knew the rules of the club business. She also knew the singer's girlfriend usually doesn't get harassed by the door people. Unless they deserve it. She was being polite. She didn't deserve Big Red's wrath.

"She's 28 years old Red. I can vouch for her. We run clubs in this city. You worked in our club. I would never jeopardize your place with someone underage. She's my girlfriend. Look! We packed your house on a Wednesday. Come on. She won't drink if you don't believe me."

My girlfriend sensed me getting pissed.

"Kev, I'll just go. Don't worry about it," she said.

I looked at my girlfriend, "Wait here a minute."

I walked back on stage. I gathered the band in a huddle.

"We're getting the fuck out of here. This lady at the door is a fucking lunatic asshole and the owner is a fucking jerkoff. I'm not playing here. We'll go to the Lion's Den. We can go on in an hour. The Brazilian band will be done by then. We'll tell the crowd to get their money back and to go there."

The band all immediately agreed and spoke at once, "Fuck this bitch! This place sucks! She's a fucking Cock-Douche!"

I got on the mic, "Ok, everybody listen up! Because the owner of this club is an asshole and the lady at the door has been rude to each and every one of you. We're moving the show to The Lion's Den. I want you all to go get your money back. We're not playing here tonight. We're going to move the show to 214 Sullivan Street. We'll begin in an hour. Meet us out front. I will personally give you cab money to get there, if you need it."

The crowd started rumbling, "Fuck her! This place sucks! She's an asshole! The owner is a cock! Lion's Den blows this place away!"

I watched Big Red's face from across the room. She was astonished. People bummed rushed her to get their money back. She looked like she was going to the electric chair. I saw her grab the clip board. She was going to take off.

I knew she couldn't give back the money. I saw the owner take it from her. He came out from behind the curtain in a childlike fit, screaming, "Who the fuck is this guy calling me names from my stage! In my club! This is bullshit! Who'd you bring in here, Red!?"

"Fuck that!! They packed the house. You made me be rude to everyone. This is what you get," Red finally back boned back.

The Owner and Big Red became overwhelmed by the crowd.

I said to the band, "I'll see you guys out front. I'm gonna go to jail if I stay here another second.

"Ok," the guys nodded. They knew I was in a dangerous mood.

I headed to the front door where my girlfriend stood to the side. It was time to let Red have it.

"You're the worst door person and promoter I have ever seen! You treated everybody that came here to have a good time and spend money, like a criminal! You treated everybody like shit! You and this club suck! Fuck you! And fuck him!"

I pointed to the owner cowering behind Big Red. I threw my next comment in his eyes.

"You! Owner guy. You shouldn't be in the club business. You have no idea what you're doing. You're a fucking idiot! And an asshole! You fucking jerkoff!"

The owner decided to get rough.

"Oh yeah! I'm a jerkoff!" He shouted.

He opened the front door calling to someone outside, "Darrell come in here."

A bouncer was in front of the club. He walked inside. He was a monster. He was way bigger than me. The owner smiled

"Let's see how tough you are now with my security here. Fuck you Asshole!" He said grinning.

The bouncer walked over to me. He was four inches taller and sixty pounds heavier than me. He looked like he could eat me for breakfast. He put up his hands. The owner smiled. I put up my hands. The bouncer reached out. I reached out. We locked arms and bro hugged.

"What's up, Kev? How things at the Lion's Den?" The bouncer asked swallowing me in a hug.

I knew the bouncer well. His name was Darrell. He hung out at The Lion's Den. I had drinks many times with Darrell after hours.

Darrell spoke to the owner, "I've know this guy for a long time," he said pointing at me. "He's the kind of guy you want in here."

Rage filled the owner's face. If he could've got away with it. He would have had me killed.

"How many days you work here Darrell?" I asked.

"Not really many. Once or twice a month. I'm a fill-in guy here," Darrell said.

"Fuck this jerkoff," I said almost foaming at the mouth.

"...If these people don't get their money back. This place is done. You better go get the cops now. Because, I'm not fucking around."

"What Happened?" Darrell asked.

"These two have been rude and disrespectful to everyone who came to see us. We've had enough. We're getting out of here and going to bring the show to the Lion's Den. I want everyone to get their cover charge back."

I could tell Darrell wasn't surprised about what I just said. I could also tell he was torn. He knew me. He knew I meant business and was a fair guy. I had worked many freelance security jobs in the underbelly the City with Darrell. We also partied after hours together with Big Rob many times.

Darrell was silent in contemplation. His wheels turned thinking of the best way to solve this problem. Fifty people waiting to get their cover charge back watched the stand-off. Everybody, including a silent Big Red and owner, looked at Darrell.

The band started rolling their amps passed the confrontation. The bartender walked over from behind the bar. She came over to me. She was an inked up hottie. I knew her from a very successful touring New York City girl band she was in. She asked me not to leave.

I could tell the inked up hottie was counting on the money from our crowd. I paused for a second before I calmly spoke to her direct, "We have to leave. Red went too far treating everyone like shit. And this owner guy here," I pointed to the fuming owner. "He's a fucking asshole. I feel bad you have to deal with this piece of shit."

The tattooed hottie didn't say a word. I looked at her face. It read, 'I hate this guy so much. I know he's a piece of shit. But I need the money and the job!'

We were past the point of no return. The rage of what jerkoffs the owner and Big Red were to everybody had taken over the night. I couldn't let it go. I couldn't do a show on the principle.

Darrell turned to the owner, "My advice is to give them back their money."

The owner snapped at Darrell, "What kind of bouncer are you?"

"The kind that doesn't work for assholes. Fuck you! I quit."

Darrell the ex-bouncer turned to me, "You guys going to The Lion's Den? Is Big Rob working tonight?"

"Yep," I replied. Not taking my eyes off of the purged, scrunched, evil face of the owner.

"Good. I'll see you over there," Darrell said. He turned to leave. I reached out grabbing his shoulder.

"I didn't see you when I came in. What time did you come on here?"

"I came on two minutes after you got here. I was across the street getting a coffee. I saw you walk in from there."

I opened my wallet. I pulled out twenty five bucks, "Here, take this for the time you worked tonight. You're gonna have to beat the shit out of this prick to get any money out of him."

"I was ready to eat it," Darrell said.

"Take this. See you at The Lion's Den. You better get out of here."

Darrell took the money and left. The bar owner was

now alone with me, Peter Cav, Captain Al and fifty *4th Floor* fans.

Aside: *This owner was an arrogant, resentful, piece of shit. He had no redeeming qualities. He wanted to bully people. I hated club and bar owners like that. They usually came from money that wasn't earned. They harass young waitresses, because they can. They hold bartender's shifts over their heads, because they can. They torment kitchen workers, bus boys, and bar backs, because they can. They know people need jobs. They know people have children and rent to pay. They take advantage of that by treating their staffs like shit, because they can. Because they hold the work. A dick bar owner is one of the lowest forms of humanity. New York City had allot of them. Most didn't last long in business.*

"Everybody line up. Show your hand stamp. Get your money back," I said.

The crowd lined up. I looked at the owner.

"Either give them their five dollars back. Or, go get the cops."

You never want to call the cops to your bar for three main reasons. First, its public record. Second, the precinct get pissed for you not being able to handle your own shit. And third, a cop can always find something to write a ticket for if they want.

I knew this guy wasn't doing something right in this place. All asshole bar owners never play by the book.

The owner looked around. His night was crumbling. He fought his thoughts. He took the wad of bills from his pocket. He handed it to Big Red. He spoke defeated, "Give them their money back."

The crowd gave a tension ending, "Aaah."

I watched Big Red fork over five dollars to everyone

who paid to get in. Kenny walked by carrying his cymbal bag. I went after him. We were the last to leave.

Outside the club the band and fifty fans were ready to move.

"Everybody meet at the Lion's Den on Sullivan. We'll go on in about an hour," I shouted to the crowd.

I jumped in a cab with Kenny, Al, and Peter May. Lee, Marcello, Peter Cav, and some stragglers jumped in other cabs.

We all arrived at The Lion's Den minutes later. Big Rob had a puzzled look on his face out front. Thirty *4th Floor* fans stood with him when I got out of the cab.

"Hey, Big Rob. We're gonna play after The Brazilian band."

"Dam, Kev! I was going to come over there and drink with you guys," he said. A disheartened tone in his voice.

"Well, you drink with us here," I said.

"Yeah, but I got to work and stand at the door."

"So what. Like twenty chicks are coming here to see us. You can have fun with that."

"What happened? Why you guys here? You should be on stage over there."

"We had a little disagreement with the way our people were treated, so we left. By the way Darrel is coming here. I want to start working him in on busy nights. He needs a new gig."

"Darrell? What happened with him?"

"He chose a side. I'll tell you later. Anybody who comes in asking for *The 4th Floor* let them in. No cover. As a matter of fact, anybody that comes here that is of age, let them in no cover. We might as well play for as many people as we can."

I walked in the club. I watched most of the crowd from the East Side enter. Everybody was happy. There was a feeling of solidarity among us all. We told "The Man" to fuck off. We were the ones in control. It felt great.

Our crowd mixed in with the one hundred dancing Brazilians. It was a Wednesday night just after 11pm. The Lion's Den was packed.

The Brazilian band finished at 11:30. We got right on stage to start setting up. *The 4th Floor* band was a machine. When we had to, we were the quickest setting up band ever. Our philosophy was get on stage fast. If you get on stage fast you're more than likely to capture some fans from the previous band. This philosophy gained us thousands of new followers over the years. There's nothing more stupid than a band that takes it's time setting up, letting an already gathered crowd walk out. I hated seeing that kind of bush league stuff. It was amateur.

We struck our first note at 11:45. Most of the Brazilian crowd was still in the house. We hit that stage hard. We were tight. We played with a level of rage and passion that was paramount. We were pissed. We were playing with a feeling of victory. It felt good. We played for over two hours.

With no-cover charge the walk-in street traffic crowd grew during the show. On our last note over two hundred people were in the club. It was great. Most of the Brazilians stayed. Our crowd never left. And, at least fifty new walk in people were there. It all added up to a great night.

I went to the front door after coming off stage. Big Rob was talking with Darrell. Big Rob spoke to me, "I got Darrell a shift on Reggae night."

"Good," I said. "That's a steady job every Sunday. Nice Darrell. One door closes. Another one opens up."

People started coming up to me. I chit chatted with everybody. I was approached by a pretty Brazilian woman. She stuck her hand out for me to shake.

"My name is Monica. That was a great show. Wow! I was sitting here watching the Brazilian band and I see you guys walk in with a mob. I said to myself, 'Who are these guys'. I was going to go home but you guys were on that stage so fast. Once you started playing I couldn't leave. What a show! Do you guys have a record deal?"

"No. Not right now," I replied.

"Do you want a record deal?"

"Of course we do!"

"I have been in the record business a long time. I haven't seen a band with that much energy since *The Red Hot Chili Peppers.*"

"Thank you," I said, becoming interested.

"I would love to use my connections to get you guys a record deal."

I have heard a lot of mumbo jumbo from people after a show. Most of it drunk talk and nonsense. I believed Monica. She wasn't drunk. She continued.

"I know I can get you guys a record deal. When is the next show?"

"In two days on Friday night at The Red Lion. We play the late 1am to 4am show," I told her.

"Man, that is late. I don't think I can get a record executive there at that time. Are there any other shows."

"If you thought this show was wild and full of energy. You should see when we play The Red Lion on a weekend. You can't move in the place. We pack it. Everybody knows the words to our original songs and sings along. The place goes nuts."

"Really," Monica said. She began thinking to herself, "Let me see what I can do."

Friday came, the buzz was in the air at The Red Lion. Monica was at the show. She told me some record people were going to be there.

I asked her a favor, "Please keep the record people away from the band until after the show."

Monica had just met us. She had no idea yet the loons

she was representing in *The 4th Floor*. It was too early in our relationship to come clean. I didn't want to scare her off. I continued, "Unless they see us. There is no reason to talk. I don't want to sound like a dick. I know that's the best way to do this. Keep the record people away from the band until after we play. Please?"

I wasn't being elusive, or pompous, by not wanting the band to talk to the record people until after the show. I worked in the club business for many years. I had seen bands get signed, and bands blow it. Most of the bands that blow it, blow it before they even play. They either kiss too much ass, or act like elitist dicks, or they get drunk and blow it.

I wasn't worried about my guys kissing ass, or being elitists. We weren't about that. I was worried about the booze factor. *The 4th Floor* liked the shots and beers. Lee, or Peter Cav, or even myself, might say or do something outrageous that might scare a record executive off. Especially Lee the bass player. He was the wild Australian. No need for the record labels to chat with a boozed up Lee or any *4th Floor* member until after we sign. I wanted our music to do the talking for us.

Monica suspiciously agreed.

That night we played an awesome three hour show. I didn't know if the record people showed or not.

When we were done Monica came up to me, "Hey, Kev! Guess what?"

"What?"

"You got offered a record deal!"

"No way! That's great!"

"There were two people here from a large independent. They have major label distribution. They stayed for most of the show. They are office people who have been up since 6am. They were here for over two hours having the time of their lives. They want to give you guys a deal!"

"Fuck Yeah!" I screamed.

I picked Monica up. I squeezed her so hard I thought I broke her. I knew her for two days. She changed my life forever.

In the metaphysical world it is said, "You are where you are supposed to be."

I thought, 'If it wasn't for that scumbag East Side club owner being a megalomaniac, we would've never been offered a record deal. That prick pissed us off. We said fuck off. And that led us to Monica and a contract. One door closes. Another one opens up.'

Every time I think of this story I count my blessings we left Big Red's club. I also count my blessing that we were a tight as hell machine of a band that had a club to go to after we left Big Red's place. If it wasn't for that we would've never met Monica on Brazilian night. If we never met Monica we wouldn't have had the record deal and all the future good things that would happen to us.

In the metaphysical world '*You are where you are supposed to be*'.

One door closes. Another one opens up!

Seven Reason Why
1996

CHAPTER 18

SEVEN REASON WHY 1996

Events That Led To Opening for Alice Cooper/Scorpions

A "Never say die performance where nothing is left behind or held back is the way my band *The 4th Floor* performed. Every show and every person in attendance was important. If the audience wasn't tired at the end of the show from cheering, head banging, dancing, singing, and fist pumping, we didn't do our jobs.

When I was in high school I played on the Madison Central football team alongside Captain Al another 4th Floor band member. Our coach was a hard ass from Yonkers, New York. His name was coach DeMarco

As my life went on I became grateful Coach DeMarco was a hard ass to us. But at the time I was on his team I wanted to slash the tires of his jalopy. His tough practices and disciplined routines had Madison Central always ranked in the top, not just in the state of New Jersey, but in America. We had a team saying, "Be The Best".

I took the "Be The Best" attitude with me to the stage. Hit hard, be in shape, write good songs, and leave nothing behind.

In July 1996 *The 4th Floor* had a record deal. Our album was complete. We were waiting for it to be released nationwide on October 8th. We were playing shows constantly.

Most of the Band lived above The Red Lion Pub on the corner of Bleecker and Thompson in Greenwich Village NYC. The phone rang one day. It was Stacy from the record label. She told me she got a call from the Ron Delsner group about us.

The Ron Delsner group was the biggest booking agent in the New York/New Jersey area. They booked all the arenas and best clubs. They handled a club called Mercury Lounge on Houston Street in downtown New York City a few blocks from *The 4th Floor's* Bleecker Street epicenter.

Stacey got right to the point, "The Delsner group just called. They asked if you guys can do a gig at the Mercury Lounge this Saturday."

"That's four days away," I said. "We have a gig at The Red Lion at 1am that night. What time do they want us to play?"

"They need you guys to start an hour set between 10:30 and 11 O'clock that night."

I thought a few seconds before I spoke.

"We could do the gig but we can't promote it. We have a show at the Limelight next week. It's not fair to them if we promote a show that just popped up a few days before theirs. We've been booked at The Limelight for months. Why are they asking on such short notice?"

"Because they'll be packed. They don't need you to draw. They have a sold out show at 9 O'clock. They want you guys to get on stage right after that show and keep the crowd in the house drinking. They heard about you guys. They said they need a band that will hold a crowd. They are offering two hundred bucks," Stacey said.

I could hear her shuffling papers around. She was at the Record Company's office.

"Yeah, we'll do it. We'll play until midnight. That will give us enough time to break down and get to The Red Lion for our 1am show."

The Mercury Lounge was about a ten minute walk from The Red Lion. A ten minute walk on a Saturday Night in New York City is a twenty minute cab ride. I knew we could walk back and forth to do both shows.

The few days passed until the Mercury Lounge show. It was a normal Saturday night in New York City. The streets were packed. People were happy.

We didn't have to carry much to the gig because Mercury Lounge had a back line. A back line is a drum set, a bass rig, and usually two guitar amps. Mercury Lounge was a prime club who knew how to run a show.

We met at our home base The Red Lion. We walked from there. Peter May, Marcello, and Lee had guitars on their backs. Kenny carried his snare drum in his hand and his cymbals on his back.

We arrived at the club about 9:30pm. There were fifty or sixty people out front trying to get in. Mercury Lounge was at capacity. No one was being let inside. The door guy knew us. He waved us over. We were escorted to a band room. There was a bucket of beers on ice waiting for us. We dove right in.

Lee the bass player exclaimed, "I'm going to check out the crowd mates."

I got a lump in my throat. If Lee, our true resident madman, went out of my sight before a gig I always became worried.

I watched Lee grab a beer and walk out of our dressing room. I blessed myself.

Lee self-appointed himself the band's representative to "check things out". Who knows what Lee will get into? There was nothing I could do except crack a beer from the ice bucket.

Five minutes past before Lee came back with his report, "There's no guys out there mates. It's packed with girls. Some of them are making out with each other and all sorts of stuff!"

"Really?" Everybody shouted as one.

"Really! Check it out!" Lee barked.

The entire band ran for the door knocking into each other to get out.

Sure enough Lee was right. There were maybe ten guys in the sold out crowd of hundreds.

I went over to the sound man. I stuck my hand out, "How ya doing. I'm Kev from *The 4th Floor*."

"I'm glad you guys are here. I heard about you guys. This is a great crowd. We'll get you guys up as fast as we can. We want to hold these people here drinking with you guys."

"No problem," I said. "What's with all the girls?"

"You didn't know who you were playing after? They're like the number one lesbian band in the world. They might be playing that Lilith Fair everyone is talking about."

There was a music tour called The Lilith Fair that was slated to begin later that year in September of 1996. It was a tour of feminine bands. It was the answer to the male dominated music tours like *Monsters of Rock, Lollapalooza,* and *Oz Fest.* It was founded by a singer songwriter named Sarah McLachlan. Even though I was a big macho rocker I liked Sarah McLachlan's music allot. Her album 'Fumbling Toward Ecstasy' I listened to it all the time along with Black Sabbath and Metallica. It was my girlfriend's CD. She played it all the time and I grew to love it.

At this point in *The 4th Floor's* history we had played

everywhere and anywhere. We played gay nights in the West Village, biker bars in Pennsylvania, Irish festivals, Woodstock reunions, ski lodges, metal shows, punk shows, and ska shows. We got along with everybody and all walks. Our album was titled, "We're All Good People, Except The Jerkoffs".

When I walked through this crowd I felt uneasy. The girls frowned and scowled at me. They turned their heads in a cold manner. I felt very unwanted. It was like a gathering of the "She-woman-man-haters club". Dejected, I went to the band room and the bucket of beers. The rest of the band followed feeling the frost too.

Peter May, the rhythm guitarist, was the first one to speak, "Dudes, I think we might eat it tonight. They despise men. They're going to hate us."

I wasn't going to listen to any of that negative stuff. I spoke, "Don't quit on this crowd. Remember the time we played in front of that hardcore punk crowd in Asbury Park? We thought they were going to hate us. Now they're regulars at our shows. We're going to rock this little rose pedal crowd into liking us."

"I don't know about this one," Lee said. "I asked, 'How ya doing?' to one of the girls. She called me a douche, told me to get away from her, and screamed for me to eat my own cock. She wanted me dead."

"That's the way most girls respond to a leering dude asking, 'How ya doing Shelia? You partying?'" I mimicked in an Australian accent.

Lee nodded his head in agreement.

I got into coach mode, "Let's not think about the hatred out there. Let's get ready to get on that stage as quick as possible and kick some ass! There are a few hundred people out there that are going to be our new fans. So let's get ready."

The other band's show stopped at 10:32pm. We grabbed our stuff and headed toward the stage. The other band had a small road crew and so did Mercury lounge. We were ready to play in twelve minutes. The entire crowd was still in the house when we hit our first note at 10:47. A sea of feminine energy stuffed the air. It was great.

Our opening song was called 'Sasquatch'. It's an epic chanting anthem about the mythical beast from the Northwest. It starts with Kenny slamming out a thunderous drum beat. Peter Cav on vocals does a high pitched, "Hey, Hey, Hey, Hey, Heyeeay! Followed by myself and Captain Al joining with guttural gang vocals, "Hey, Hey, Hey, Hey, Heyeeay!"

Marcello, Peter May, and Lee pounded on their guitars like tribal warriors. 'Sasquatch' never failed inciting people to jump around. It always lured strangers into our musical spell.

But not this time.

I saw the faces of every woman in the place fill with disgust. If they could've, they would've sprayed us with bullets. The mass exodus was on. You would have thought someone yelled, "Fire!"

The crowd herded itself to the door. It was as if they planned an orderly drill to get away from us. A drill they practiced. By the end of 'Sasquatch' - a four and a half minute song - the room was empty. The hundreds of people that were in the room at the beginning of the song were gone. Every one of them. They saw seven reasons why they were lesbians and they left.

The only people in the room were the soundman, three of our giggling girlfriends, our friend Jeff Larkin who thought it was hilarious we emptied the room, two angry waitresses, a few Mercury lounge staffers, and a drunk gay guy who was too bombed to get up from his seat.

The eyes of the guys in *The 4th Floor* wore of astonishment. Lee was laughing his ass off. Marcello didn't know what to think. Peter May said, "I told you they were gonna hate us."

Peter Cav got on the Mic, "Was it something we said?"

Kenny yelled out to me, "Let's get the fuck out of here. Go back to the Red Lion. Fuck this."

I stood silent for a second. I was overtaken by a humbling sensation. I thought about my High School football team's saying, "Be The Best".

I turned to the band, "We're getting paid to play this show. It's easy to play in front of a huge home crowd. Let's see what we're made of! I'm not going to die on this fucking stage right here tonight!" I shouted.

Captain Al, my High School football teammate, had the "Be the Best!" approach to life embedded in him too.

Al chimed in, his voice echoing in the empty room, "Fuck this! Let's see what we're made of *4th Floor*! Let's kick some ass! Kenny count us in!"

The next song was "Earthling". A song about the highs and lows of humanity living on our planet. We hit it hard and furious. We did the same for the next song, and the song after that, and the song after that, and the song after that, until our agreed hour set was done, and then we played more.

We played until 12:30. An hour and forty five minute set. The drunk gay guy woke up with a second wind. He started dancing around forty five minutes into the show. A few people came in during our performance but no one from the ex-crowd. It was a shame. They would have danced and had fun but they left.

The soundman came up to me after the show. He said it was a great performance. He also said he never saw an audience run out of a club as fast as the crowd did for us. We thanked him for the great sound he gave us for the show.

We packed up our stuff and walked to the Red Lion for our three hour 1am to 4am show. The drunk gay guy tagged along with us. I was never more proud of my band guys. They all played like we were in Madison Square Garden with a packed house.

We arrived back at the Red Lion three minutes before 1am. It felt good to get greeted by people who liked us. People who supported us. People who made us feel wanted. I was hugging fans like I was just pulled out alive from a mine collapse. It was nice. We started our show about 1:15am and played straight through until 4am. All tolled up that night we played four hours and thirty minutes. One of my favorite nights of my life.

A week and a half went by. The phone rang at our apartment above the Red Lion. I answered it, "Hello."

"I'm looking for Kevin from *The 4th Floor* band."

"This is Kevin."

"This is James from the Mercury Lounge and Ron Delsner's booking office. We want to know if *The 4th Floor* can play The Garden State Arts Center opening up for Alice Cooper and The Scorpions this Saturday August 4th."

"You are from the Mercury Lounge? We emptied that place. Nice try Larkin!" I hung up the phone.

The phone quickly rang again. There were no caller ID's in 1996. I answered it, "Hello."

"Kevin this is James from Ron Delsner's office."

"Blow it out your ass Jeff! Quit being a jerkoff!" I hung up the phone again.

Captain Al and I grew up with a guy named Jeff Larkin. He came to allot of our city shows. He would stay at our place when he did. He was at Mercury lounge the night we emptied it. He got the biggest kick out of it. Jeff was always prank calling our apartment and pulling tricks on myself and Al. I wasn't going to fall for any of that. I hung up on him.

Ten minutes later the phone rang again.

"Hello," I answered.

"Kevin this is Stacey."

Stacey our representative from the record label.

"What's up, Stacey?"

"Did you just hang up on Ron Delsner's office?"

"Ahh. Did I?" I mumbled.

"James from Ron Delsner's office just told me you hung up on him twice. That you told him to 'blow it out his ass!' He saw you guys at Mercury Lounge."

"We emptied the house over there. I never saw anything like it in my life. I thought he was my friend Jeff playing a joke on me."

"No! It was James from Ron Delsner's office. He said he saw you guys play like animals that night. And you guys were one of the best bands he'd ever seen. He said you guys got better when everybody left. He said it was a great show. They have an opening spot in front of Alice Cooper and The Scorpions this Saturday at the Garden State Arts Center in New Jersey."

"Really?"

"The band that was supposed to open the show had to back out. The Delsner group wants *The 4th Floor* to do the slot and open up the show."

"Holy Shit! Fuck yeah! We'll do it. Call him right back. Tell him I thought it was a joke. I won't hang up on him."

"Ok," Stacey said. "Stay by the phone. I'm calling him now."

I hung up the phone. I was amazed at what I had just heard. James called back. I apologized for hanging up on him. He was very nice and complimentary.

"I was at the Mercury Lounge show," James said. "We shouldn't have teamed you guys up with the most effeminate band in the world. It was a bad match. But you guys didn't get fazed, or frazzled, and you played in front of basically no one as hard as you could for almost two hours. It was amazing. I know you guys will go over big with the Alice Cooper and Scorpions crowd. You only have to play for thirty minutes."

"Of course we'll do it! Thanks for the opportunity," I said.

"Don't thank me. Thank yourselves. You guys deserve it," James replied.

I hung up the phone. I ran around the Village looking for my band guys to tell them the good news. We did the show on Saturday, August 4th 1996 at the Garden State Arts Center (now PNC Bank Center) in Holmdel, New Jersey with a capacity of 17,000 people. The bill was The 4th Floor, Alice Cooper, and The Scorpions. We also played our 1am to 4am slot at the Red Lion that night. It always pays to go out and "Be the Best".

The Phone Call Day 1996

CHAPTER 19

THE PHONE CALL DAY 1996

Finding out about opening for KISS

In 1996, New York City was evolving from an untidy 'Free for all' to a stroller friendly welcome center. Rudy Giuliani was heading toward his second term as Mayor. My band, *The 4th Floor* had a major record deal and was performing all over New York City and the North East Coast; from Portland Maine to Philadelphia Pennsylvania.

I was living above the Red Lion Pub on the corner of Bleecker and Thompson Streets in Greenwich Village. My apartment was on the second floor right above the bar. If I cut a hole through my bedroom floor I would fall onto The Red Lion stage.

Five out of seven *4th Floor* members lived in that same building. I had two living with me in my apartment. Two more living in apartments above mine. The other two band mates were a few blocks away. It was a great time. We were on a great run.

The 4th Floor headlined every Friday and Saturday night at the Red Lion. My commute to the stage from my bed was 37 seconds. Our shows started at 1am and finished at 4am. The place was always packed.

Through hard work, an ignorance that the impossible can't be done, and practicing our craft was surmounting into favorable events for *The 4th Floor* band this day. The phone rang. I answered.

"Hello!"

"Kevin, its Stacey. I have great news for you."

Stacey was the A&R Rep from our record label. An A&R Rep is the link between the recording artist and the record company. A&R people help with the development of a band. We all loved Stacey. She was our number one supporter.

"Oh yeah! Good news?" I asked.

"Bobby Held got you guys an opening slot on KISS's reunion tour. You guys are going to do the Northeast leg!"

I paused for a second. Bobby Held was our record producer. It was two in the afternoon. We played the night before. We didn't get home until after 5am. Band guys were asleep all over the apartment.

When I was a kid I watched a cartoon called "Peter Potamus and His Magic Flying Balloon". Peter Potamus was a hippopotamus that would go on adventures with a little monkey friend. Peter Potamus would let out "The Hippo Hurricane Holler" whenever he was in trouble. The holler was so loud Peter Potamus's enemies would get blown away like a giant turbine jet engine was screaming on them.

Hearing the KISS news. I decided it was time for a recreation of the "Hippo Hurricane Holler".

"Whaaaaaaaaaaaaaaaaaaaaaaaaaaaaaaaaaaaaaaaaaaaaaaaa! Who

ooooooooooooooooooooooooooooooooooooooooooooooooooo
oo!Weeeeeeeeeeeeeeeeeeeeeee!"

I ran out of breath. I took in another deep inhale. I let
out another "Hippo Hurricane Holler".

"Waaaaaaaaaaaaaaaaaaaaaaaaaaaaaaaaaaaaaaaaaaaa!
Whooooooooooooooooooooo!   Weeeeeeeeeeeeeeeeeeee!

I could hear Stacey laughing.

"Stacey can I call you back later. I got to tell the guys."

"Sure. Don't go too Crazy Kevin, " Stacey said, stern.

I was laughing uncontrollably. Stacey knew me well.

"Ok. I'll behave. Talk to you later. Thanks Stacey!"

I hung up.

Peter May, guitarist, was an anomaly.

He was hung over lying on the floor.

He grumbled low, "Dude, what is wrong with you?"

He threw a half full beer can at me.

"Why you screaming like that? Man!"

Captain Al, another singer in the band, was asleep in
his room. I kicked his door in. He rolled over pissed off, "What
the fuck man! I heard you screaming! Why you screaming? Are
you a dick!?"

"We are going on the road with KISS Mutherfucker!
Wake up all you Bitches!" I screamed.

I grabbed a broken guitar that had been propped
against the kitchen wall for a year waiting for Peter May to fix. I
ran into my bedroom. I started banging the busted guitar on the
ceiling.

Kenny our drummer lived right above my bedroom. I
could hear him rustling after a few hard bangs. I put a small hole
in the ceiling. Plaster dust fell into my mouth.

I screamed again, "Wake the fuck up everybody!"

I ran out toward Peter May. He was standing with
a broken mic stand in his hand. He was supposed to fix it two

years earlier. He looked like he meant business. He wanted to hit me.

"Come over here!" Peter May yelled.

"Stacey just called. We're going to open up for KISS!" I hopped around like a contestant on the "Price Is Right".

Peter May was puzzled, "What? How? No way," he questioned. His rage calming down.

Peter May's face changed from anger-filled to astonishment, then to glee filled. He threw the broken mic stand aside.

Peter gave his best version of the "Hippo Hurricane Holler", "WhaaaaaaaWhooooooo!"

He began to cough and choke. He was a big smoker.

I decided to smash the busted guitar on the floor like Pete Townshend from The Who. The guitar didn't break. Peter May ripped the guitar from my hands.

"Give me that! I'll show you how's it's done," he said.

Peter May raised the guitar over his head. He swung it toward the floor smashing it into a million pieces.

We both screamed, "Fuck Yeah!"

I ran to my bedroom. I went out the window onto the fire escape above Bleecker Street. I rocketed up to Kenny the drummer's room right above mine.

I looked in the window. Kenny was lying spread eagle in his underwear. He was groggy. He was semi-awake. He heard all the "Hippo Hurricane Hollers", the hooting, the hollering, the banging, and the guitar smashing.

I open palm pounded on his window. He waved for me to go away.

The window was cracked opened. I pulled it up. I crawled in like a cat burglar. Kenny wasn't happy. Kenny started screaming.

"What the fuck! You're an asshole, man! What is wrong with you!"

"Wake up douche! Stacey just called. We're gonna be opening up for KISS!

Kenny didn't say anything. His face became perplexed. He was in disbelief. He looked at me with suspicion.

"What! No way. How did that happen?

"Bobby Held set it up somehow."

"Really?" Kenny questioned. Still in disbelief.

"Really! No joke bloke. Get ready to kick ass!" I yelled back.

Kenny jumped up from his mattress on the floor. He was in his tighty whities. He started dancing around. I started dancing around too. We were jumping up and down hugging each other when I realized I could feel his mule on my leg through his tighty whities. I was wearing boxer shorts. My legs were exposed. Kenny's mule was rubbing on my left thigh. I pushed him away like we were about to fight.

"Get off me! I just felt your mule! I'm gonna puke!"

"Fuck that! You're the one that busted in here. It's good you felt my mule. You deserve it," Kenny shot back, "Let's go tell Peter Cav the news."

"That I just felt your mule? I'm not telling him that!"" I barked disgusted.

"No dickhead! I don't want to tell anybody bout that either! Let's tell him about KISS."

Peter Cavanagh lived in the back of the building two floors up. Kenny and I rushed into the hallway forgetting we were in our underwear. The tenants of the building knew us. They were used to our shenanigans. Nobody was in the hallway anyway. We sprinted up the two floors. We banged on Peter Cav's door. I could hear muffled yelling coming from inside, "Go away! I just went to sleep! Assholes!"

"Open up man! It's Kev and Kenny!" I screamed.

"Go away! Don't be dicks!" Peter Cav yelled back, growing angrier.

I heard a door on the floor below open up. It was Anthony a twelve year old kid from the building. He looked up the stairs. He saw me and Kenny in our underwear. He started laughing, "You guys are in your underwear."

Anthony's father knew us. He poked his face out of the doorway. He saw us in our underwear. He was pissed. He pulled Anthony inside, "Come on Kev and Kenny. My kid don't need to see you prancing around the building in your skivvies!"

"Sorry man! We just found out we're gonna be opening for KISS. We got a little carried away. We want to tell Peter Cav," I replied, turning red faced.

Anthony's father shook his head. He stepped inside. He slammed his door. Just as his door slammed closed, Peter Cav's door swung open. He was in his tighty whities, "What did you say? We're going to be opening up for KISS!"

"Yep," I said, "Stacey just called. She told me Bobby got us on the tour somehow!"

Peter jumped on Kenny and me. We were in the hallway of 205 Thompson Street, on the corner of Bleecker Street, jumping up and down like we just won the Super Bowl in the last second. I didn't even care that Kenny and Peter Cav's mules were grazing my leg through their tighty whities.

We went down to the Red Lion to start celebrating. We did put our clothes on. We called Lee and Marcello. They didn't answer their phones. We kept leaving messages with unholy vitriol until they picked up. Soon they were at the Red Lion with us drinking. The entire band was filled with happiness and on our way to open for KISS. A Great Day To Be Alive!

20

Opening For Kiss December 28th, 1996

CHAPTER 20

OPENING FOR KISS DECEMBER 28th, 1996

It was December 28th 1996, our first day on the KISS tour. It also was my birthday.

KISS, the legendary face painted band with such hits as *'I want To Rock N' Roll All Night And Party Every Day'* and *'Beth'* had asked us to open up the last week of the 1996 tour. We arrived at The Centrum in Worcester, Massachusetts at 2pm for load in. We received our credentials and were walked toward the monstrous KISS stage.

Everyone in the band was so excited until we were stopped by a big guy dressed military, but rock n roll. He looked like a biker Louis Gossett Jr. from the "An Officer and a Gentleman" movie. You could tell this guy was tough. He was very confident.

He introduced himself, "I'm the head of security for

168

KISS and we don't tolerate any crap! Who works at The Lion's Den Club on Sullivan Street?"

Not expecting that question we all looked at each other. Peter Cav, Captain Al, Bryan the soundman, and myself raised our hands bewildered and slow. All four of us worked at The Lion's Den. I thought, 'Why is he asking this?'

"You guys know Ace? Right?"

In a simultaneous shrug we responded, "Yes" and "No".

We knew that Ace was the lead guitar player for KISS. None of us personally knew the guy though.

I thought, 'Ace might know our faces from the Lion's Den where he occasional hung out. But I doubted it'.

Deadpan, I answered, "No. We don't know him. We are not friends with him. If that's what you're asking."

Once in a while Ace drank at The Lion's Den. He would come around for Jerry Adams Monday Metal Nights, like many rock stars.

We never bothered celebrities at The Lion's Den. As long as they had money on the bar and didn't act like jerkoffs, we never cared what they did. Ace and his crew all knew how to handle their business. They were always cool.

The Security Guy continued, "I know what goes on at your club. I know Ace knows you guys are here. There are four more shows remaining on this tour. Ace has been sober the entire time of this run. I heard how wild your shows can get. I know you guys are rowdy. Listen to me! You give out any rowdy stuff! You are instantly thrown off the tour."

We all stood astonished. The only time *The 4th Floor* band ever stood in any kind of order was when we were on the side of a Highway stopped by the cops. Like a drill Sergeant Kiss's giant Security guy started laying into us.

"*The 4th Floor*, Huh! I heard about you guys. You guys are from New York City, right? From Bleecker Street in the Village, right?"

We all nodded, "Yes."

He spoke louder, "If Ace comes into your dressing room and you let him have anything like weed, or coke, or beer, or booze, or even a fucking cough drop! You guys will be waltzed out of here on the spot. I heard how rowdy you guys can get. You give out any of that rowdy stuff and you are gone! You got me!?"

The entire *4th Floor* band again nodded affirmative.

The Security Guy was right. We were a rowdy band. We were sponsored by Bass Ale. We had two kegs of it in our van. Thank God we decided to leave the kegs in the vehicle and check out the lay of the land before we wheeled them in the arena. I can only imagine "The baby" this guy would've had seeing us gleefully rolling two kegs of beer into our dressing room.

Unbeknownst to everybody, except Captain Al, I had a case of beer in the roll-able suitcase that was in my hand. I was glad the Security guy didn't hear the clanging aluminum when I was dragging it around. He continued to berate us. We took it like first day recruits at boot camp.

"If Ace comes into your dressing room and asks for alcohol, or whatever else you guys might have. And, you give it to him. You guys are out on the spot. So, you better watch it! Cause, I'm watching it!"

I couldn't believe Ace would come to our dressing room. We weren't buddies at all. The news of Ace having to be sober for the tour was in all the music magazines. A scenario started to become clear to me why we were getting the anti-Ace booze speech

KISS was a New York City band like us. Allot of the late night New York City club crowd I was friends with; were also friends with Ace. Someone I know must have told Ace the guys from The Lion's Den, a place he had partied hard at many times, were opening up for him the last four shows.

I spoke back with caution, "We won't let him have anything. I promise. We don't want to be kicked out of here."

"Another thing," the Security Guy continued. "There are a lot of fans who have their young kids with them. So there are seven, eight, nine, and ten year olds out there. If you guys say one curse on stage. You are fucking gone! I had a band that was getting booed hard. They started cursing back at the crowd. We got a lot of complaints from parents asking for refunds. That band was thrown off the tour on the spot. So keep it clean or you're gone! You got it!?"

We all nodded, "Yes Sir."

The Security Guy burned a fierce silent stare into our souls for a few seconds. He turned and walked away. The entire band looked at each other. Lee, in his crocodile Dundee accent spoke first, "I guess we can't bring the kegs in now mates, huh?"

"No way," I said.

"Well what we gonna do now? We got no beer!" Lee continued.

"I packed a case of beer in this suitcase. We are good for a while. We just got to watch out for Ace. Sasha you got to be the lookout."

Sasha was our friend from another band called Yowsa. He asked to be our roadie for the KISS tour. He was from Yugoslavia. He was a great guy and he always hung around with us.

We started walking toward our dressing room. We were all a little timid after the scolding we just received from the head of security. Our sound engineer Bryan had a long head of blonde hair. He looked like he could've been in Motley Crue in 1985. We walked past a few roadies standing by giant amps. I saw their eyes light up.

"Hey Bryan! What's up? What you doing here?" The tallest roadie asked.

"I'm running sound for tonight's opener *The 4th Floor*," Bryan answered. He was gang hugged by three road crew guys.

I realized Bryan knew most of KISS's roadies. A welcome relief after getting hollered at by the head of security. Bryan knew KISS's sound engineer as well. They were old pals and worked together in the 80's on the road. This was good news. We weren't going to be treated like a bar band, which we were at the time. We were taken to our dressing room. It was the locker room for the visiting hockey teams to the Worchester Centrum.

I gathered everybody around and spoke, "We go on at 8pm. That's over five hours from now. Let's not start drinking until 6pm. We don't want to get too fucked up! Ok?"

All the guys agreed.

The Louis Gossett Jr. Security Guy heard right. We were a hard partying band. We could always handle it though. There were no pussies amongst us. We always showed up on time. We always rocked the house.

It was a Godsend to have gotten the no cursing speech from that security guy. I always let F-bombs rip. So did Captain Al and Peter Cav. I was glad we were warned. Most definite an F-bomb would have been shouted in some sort of merry filled rock-n-roll statement like, "Fuck yeah! You guys Fucking rule!" or "This is Fucking great to Fucking see all you Fucking people!" or "Fuck all right! You Fucking guys Fucking rock! Fuck Yeah!"

There was a 100% chance of F-Bombs. I was so glad to be warned. That warning saved us.

Peter May spoke, "Dudes let's get some food. It's free."

One good thing about being on a big tour is craft services. Craft services is the food that is provided for the crew and band members. We had time to kill. We decided to check it out.

When we got there Lee's eyes bugged out. He whispered out loud, "It's a candy land mates."

There was a carving station with roast beef, there was *chicken* franchisee, mashed potatoes, lasagna, and cold cuts of all kinds. The entire bands eyes lit up like we were just released from a North Korean prison camp and stumbled upon an all-you-can-eat buffet.

I looked around. Road crew guys were eating and talking at perfectly lined foldup tables. There was a desert station. There were a bunch of good looking women at a table to the far right of the room.

Bryan wasn't with us. He was out at the sound board working with KISS's crew. We sat at an empty table to the far left of the room. After a few minutes I noticed someone was missing. I had the entire band with me. Bryan was on stage. Who was missing? It was Sasha.

I asked Peter Cav, "Where is Sasha?"

He shrugged his shoulders, "I don't know?"

We all looked around. I saw him walk in with us.

In a horrified voice Peter May pointed as he spoke, "Oh no Dudes! Look where he is!"

I turned to look. Sasha was standing at the table of pretty women. You could tell the ladies didn't want to be bothered with anybody. Peter Cav jumped up and with an invisible rush sauntered over to Sasha whispering in his ear. I don't know what he said but Sasha walked away immediately.

We had no idea who those ladies were. They could be KISS's wives, or the promoter's sisters, or the road crew's girls, or police mistresses. One thing was for certain, they were somebody important's women and Sasha was about to start his shtick on them. Lucky for us Peter May spotted him before any major damage was done.

Back at our table Peter Cav started giving it to Sasha.

"What the fuck is wrong with you! They're watching us! They think we're rowdy. We're being watched. What if they are KISS's girls? You heard that guy yell at us."

The whole band nodded their heads in solidarity. Except Lee, he thought it was hilarious. He was giggling and cackling like a hyena over his prime rib.

Sasha was getting paid to be our roadie. Beside helping us lug our gear around we needed him to stand in front of the door while we drank and keep an eye out for Ace Frehley. It was his job.

We all ate like animals then headed back to our dressing room.

At 4 O'clock we were called to the stage for sound check. Our gear was set up perfect. Bryan was worth his weight in gold. Kenny made a few adjustments to his drums. Lee, Peter May, and Marcello plugged in to get their sounds. It was amazing to be on that stage. The giant KISS logo beaming over us like a full moon on a clear night.

Kenny's kit was set up in front of Peter Criss's drums. Marcello and Lee were set up in front of Ace Frehley's and Gene Simmons' massive guitar cabinets. Peter May was set up in front of Paul Stanley's massive guitar amps. My mic stand was stage left, Peter Cav's center, Captain Al's stage right.

I noticed the lyrics to 'Detroit Rock City' taped to the floor in front of my mic. The soundman, who mixes the monitors on stage, noticed me looking at them.

He made a crack, "Don't be ripping up my tape job now."

He knew Bryan. He said it smiling.

"No, I won't," I said. "They still need cheat sheets after twenty years of singing these songs?"

"These guys play a lot of shows. Sometimes they decide to play a song they haven't done in a while. Sometimes the miles and countless shows takes a toll on a man's memory. In my opinion these guys could do whatever they want. They put on a great show. They give a shit about their fans. They always give it their all and they leave nothing behind. If KISS wants the whole set taped on the floor. That's my job. I'll happily do it. You'll see when you get older."

He was right. Taping lyrics to the stage has been part of my routine to this day. I never forgot what that monitor guy said to me. Not about the lyric taping but about KISS giving a shit about the show they put on for their fans. I always gave one hundred and ten percent when I performed even before that talk. I learned that from my high school football days. But the never ending caring to give fans the best, no matter what, was great to witness and melt into my mind.

On the very rare day I might not have been feeling it, I always thought about what that monitor guy saying, "KISS leaves nothing behind. I see it every night."

That statement got me through some flu stricken shows over the years.

It was time for us to sound check. We were ready to blast. Bryan spoke over the monitor speakers from the sound booth in the middle of the arena, "You guys ready?"

"Yep!" I replied.

Hearing my voice throughout the eighteen thousand seat empty arena was an awesome feeling. Kenny counted us in 1,2,3,4. We kicked in with 'Sasquatch'.

Hearing 'Sasquatch' through the massive KISS sound system was a trip. It felt like a jet plane taking off. We were so happy. We were so tight. We had played at least three to four shows a week for the past two years. Our weekend shows were three hours long. It made us very tight as a band. We knew each other like supernatural science on stage. We read each other's thoughts.

I could see the road crew banging their heads. They were very accepting to us. Thank God for Bryan doing sound.

After sound check we went back to our dressing room. A few of the road crew guys came to visit with Bryan. We got to know them.

"What time does Ace get here?" I asked the tall roadie.

"He gets here a few hours before the show to put his makeup on. He should be here soon," he replied.

Most of my *4th Floor* guys were drinking already. It was just after 4:30pm. None of them could wait until six. I wasn't worried about any of my guys drinking. I was worried about Ace drinking.

"Sasha you got to post up out front of the dressing room door. You need to be our lookout. You are getting paid to be here. So you got to do it."

I walked with Sasha out the door.

"Sasha, if you see Ace heading our way, come in and warn us."

I walked back into the dressing room where Lee found three steel buckets. They looked like they came from the corners of a boxing ring. The kind a fighter would spit in between rounds. I had no idea what these buckets were used for. Hockey players bloody teeth, maybe? Lee rinsed them out and filled them with beer. Peter May went in search for ice.

We had to Ace proof the room. I put the buckets in lockers at the farthest place from the front door. I grabbed a bunch of coffee cups earlier from craft services. I handed a cup to each guy. I gathered everybody around.

"Don't drink from a can. Pour your beer and booze into a coffee cup. If Ace comes in, talk about how good the coffee is in Massachusetts. Ok? We are going to have an Ace fire drill right now."

All left eyebrows in the room got raised in a questioning manner.

"What's an Ace fire drill?" Everybody asked.

"I'll show you. Lee go over to the door and say 'Ace is coming'."

Lee went to the door cackling and giggling. He sounded like a diabolical pirate. He looked out the door snickering. His eyes bugged out of their sockets instantly as he peered out. He spoke fast and nervous in a loud whispered scream, "Ace is coming! He's right there! I'm not kidding. This is not a drill."

I thought, 'Man, Lee is a great actor'.

"This is no joke, Kev! He's coming," Lee whispered.

"For real?" I questioned, filled with sarcasm.

"For real, Kev."

Lee look stunned. He was always laughing. This was the first time I ever saw him not laughing. I could tell he wasn't joking.

"What the fuck! Where is Sasha?" I barked.

Lee looked around outside the door. He saw Sasha.

"Shit! He is talking to a girl dressed as a pretzel. Fuck Mates! Sasha's chatting up the pretzel girl!" Lee reported back.

"Are you serious?" I whispered.

"I'm serious! Ace is coming this way!"

"Dammit! Everybody chug!" I shouted.

We all started pounding our shots and beers down. I threw coats over two of the beer buckets in the locker. I looked for something to throw over the third. Nothing was handy. In a panic I took off my shirt. I threw it over the third bucket.

Peter Cav threw guitar cases over the garbage bin that held the empty beer cans and pint bottles. We tried to hide any evidence of drinking. Everybody ran around looking for stray cans and bottles. It was a mad scurry.

Figuring the best defense is a good offense. I stepped outside the dressing room. Lee was right. Ace was heading right at us and Sasha was chatting up a girl in a pretzel outfit. I popped my head back inside.

"Ace is coming! Make sure everything is out of sight!"

I pulled my head back outside. I needed to make up an excuse for Ace not to come inside. I had to do it quick. I didn't want him rummaging around our dressing room like a hungry grizzly bear. Fast thinking I came up with, 'A band member shit himself and the room stinks'.

I stood shirtless in front of the dressing room blocking the way in. I could hear moving guitar cases and the clamor of empty beer cans being thrown. Ace was fifty feet away, forty feet away, thirty feet away, twenty feet away, ten feet away, five, four, three, two, and one. Ace was right on me. I took a deep breath ready to begin the shit story. I was about to speak but Ace spoke first. He looked me right in the eye.

"How you doing, man?"

"I'm good Ace. How are you?"

"I'm good. Thanks for asking!"

"Ahh... One of our band members had an accident..."

Ace didn't notice me talking. He never broke his stride. He walked right past me. I stopped the nonsensical shit story. I was now looking at Ace's back moving away from me. Absolute relief and joy over took my body.

Ace had no idea I was one of the guys who let him do whatever he wanted at The Lion's Den in New York City. I was just some shirtless guy in the middle of the winter hanging out in bowels of the Worcester Centrum. We were safe - for the moment.

I waved Sasha over as the pretzel girl handed him a napkin.

As a roadie Sash might not have been a great choice. He was a great front man from a great Bleecker Street group. The entire 4th Floor band was guilty of letting him talk us into letting him work the tour. We all loved Sasha.

He walked over smiling while looking at the number.

"Come on man! You're supposed to watch the door." I snapped.

"I was watching the door. I was watching for Ace. I saw you see Ace. Ace walked by. No problem," Sasha said in a halting Eastern European accent.

"There's three hours before we go on. Ace is still lurking around. You can't let up! Keep an eye out Sash. There's a long way to go."

I walked back in the dressing room.

Delighted that Ace walked by, I spoke, "Drink up boys! He's gone for now."

Everybody pulled their drinks from their hiding spots and started sipping.

Things were going smooth an hour before the show. Ace was nowhere to be seen, yet. We all took turns looking out to give Sasha a break.

I had gotten tickets for the show for my friend Wayno Draino and his wife Sharon as a wedding present. They were on their honeymoon in the mountains of western Massachusetts. They were visiting us back stage. I asked Wayno if I could look at his ticket. I wanted to see our name along with KISS's. The ticket read, 'Kiss December 28, 1996 Worcester Centrum Arena Showtime 8pm'. We were not on the ticket.

I thought, 'We're screwed!'

People are going to think KISS is on at 8pm. The place is going to be filled to capacity when we take the stage. The audience is going to be pissed to see us and not KISS.

I decided to keep the news quiet.

Ten minutes before show time the stage manager came to get us. I could hear the roar of the crowd. Drunk Massachusetts people were screaming for KISS. We walked through the underbelly of the arena past roadies and photographers. The photographers started snapping away not even knowing who we were. Adrenaline flowed through my veins.

Three minutes before show time we were behind the backstage curtain. I could see the crowd past the giant KISS sign. The arena was packed. Not an empty seat. I knew everybody thought KISS was coming on at 8pm. That's what the ticket said. If it said 'The 4th Floor' at 8pm. The arena would be half full. The people of Massachusetts would still be drinking in their cars or the local bars of Worcester. Nobody cares about an unknown opener from New York City in Worcester, Massachusetts.

We had played Boston many times before this show. The Rathskeller, the CBGB's of Boston, was a great place. We also played Mama Kin's, the club partly owned by Aerosmith. Mama Kin's was on the other side of the "Green Monster', the giant left field wall at Fenway Park, where The Boston Red Sox played.

The first time we played Mama Kin's we were scheduled for 11pm. The crowd in the club was light at 10pm. Nobody cared about us.

That night the Red Sox were home. They lost a game that ended at 10:15pm. By 10:30pm the club started filling up. By 11pm you couldn't move in Mama Kin's. The crowd wasn't there to see us. They were drunk pissed off Red Sox fans looking for a beer after a loss.

The MC introduced us, "From New York City! The 4th Floor."

We were booed automatic. The never ending fued between Boston and New York City. We did what we did and won the crowd over in the end. It was great.

We always went over well in Boston and in New England. It was always the same thing. First walk in, nobody gives a crap about us. It happened in Providence, Rhode Island. It happened in Portland, Maine. It happened every first gig we ever played in any town. Once we hit the stage we won them over. The next time we went to that town we were always greeted with open arms.

On the club scale we would use tricks like telling funny f-bomb laced stories, drinking shots with the crowd, and heavy tipping the bartender before we go on. Those tricks always help win a crowd. But it was the performance that eventually won the people over.

We couldn't use any f-bomb laced stories or club tricks on this KISS arena level. There were no bartenders to pay off to help get the crowd on our side.

We were about to walk plank in Worcester.

My guys were happy at this second. They didn't know about not being on the ticket. There was no reason for the entire band to be worried. Worry does nothing. The onslaught of hatred we were about to receive was inevitable. No need for everybody to dwell on it.

At one minute to 8pm the house lights were clicked off bringing an enormous roar from the crowd. The roar was tremendous. All my guys started to get pumped.

We were herded to the side of the stage.

When we got to the bottom of the stairs to go up on stage the cheers turned to jeers. People saw us. They quickly realized there was an opener.

The entire arena started booing. There were a couple hundred people within thirty feet of us screaming like we murdered their children with our bare hands.

"Fuck you! We want KISS! Go home assholes! You fucking suck! Go home! We want KISS!"

Two big fat drunk guys were leaning over the hockey boards giving me the finger. They were less than two feet from my face. My instinct was to throw a punch. I thought about the security guy's lecture. I held my fist. I didn't want to get thrown off the tour before we even stepped one foot on stage.

I looked at my guys faces. They were perplexed. Except for Lee and Captain Al, they were laughing. People were yelling obscenities. I decided it was time for a speech.

I called my guys in for a huddle. All seven of our heads were inches from each other. I spoke, barely audible, through the taunts, jeers, and boos.

"Peter Cav, when we go up there get right on the mic and say, 'We would like to thank Gene, Paul, Peter, and Ace for giving us the opportunity to open for them'."

I knew saying the names of KISS band members would get cheers. The crowd would stop booing for the eight seconds it took Peter Cav to say them all.

I continued, "When Peter's done talking. Immediately come in with the first note of 'Sasquatch'. Got it?"

Everyone nodded. The stage manager yelled at us to get on stage. I kept talking.

"Listen, we're going to win this crowd over. Fuck this! We are here for a reason. Because we kick ass! Remember playing those dives in Jersey and Pennsylvania opening for the local band that knew everybody in the town. Those crowds hated us before we ever even played. They looked at us like competition for their friend's band. We are not competition! We are here to give! Did we always win every crowd over by kicking ass and rocking!? Yes! We fucking did! Those gigs were harder than this one! Now let's go and murder this crowd!"

Rage red the faces of *The 4th Floor* turned. We rushed up on stage. Peter Cav went right for his mic. Eighteen thousand people were booing with no mercy. The boos were filled with hate. Peter Cav spoke into the Mic.

"What's up Massachusetts?"

"Fuck you! Get off the stage asshole!" Was screamed from all angles.

"We would like to thank Gene..." Peter Cav shouted.

The angry boos in an instant turned to a giant happy roar.

"Paul..."

The crowd got louder, cheering.

"Peter..."

Still the crowd cheers grew louder.

"And Ace..."

Eighteen thousand people cheered like they each won a new car.

"We would like to thank all the members of KISS for giving us this opportunity to open for them."

The band hit the first note in perfect time like a giant thunder ball. Homage to the years of playing together. We were off.

Only once in the hundreds of times we play 'Sasquatch' did it not go over. I watched the crowd as I grunted into the mic. They wanted to start booing but they didn't. They were bopping. They were digging us.

We sing three man gang vocals in the beginning of 'Sasquatch'. Kenny's drum beat makes people move even if they don't want to. 'Sasquatch' is a song steeped in human nature. Lee, Marcello, and Peter May are an in-sync wall of sound. Peter Cav sings a high pitch tone that brings the crowd to its feet.

At one minute into 'Sasquatch' most of the crowd were bopping with us. Others wanted to join in, but they fought themselves out of the unwritten code of not being accepting to KISS openers.

At three minutes into 'Sasquatch' we were winning the crowd. The middle fingers were pretty much all gone. A few lingering ones were scattered about the arena. We had almost the whole place on our side. The test would be when we finish 'Sasquatch'. Will they boo? Will they cheer?

We always made sure that between songs there wasn't much dead air. The last note of 'Sasquatch' was hit. It rang through the arena. The crowd was silent. I couldn't believe it. Total silence. No booing. No cheering. Nothing but silence. Four minutes earlier it was so loud with booing, taunts and hate filled jeers you couldn't hear the guy two feet away. Now it was as silent as a library. I thought, 'With this silence... We might win the crowd'.

This Massachusetts crowd didn't know how to react to

not hating us. They didn't want to clap. But they weren't booing. They did nothing. I considered that a victory. I didn't want
to take the non-boos for granted. We had twenty five minutes
and six more songs to go. Anything could happen.

Peter May turned to Kenny. He gave him the eyes.
POW, 'Earthling' the next song was pounded in perfect time.
Total time between 'Sasquatch' and 'Earthling' 1.5 seconds.

The riff of 'Earthling' was another automatic head bob-
ber.

It was a song about, 'Why doesn't all of Earth get together and get along'.

Musically we had the same message as KISS, which was
to *Rock n' Roll All Day and Party Every Night*.

It was my turn to sing lead. Peter Cav and I went every
other song for the KISS short set. I began to sing and stalk the
giant stage. The crowd was still on our side. I was in great stage
shape. I learned earlier in the year opening up for Alice Cooper
that you needed to be in shape for the bigger stage.

We all learned allot from doing the Alice Cooper show.
We were used to small club stages and New York City Irish
bars. These arena shows you need to cover allot more space.

We had a while to prepare for this tour. I worked out
like I was training to make The New York Giants.

I ran around the KISS stage like a rabid raccoon trying
to figure out a way to escape some family's garage. The crowd
was bopping. I finished the lyrics to the second verse. It was
time for the lead guitar section where Marcello showed his
chops. He began wailing.

I moshed - arms flailing - to the middle of the stage.
Things were great. We were winning the crowd. I looked up. I
didn't see any middle fingers in the upper deck. It was magnifi-
cent. Things were great. Until, I looked down at the front row.

I said to myself, "Fuck!"

Like an illuminating beacon, two enraged guys were

screaming at me. They stood upright, extending their middle fingers as high as they possibly could. They were in the best seats. They strained their muscles pushing their vulgar gesture at me.

"Fuck you! You suck! We want KISS! You suck!" They yelled looking me dead in my eyes.

All eighteen thousand people saw these two guys. You couldn't miss them. They were front row and center. There was a spotlight coming from the back of the arena. It silhouetted their middle fingers onto the giant KISS logo behind Kenny's drum kit.

I looked down at these two guys. They both waved their middle fingers harder now they had eye contact with me. They shoved them toward my face with all their might and hatred. They were looking me dead in the eye shouting, "You suck! You fucking suck! Go Home!"

My New York City hardcore/punk club instinct took over my body. Without hesitation, I lunged off the stage. I didn't think at all.

I just reacted.

I snapped.

And an automatic regret filled my being.

I was now ten feet in the air flying at the guys with the best seats in the house.

We had done hundreds of shows. Some of them were in rough spots. Once in a while we had a brawl.

One million thoughts went through my brain as I floated toward the arena's floor. My body was in suspended animation. My mind raced. I heard the security's guy's voice ring in between my ears.

"I heard you guys were rowdy. You give out any rowdy stuff! You are instantly thrown off the tour!"

I couldn't defy gravity like Lee. I couldn't be bungee corded back on stage. I was in full commit with my snap. It was our second song and we were going to be thrown off the tour. The last thought I had before hitting the ground was, 'I hope these guys are pussies'.

I landed on my feet like superman from the ten foot jump. I crouched down as I hit to lighten the impact and not break my leg. I popped up quick and stood straight. I was taller than these two guys. I still had the mic in my left hand. I shuffled the two feet to be right on the angry KISS fans.

I was face to face with them now. I saw the utmost fear overtake their eyes. Their middle fingers were put down and at their sides. It was like they were standing at attention.

I spoke into the mic for the eighteen thousand people to hear, "You two guys have something you want to say to me?"

The guys were terrified. Their jaws dropped to the basement of the arena. They were quivering. Marcello was wailing out his lead. The band was rocking hard. I held the mic in their faces waiting for a response like a news reporter. They didn't answer. I spoke into the mic again.

"Well, do you?"

I shoved the mic back in their faces.

"No," they both stuttered on the one syllable word. I put the mic back to my mouth.

"Well than! Do you want to sing with me?" I asked.

Their voices quivered as they replied in unison for the entire arena to hear, "We don't know the words."

I heard a roar of laughter come from the crowd.

One of them stuck out his extra giant popcorn tub. I saw he was about to speak. He was filled with nerves. I stuck the mic back in his face again.

"Do you want some popcorn?" He asked.

I swung my arm screaming "No" into the mic while bitch slapping the popcorn tub. It exploded like a firework on the 4th of July. Popcorn splattered all over the first few rows. I heard the security guy's voice in my head, "Any rowdy stuff and your gone!"

I estimate some kernels went up as high as twenty five feet. All Eighteen thousand people in attendance went crazy. The crowd loved it. There was a giant roar. People in the front row started patting me on the back saying, "Fuck yeah! Fuck Yeah! You're awesome!"

The roar of the crowd got louder and louder. Marcello wailed. The band was on fire. My third verse was coming up. I had to get back on stage.

I always sucked at basketball. The movie 'White Men Can't Jump', when it first came out, I thought was written about me. I never came close to dunking a basketball in my life. A basketball rim is ten feet, the stage was about that.

I crouched down the way a monkey would before jumping from tree to tree. I knew if I didn't make this jump it would reignite "Boo city". We had the crowd at that second. If I make the jump I know we'll have them forever.

I said to myself, "Here we go!"

I leaped, flinging my body upwards. I was airborne again. This time going up. My adrenaline fueled inertia took me up higher than I ever jumped in my life. But that wasn't good enough.

I was four inches short. I wasn't going to make it. I was about to be booed like no one else in years.

"Shit!" I said to myself. "Why didn't I just stay on the stage? Why didn't I ignore those dicks?"

My mind raced.

I started to go back downwards.

The Security guy's voice again haunted my head, "I heard you guys were rowdy!"

That's when the miracle hit.

I felt my waist being grabbed.

I looked down.

There was nothing but I could feel hands on my waist.

I was now heading back upwards again.

I felt hands on my waist like when I was a baby and my father would chuck me in the air.

It was like I bounced off a trampoline and was hurled toward the sky.

I flew higher and higher until my fingers barely clutched the stage.

With "Grandma pulling the refrigerator off the child" strength my fingers held on.

The crowd going wild roared louder. I was holding on for life.

I began to slide down. The sweat on my fingers slimming my grip. I put all my might in my fingers. Gravity was winning. I was slipping.

At that instant, the hands on my waist feeling came back. I was boosted again upward onto the stage. The force of the propulsion flinging me into a somersault. I popped to my feet at the exact time I was to start singing the final verse. The crowd cheered extremely loud. The roar was immense.

The band never stopped rocking hard. They acted like nothing happened. Every band guy was giving me the side eye, telepathically saying with their glances, "Wow you were lucky there."

Even Lee gave me a look of, "Wow that was close".

We finished the song. Some of the crowd was standing on their feet clapping. Eight minutes before it was raining torrential boos on us. Now we were getting claps and some people were even standing cheering.

I looked back toward Kenny. He gave me the eyes. I noticed two KISS members in full uniform back stage behind his drum set. They were in the shadows hidden from the crowd's view. The stage lights were in my eyes. I couldn't tell which members they were.

Every song we played that night was given a cheer and applause. We left to cheers.

I looked down at the stage floor as I left. I decimated and trashed the 'Detroit Rock City' KISS lyric cheat sheet. I went up to the monitor guy.

"I'm sorry man. I trashed the cheat sheet. I'll tape them back up if you have another copy."

"Don't worry about that," he said. "You guys were awesome! That was a great show, Holy Shit! I got more lyric sheets and tape. Don't worry about it."

After the show we walked through the backstage corridors. Photographers snapped away asking who we were and where we were from. In our dressing room at least ten roadies came to visit us. Sasha brought one of the kegs in from the van while we were on stage.

He said, "I looked like a regular beer guy delivering to the stadium. No one knew it was for us."

Now I remember the reason we hired Sasha.

KISS went on stage to thunderous applause. Ace was up there kicking ass. We still had three more shows to go.

The next night we were at Nassau Coliseum in Long Island, New York. It was a hometown crowd. Most of them knew us and gave us a huge welcome. The day after that show we were back in New England in Hartford, Connecticut. We had a local Connecticut rock-radio station turned on in the van when we pulled into town.

The DJ said, "If you're going to the Hartford Civic Center to see KISS tonight, I recommend you get there for the opening act *The 4th Floor*. I saw them in Worcester, Massachusetts a few days ago and they were awesome. One of them jumped off the stage. They're all wild men in that band! So much energy was reeling off the stage, it was fantastic. And their music was great too. They are from New York City. So, do not blow off the opener at the KISS show tonight. You will not be disappointed."

    We all started screaming and punching the ceiling of the van.

21

People Grow Apart
1997

CHAPTER 21

People Grow Apart 1997

In the springtime of 1997, after over five years together, The 4thth Floor decided to go their separate ways. Five years was a long time for seven people to be with each other in one form or another. I loved being in The 4th Floor but we all were changing. We all were getting older and wiser and it showed as our musical tastes evolved in different directions.

I was sad to have it end. I had some of the best times of my life with Captain Al Batenko, Kenny Kramme, Lee Matheson, Marcello Capparelli, Peter Cavanagh, and The Dude Peter May. There is a special space in my heart for each one of them.

After a three week bender from the day The 4rth Floor broke up, I started to put a new project together. I was dead set on rebuilding a new band. I starting putting together Weedkiller.

Nowadays *The 4th Floor* gets together for reunion shows once every few years. I love seeing all the guys and telling old stories. I look forward to the gatherings. They are allot of fun. Between reunion shows we all communicate through social media and make each other laugh.

Randall's Island Lollapalooza 1997

CHAPTER 22

RANDALLS ISLAND LOLLAPALOOZA 1997

Snoop Dogg and the human bullet wall

In July of 1997 I didn't have a band. I was working as a bartender and a bouncer in Greenwich Village. I was approached by the legendary NYC bouncer Jerry Adams to work security for The Lollapalooza tour when it came to New York City at the stadium on Randalls Island.

Randalls Island is in the middle of The East River in between The Bronx, Queens, and Manhattan. It is the place where I played Rugby with The Village Lions.

I took the job because I needed the money. The 4th Floor had broken up two months before. I was sad over it.

I told Jerry, who was also my friend I had worked with for years, that I would do the job. He told me to meet him at 125th street and 2nd avenue in Harlem. There would be a shuttle bus that would take us and the security team to the stadium.

When I arrived at 125th and 2nd I saw twenty huge black guys standing on the corner. I knew I had to be in the right place. I walked over to the crowd of humongous men. I didn't know a single soul.

"Is this the bus to Randall's Island for Lollapalooza security?" I asked.

All of a sudden it was quiet. Everybody stopped talking. I scanned around for a friendly face to answer but there was none. There was nothing but silent stares to the sky. I knew I was where I was supposed to be. It was a bouncer crew call. Only if the New York Football Giants were having a team meeting, on the corner of 125th Street and 2nd Avenue in Harlem, would explain the twenty huge black guys standing there.

I knew full well every one of these guys thought, with my Irish mug, I was a cop. I saw all these guys laughing and yukking it up when I was a half a block away. Now they're in total silence. It was as if someone clogged my ears. I couldn't hear anything. The squeaky braked New York City buses on 125th street were even silent.

I joined in on the quiet and stood in place. I could not wait for Jerry to show up and break this eiree hush.

When he gave me the job Jerry laughed, "Kev, I am hiring an all-star team of the best bouncers in the city."

These guys were definitely All-Stars because they knew to be quiet when a strange white guy nonchalantly stands in the middle of twenty black guys. Only a cop looking to stir up trouble would do something like that. I did not look like a broke musician looking to make a few bucks doing security at Lollapalooza. I looked like a cop. I totally understood. I would have been silent too.

It was a long two minutes of silence before I heard a familiar voice calling my name.

"Kev! Over here! Hey Kev!"

It was Jerry. Thank God.

Jerry was the black Sparky Anderson (Famous Baseball Manager) of the bouncer world in New York City. Jerry hugged me the way only mutually respect filled friends do. Guys who have been through the shit together. Guys who have had each other's backs in the past. Everybody saw that.

Jerry did the display for a reason. He wanted all the black guys to know this white cracker was all right. The silence stopped. We all became one. It became loud as hell.

It was an all-star team ride over the bridge to Randall's Island. We all talked. We all knew each other's boys. We arrived at Randall's Island after the twelve minute journey from Harlem. No more yukking it up when we got there. It was all business once we stepped off the bus.

There were another twenty security guys on Randall's Island waiting to work security when we arrived. I knew a few of them. I met the Security boss. He was the guy who made one phone call to Jerry and bam we were all here. He handed us shirts with the word security in big letters on the back and small letters on the front.

Jerry drew up squads. I was put in the pit with the biggest of the black guys. Jerry told me to be the grabber. The grabber 'grabbed' people that were getting crushed in the mosh pit.

At 6' foot 2" and 195 pounds I was the smallest guy in the squad by inches. Except for the only other white guy. He was about five-foot-ten and two hundred pounds. He had a buzz crew cut. He looked like a cop too.

The other white guy came right for me. He stuck out his hand. I stuck out mine. We shook.

Feeling his shake I thought, "This guy's way too pumped up."

He smiled a devil's smile.

"It's gonna be great!" He said moving his shoulder like he was going to ram it into someone's back.

I said nothing.

"Anybody jumps on that stage. I'm gonna do the job," he said nodding.

He kept shaking his head enticing me to join in on the goon parade. This guy was way too excited. He acted like we were going to play in the super bowl. I could tell he wanted to hurt people.

Aside:

At the Lion's Den I was in charge of hiring bouncers. When I'd interview a guy I would ask two questions and make two statements. If they answered both questions right and reacted to the statement correctly. I offered them the job. The first question was, "Do you like to fight?" If they answered, "Yes." They were eliminated automatic. I would run through the hiring process to save face, but they were out. If they answered, "No." The next question was, "Can you fight?" If they answered "No". They were eliminated. If they answered, "Yes". I would look right into their eyes to watch how they reacted when I spoke my statement. "If you throw a first punch. You're out. Fired." My stare would go deep into the soul behind their eyes of the interviewee. Real tough guys would never break eye contact. I'd listen for their tone and watched their face, eyes, and body very close. If they were nonchalant in replying, "I got no problem with that." They got the job.

This only other white guy on the Mosh pit crew would never pass the first question. I could tell he liked to fight. It wasn't hard to spot. He wanted to inflict pain on people. The other guys saw it too.

I knew two other guys on the pit security team from

working with them in other clubs. A lot of these guys never saw a mosh pit before. They were big black guys from tough black neighborhoods. They knew rap and R&B. They never saw a group of white kids kick the shit out of each other. I knew when Heavey Metal Band KORN or Tool hit the stage this place was going to explode. These guys had no idea the violent energy that was about to go down.

Jerry knew I could handle a pit from being in a band and working shows at the Lion's Den. Jerry also knew some of these guys had no clue what awaited them.

We all marched to the pit behind the barricades in front of the stage. Fifteen New York City Cops were already there. These were uniformed NYPD. I knew two cops from Bleecker Street. The cops were behind us facing the crowd with their backs on the stage.

The first few acts were rave type house music DJ's: The Orb, Prodigy, and Orbital.

It was a hot 80-degree day. We pretty much stood and watched kids dance by themselves to the pulsing beat the first few hours of the show. The only problems I saw were dehydrating kids hyped on ecstasy. Their friends usually carried them to the first aid stations at either side of the venue. There was also a triage unit backstage for really hurt kids. This wasn't common knowledge for many people in the crowd. Security and vendors knew it. Backstage was only for seriously injured kids.

After the rave portion of the show was over it was time for KORN.

KORN was a heavy loud aggressive band from California. They had hip hop beats mixed with heavy metal guitars. They were a favorite band of mine at that time. I was happy they were playing.

When Korn stepped on stage the temperature was somewhere around 80-degrees. That meant it was going to be well over 100 degrees in the pit when you calculate the mass of people packed in the hot sun. When the crowd would start to dance and slam, the temperature will exceed 120 in the crush. People are going to get sick.

I turned to look at KORN five feet from me. I was pumped to see them. They hit their first note and that was the last I saw of them. The place erupted. The mosh pit swelled instantaneously like a molten lava explosion. Kids started slamming into each other with the violence of a medieval battlefield.

The jaws on some of the black guys in the crew dropped. Their eyes went wide. They looked at each other in amazement as the few thousand kids within fifty yards of them started bashing into each other.

A few of the rave kids on ecstasy got caught in the mosh pit. They couldn't get out. Fear and panic rolled in on them. I saw terror in their eyes. Twenty feet away I saw a desperate kid put up his hand as if he was drowning. He looked me dead in the eye. Big Dee was next to me. I knew him from Don Hill's Nightclub. I yelled to him, "I'm going to get that kid and pass him to you."

"What are you talking about?" He shouted as KORN's thunderous guitars blared.

"Just keep an eye on me!" I yelled in his ear.

I jumped up on the barrier. I dove on the crowd. I was sustained by the shear mass of humanity. I crawled on heads and shoulders. The rave kid was getting crushed. I skimmed across the mass of people like a mosquito on a country pond.

When I got to the rave kid his eyes glowed liked a sea survivor when the coast guards arrives. I reached down to the back of his pants. Bracing myself on the top of the crowd I pulled the kid up to the top of the bouncing mound of humanity with one hand. I pushed him toward the six-foot-five Big Dee's out stretched arms. Big Dee grabbed the kid. He put him on the ground between our crew and the NYPD. The kid was safe.

I saw two fifteen or sixteen year old girls put their hands

up about 40 yards away. They were getting crushed too. Hard-core Metal Dudes where bashing into everything at a hundred miles an hour like the war of forever was being fought.

The girls were gasping for air taking a beating. Like a skipped rock I skidded over heads and shoulders to them. I reached down and grabbed the back of the first girl's shorts by the belt area. Again, one handed, I ripped the first girl up. I pushed off the moving mass for support. I shoved her toward big Dee. I did the same to the other girl. Big Dee grabbed them both. He gently put them on the ground. They were safe.

The saving of people getting crushed never stopped. Ten minutes into the show I noticed the other white guy pushing, shoving, and punching every kid that I saved. Big Dee would put them down and he would yoke them up.

Another few minutes went past. The pit slowed for a couple seconds during one of the few mellow parts of *Korn's* catalogue. I knew the song. I had about thirty or forty seconds before another eruption. I used that time to crawled over heads and shoulders back to behind the barrier and the other white guy. He was nodding his head all amped up. I rushed at him as fast and hard as I could. I gave him a two-handed chest shove.

"What the fuck are you doing? These kids paid to see a show. Not to get beat up by you! You fucking jerkoff!"

He came back at me. We started fighting. He wasn't an easy go. Three or four guys separated us.

The NYPD guys were right there. I looked up. I saw a cop I knew from Bleecker Street. He nodded affirmative at me. KORN's mellow song part was over. They went on to their next heavy angry rant. The pit kicked up again. I looked at Big Dee. He was huffing and puffing. He nodded to me. I jumped up on the barrier. I noticed some NYPD talking to the other white guy in his ear.

I scanned the crowd like a lifeguard does the water. Thirty seconds went by until I was crawling over heads and shoulders to the next victim of the crush. I grabbed a guy who must have been sixty. He was drunk. He thought he could handle the pit. He was wrong. The smile he had when he went into the bouncing mass was turned to terror. He was a load. Pit slammers stopped killing each other for a second to help raise the sixty year old in the air. They assembly line carried the older guy over their heads to Big Dee's waiting arms.

The pit was nonstop again. This round the other white guy did nothing. He just stood motionless with a puss on his face. He never hit anyone again. I could tell it was hard for him not to assault the kids.

When KORN was finished I crawled back to my position. I looked for the other white guy in case he was coming for me. I saw an NYPD cop heading toward me. It was the same one I knew from Bleecker Street. He pointed to the other white guy.

"Kev, that guy who was beating on kids, the one you had a fight with. If he's not thrown out of here immediately the Captain is going to shut down the show. That would cause a riot. I don't want to be in no riot today. This is a side job."

I waved Jerry over and told him the news. Jerry knew the cop too. Jerry got on his walkie. The Security boss was there in less than a minute. The cop spoke to him pointing at the other white guy, "That guy is beating on kids. If he's not thrown out of here right now, the show is going to be shut down."

The Security boss called over the other white guy. He started screaming, "Get the fuck out of here now! You're fired! Give me that fucking shirt back!"

"What did I do? Those kids were coming too close to the stage. We can't let that happen."

The cop jumped in, "If you don't get out of this stadium right now! I'm going to lock you up for assault!"

"What! Really?" The other white guy said in disbelief.

The cop went for his cuffs. The other white guy backed up. He threw his security shirt on the ground. He was gone.

The cop said to the Security Boss, "That guy was a dick! Watch who you hire."

The Security boss nodded.

Jerry told me later, the other white guy got hired as a favor to a New York State trooper who knew someone, who new someone. He wasn't on the all-star team. Jerry didn't know who he was.

The cop whispered in my ear before we went back to our posts, "Nice shot you gave that dick. Good one."

"I wish they didn't break it up," I said.

I walked toward Big Dee. The entire front row gave me high fives on my way over. They saw what I did to the dick.

"What you think of this, Big Dee?"

"Holy Shit! White people are crazy. We don't do that at our shows. People would get shot."

"It's the rage of the ages coming out, Big Dee. The energy has got to go somewhere."

"I don't know about that shit. Your people are fucked up!" Big Dee said, shaking his head.

The Security boss came over. He waved us in for a huddle. He spoke like a coach.

"The cops said Snoop Dogg had a death threat. Some asshole called them and said they were going to shoot him when he gets off his bus today. That's one reason you see all the cops here."

Aside:

At this time in history Rappers were killing each other. Tupac Shakur, Biggie Smalls, and a lot of rappers were getting shot and killed in those days. This threat on Snoop Dogg was taken serious.

The Black Panthers were hired by Snoop Dogg to do his private security.

Our Security boss continued, "We're going to form a human wall from Snoop Dogg's bus to the stage. Let's go."

My entire crew was black now. They seemed to get happy. They all rose up. They couldn't wait to do it. I saw a friend I worked with I knew from downtown pass in front of me. I grabbed him.

"What the fuck. We're making a few extra bucks for a one-off. Fuck this. My mother didn't raise me to take a bullet for Snoop Dogg. Did yours?"

"Fuck that Kev! I'm going," he said, pushing me away.

Jerry was rushing by. I grabbed him.

"Jerry, what the fuck! Are you kidding me? A human bullet wall. Don't go. Snoop got the Black Panthers doing security. Let them do it. You gonna take a bullet for a guy who doesn't even know your name. What the fuck!"

"Let go of me, Kev. It's our job. I'm going."

Jerry went off. I was now alone behind the barrier.

Snoop Dogg had his own security on this day - The Black Panthers. They were everywhere.

The Black Panthers were formed in the 1960's. They were a radical group assembled to combat race inequality in America. I understood their stance. I also knew they couldn't give a shit about me. They were the opposite of peace protesters. They were there to protect Snoop Dogg from assassination.

The threat on Snoop Dogg was very, very real. It was July 11th, 1997. Four months earlier in March Biggie Smalls - a New York City rapper - was assassinated. Many think Biggie Smalls' killing was in response to the murder of California rapper, Tupac Shakur in September of 1996. These guys weren't playing around. The threat and the New York vs California Rap war was very real and not a joke.

Snoop Dogg was a California rapper in the heart of New York City. Biggie Smalls' territory. Some of Tupac's family were Black Panthers. The Black Panthers were in New York to keep an eye on, and protect Snoop Dog. I wasn't about to be a white martyr in a rap war that nobody would care if I got killed. Some people would even be happy if a white guy got killed. For some black Guys it would be a badge of honor to take a bullet in the rap war. For me; Whitey Mick Whitey it would be plain stupid.

I walked on the stage. I noticed a few black guys dressed in black fatigues. It was the Black Panthers. Snoop Dog's private security.

The Black Panthers stopped me. I told them I'm stage security. They looked at my laminate and shirt. They got out of my way. I went to the back of the stage to get a vantage point of the human bullet wall. I had a direct line of sight to Snoop's bus from where I was. Snoop's bus was about a hundred and fifty feet away. I figured I might be able to spot a shooter and get him from behind before he got to my guys. I saw Big Dee, Jerry, my downtown buddy, and the other guys I just met form the bullet wall. It led from Snoop's bus right up to where I was.

At that second Perry Farrell from the band Jane's Addiction came walking up the stairs. Perry Farrell is the man responsible for the Lollapalooza show ever happening. He was the creator of the tour. He is the reason everybody was there.

Perry got to the top of the stairs where the Black Panthers stopped me. They stopped him. They told him he couldn't come on stage. Perry didn't have a laminate. Perry didn't need one. He looked at them. I could see him step back a little, but he was very cool.

"Ok, man. That's ok," Perry said. Perry could tell these guys didn't know who he was. He started to go back down the stairs.

I walked over to the Black Panthers. I spoke to them,

"That's Perry Farrell. He's the creator of this event. None of us would be here if it wasn't for him."

"So what!" The Black Panther replied.

I couldn't see his eyes from the dark sunglasses he wore. I knew he meant business. He wasn't going to be swayed.

I went back to watching for the potential shooter of one of my friends, or Snoop Dogg. The Security boss saw me standing alone on the back of the stage looking out toward Snoop's bus. He walked up to me. He asked, "How come you're not in the human wall."

"I ain't taking no bullet for Snoop Dogg. That's why."

"Oh yeah. Ok. Why don't you go work the V.I.P. door? Relieve the guy over there. Tell him to switch with you."

I said nothing. I looked this guy in the eyes. I was just demoted to V.I.P. door, the worst job in the security business. The job where all you do is be a dick and deny everybody entrance. I took my stare off him. I put it back on my friends in the human bullet wall. At that instant, someone radioed for the Security boss.

"We have ten guys fighting back by the sound board." I heard the radio voice say.

"Go to the V.I.P. door," the Security boss yelled at me.

I was thinking on punching him in the face. But, I didn't. He ran off to the fight. I held my position watching my friends and for any sudden movement coming from the wings. Three or four minutes later Snoop Dogg came off his bus. He walked through the tunnel of humans towards me. I watched for sudden movement from anybody. Thank God nothing. Snoop Dogg walked through the human wall. He walked passed me and made his way to the front of the stage. I saw everybody was safe. I was very relieved. I turned to walk to my banishment at the V.I.P. door.

A Rolly Polly fat guy was working the V.I.P. door just off stage left. I told him the Security Boss wants him in the pit.

He looked at me with terror. He just realized he had to go where the Big Boys played.

V.I.P. stands for "Very Important People". The V.I.P. entrance is where celebrities show up to get backstage. The trick is you have to know who they are. If you don't know who they are, and they're famous, an argument usually happens, where the words, "You don't know who I am?!" are screamed at you over and over again. The job is horrible.

I stood at the V.I.P. door. The backstage triage unit - where severely hurt people get taken - was about fifty feet away. If you're a celebrity, or really hurt, I can let you in. A feeling of sadness overcame me. I thought about not having a band. I was surrounded by music and I was not participating in any of it. In the pit I had no time to think about anything. Now I was stuck in my own thoughts standing at the V.I.P. door. Not having a band was a saddening burn in my thoughts. I became depressed.

A few minutes went by when I heard a voice call to me from behind two feet away.

"Hey Man! How you doing?" The voice was unfamiliar. I turned to it. It was Fieldy the bass player from *KORN*. He was carrying a Heineken beer.

"You want a beer, man?" He asked.

I thought for a second, "Yeah man. I do."

"Ok. I'll be back in a second."

I watched him go to the KORN tour bus parked by the triage unit. He walked onto the bus. He came out twenty seconds later with two Heinekens and a red plastic cup. He was pouring a beer into the cup as he walked toward me. He handed me the cup.

"You got a bottle opener on you?" Fieldy asked me.

"Yeah," I replied.

"Good."

Fieldy put the other Heineken on its side up against the fence by my V.I.P. door.

"That one is for later. I'll be by in a while to check on you."

"Ok, Fieldy. Thanks, man."

"What's your name, bro?" Fieldy asked.

"Kevin."

"Glad to meet you, Kevin."

Fieldy walked off.

I started drinking. It tasted great.

'What was that all about? Why did Fieldy give me beer and ask my name?' I thought.

I didn't care though I started sipping. It was one of the best beer I ever had.

Snoop Dogg was rocking it up on the stage. I always liked Snoop Dogg but not enough to take a bullet for him. The crowd bobbed their heads and coolly listened. There was no moshing. My pit crew was having the time of their lives listening to Snoop.

Jerry had free reign to go anywhere he wanted. He saw me at the V.I.P. door. He walked over.

"What are you doing here?"

I held my red cup up to Jerry's face.

"Drinking." I replied.

"Why aren't you in the pit?"

"Big Security Boss wants to punish me for not getting in the human bullet wall. Made me V.I.P. door guy."

Jerry started laughing. I put my beer in his grill again to make sure he could smell it.

"I'll make the best of it." I spoke and sipped at the same time.

"I know you hate it. I'm going to cover stage right V.I.P. for a while right now," Jerry said.

"Good for you Jerry. Have fun."

I reached down to grab my other Heineken. I poured it into my empty cup, making sure Jerry saw everything. I tipped the cup toward him. Jerry laughed and went on his way.

A few kids came up to try to get in. I hated to see the look in their eyes when I turned them away. I just finished my second beer when Fieldy walked up.

"Hey Kev, you ready for another round?"

"Yeah, I am Fieldy. Thanks!"

"I'll be right back."

Fieldy left for his bus. He was back three minutes later. This time he had a bucket with ice and five Heinekens in it. I couldn't believe my eyes.

"Here you go, Kev. Thanks!"

"Thanks for what?" I asked.

"I saw you saving those kids getting crushed in the pit when we played. I saw you go after that bully. Thanks. I was waiting for someone to do something. I was about to point him out. It would have caused a riot if I did. But, you handled it. Thanks! I wish every place we played had guys like you."

I didn't reply. I didn't know what to say. To do what I did was so natural. I didn't need praise.

"Thanks for the beers Fieldy. *Korn* just broke into my top-ten favorite bands of all time."

He laughed. I raised my cup to him. He cheers'd me and walked off.

Snoop Dogg was great. I sipped beers. I watched the show for the next thirty minutes. Tool, a progressive metal band was coming up later sometime after Snoop. While Snoop played, I let two kids in the door for triage who were suffering from heat stroke. The pit wasn't aggressive for Snoop Dog. That would change for *Tool* in a little while.

It seemed to be a great turn of events. A bucket of beers, a sunny day, and great music. It was time to pay back the universe for blessing me. Two non-hurt kids approached me. With trepidation, one spoke.

"I think our father is backstage working. Can we go see if he's back there?"

I looked at both of them silent for three seconds.

"Sure! Come on in."

I opened the door. They looked at each other surprised at how easy it was to get backstage. They didn't hesitate to come inside. I sipped another beer. Minutes went by before a group of five kids came up to me. The leader spoke.

"I have to get backstage to check the fuel pump on the generator for Kraft services."

Kraft services is catering for the artists and crew back stage. I was impressed he knew the word. Kraft service people wear laminates. A laminate is a badge with the date and tour on it. To get back stage you need an official laminate.

"Where's your laminate?" I asked, taking a sip from my red cup filled with beer.

"I ahh, I left it in the car."

"You left it in the car?"

"Yeah. I'm a dummy."

"Well, dummy. Come on in."

I opened the door. He walked through. His four friends stood there not knowing what to do. The leader, now inside, looked to his friends then back to me. He spoke cautiously.

"I need their help. Can they come with me?"

I looked at his friends. Another guy, and three hot chicks in short shorts. They didn't look like they could help fix a fuel pump, or anything at all.

"Are your laminates in the car too?" I asked.

They all nodded their heads weakly, "Yes".

"Ok. Come on in. Kraft services is on the other side of the stage."

These kids were the worst actors ever. They were astonished I let them in. I opened the door. They walked in awestruck.

For the next hour anybody that had any excuse to get backstage I let in. I must have let twenty or thirty kids backstage.

It was time for *Tool* to perform. They were another of my favorite bands at the time. The pit was fierce again. I got serious with the door while *Tool* was on. Kids were getting pummeled in the pit. Some needed to be let in for triage.

I let another ten or twelve bleeding kids backstage to get patched up. I was scanning out front of my V.I.P. door. I saw two kids carrying another kid who was bleeding from his head. It looked like they were coming off the battlefield at Gettysburg. I opened the door to let them in.

I looked at the kid's t-shirt holding up the hurt guy. He was wearing a t-shirt of my old band - *The 4th Floor*. There it was, a picture of me on this kid's chest. The hurt guy was in real pain. He was bleeding from his head. I didn't say anything about the shirt. Seeing my grinning face on this kid's chest was surreal. I became sad again.

Seven months before this day I had a great band that was touring arenas. Now I was the V.I.P. door guy at Lollapalooza, with no band. A sudden turn of events. My face going by on a t-shirt was a reminder of how fast life can change.

The 4th Floor had broken up two months earlier in May of 1997. We had a record deal. We got all the good opening slots in New York City. We opened for *KISS* at The Meadowlands for Dick Clark's New Year's Eve show seven months earlier. Reality hit me. It was over.

I grabbed a bottle from Fieldy's bucket. I chugged it. No cup. I didn't give a fuck who saw me. More hurt kids came to the door. I snapped out of feeling sorry for myself. Kids needed help. I forgot about my ex-band and did my job.

Tool had the pit swelling with rage. The bounce was as fierce as Korn's. I knew they needed me in the pit, but I was being punished for not forming the human bullet wall. I knew that me not being in the pit was why so many bloody and heat exhausted kids were coming to the door for care. The pit crew guys were all too big to crawl like a spider over the crowd.

It was real busy for *Tool*. When they came off stage a smattering of beat-up kids trickled in for triage. When it died down I looked back toward the tour buses. Kids were running everywhere. I must have let fifty or sixty kids in. Twenty or so for legitimately being hurt. The rest for any reason at all.

The Security boss was running around crazy. He came up to me screaming, "Who let all these kids back here?!"

"I don't know. Wasn't me. Maybe, it was the other guy." I replied, knowing my friend Jerry was the other guy.

The security boss got on his walkie.

"Jerry, are you letting all these kids in?"

While he was speaking into the walkie. I spoke at the same time.

"It's Jerry letting everybody in."

Jerry heard me. I wanted Jerry to hear me. It was a one day job and we we're supposed to risk it all. Fuck that!

Jerry replied. I could hear him through the speaker.

"It's not me! Fuck you, Kev!"

"I don't care who it is. We got to get order back here."

The Security boss went running around grabbing kids. I saw him get the fuel pump fixers. He escorted them out. I sipped more beer from my red cup. I looked over by triage. The kid who was wearing a *4th Floor* t-shirt and his two friend were looking at me hoping to not be seen. I pointed at them.

"Hey, you guys! Come here!"

They were bummed I caught them.

The Security boss saw me yell at them. He gave me the thumbs up and ran into the fury of running wild backstage kids.

The guy wearing *The 4th Floor* shirt and his friend were walking toward me. The hurt guy had a giant bandage on his head like the piper in the Spirit of '76 painting. They took their time. They started to go out the door thinking they were getting tossed. I stopped them. I spoke to the kid wearing *The 4th Floor* T-Shirt. I pointed to the shirt.

"You like that band?" I asked.

He looked down at his shirt.

"No. Not really."

Another blow for my ego. He continued.

"My brother does. This is his shirt."

"Oh Yeah! Take a look at that guy on your shirt."

I pointed to myself grinning in the center of his chest. It was a shirt designed by my friend artist Dave "Road Hog" Ryan. The kid looked at his shirt. Then he looked at me. I made the grinning face I had on the shirt. He was puzzled. I kept making the face. Then it hit him.

"Holy Shit! You're the 4*th Floor* Guy! My brother loves you! I've seen you guys play before. Are you playing today?" He asked.

"No. I'm working the door here."

I saw the kid's face become perplexed. He couldn't comprehend the life of a rock n' roller. He knew I was just playing arenas and the best clubs, so he thought I was performing.

"Too long of a story. Tell your brother I said thanks for the support. Come with me guys."

I led The 4th Floor shirt wearing kid and his friends toward Big Dee and the pit guys. I watched the door with my side eye as I walked to behind the barrier I was banished from. I saw Big Dee.

"Hey Big Dee. These are my friends. They're gonna stand here and watch the show."

"Ok, man," Big Dee replied.

I left the three of them behind the pit security crew in front of the NYPD. I winked at the cop who knew me. The only better seat in the place was to be in the band. The kids couldn't believe it.

"You guys stay here. Watch the show. If anybody asks who let you in here. Don't say anything. Just leave."

The cops nodded to me laughing.

"Ok. Thank you," the kids said.

I went back to the V I P door.

The next two hours were mellow. No one came in hurt. The bands weren't angry mosh pit bands. The day was long and hot. Most of the kids were spent.

Fieldy came by to freshen my bucket with another three Heinekens. He stopped and we bullshited for a while. I told him about the New York City music scene. Our peaceful conversation was interrupted by the Security boss guy. He was screaming again.

"Hey! How did these kids get behind the barrier?"

He had the kid wearing *The 4th Floor* t-shirt by the back of the collar in one hand. He had his other friend by the back of the collar in the other hand. The Spirit of '76 kid was trailing behind.

"I don't know?" I said looking at the kid wearing me on his chest. I eyed him to not say a word. The Security boss walked them outside. On his way past me, the kid wearing *The 4th Floor* t-shirt mouthed silent, "Thank you so much."

I nodded at the kid. I thought to myself, 'I bet he likes *The 4th Floor* now.'

The show ended uneventfully. I was pretty drunk from Fieldy's bucket. I got paid and went home.

The next day I woke up and went back to searching for a new band.

23

Ass Grabbing Santa Gets His Ass Kicked 1997

CHAPTER 23

ASS GRABBING SANTAS

GET THEIR ASSES KICKED 1997

Every year drunk and unruly people dressed as Santa Clause gather in New York City. It is called SantaCon. I will always remember the one in 1997. I think it was the first one ever.

It was mid-December, the Christmas parties held in the back rooms of restaurants, bars, and hotels were letting out. This particular night I was managing The Lion's Den at 214 Sullivan Street in Greenwich Village, New York City.

Men with undone ties waltzed disheveled work dressed women along Sullivan Street. One after another they staggered on zigzag strolls toward Bleecker Street. A common smile on each face. A common look of corruption in the back of their eyes. I call it "The backward-eyed-forward-glare". It's a look brought on from consuming cocktails filled with liquor a person would not normally drink, except if it is free at the company Christmas party.

The Company Christmas party - an affair where coworkers, who have been hating each other all year long, stand side-by-side over indulging in free booze.

The Company Christmas party - the place where a drunk employee might say to oneself, "Now's the right time to bury the hatchet with this coworker. Bury it right in their head!"

The Company Christmas party - an event where a drunk employee might think it's a good time to stick their hand down a coworker's pants. After all, it is the season of good cheer and love. And a graze of a coworkers genitals is what the togetherness of the Holidays are all about.

The Company Christmas party - where 24 hours after its Human Resources busiest day.

The Company Christmas Party - a phenomenon that happens every year.

All over New York City and the world boozed up people run amok during the Company Christmas Party Season. Extra mayhem and stupidity occur in the streets. Like the spring equinox, the summer solstice, and geese flying south for the winter it rolls around as fast as it disappears. It's the season for office coworkers, siblings, families, and couples to rethink their relationships. It's also the season for people in Santa Suits to think they have diplomatic immunity.

It was about 10pm. The Lion's Den hadn't done much business so far this night. Big Pete, a giant white monster, was my door guy. Big Pete looked like he just stepped out of a civil war battle with his big bushy mustache. He was six-foot-four and close to three hundred pounds. Alejandro, the thick accented Argentinian, was behind the bar. Bryan, the long haired rocker soundman, was behind the audio board. Kahn, the Pakistani immigrant, was the bar back. There was a pretty New York City girl waitressing. It was her first and only day. I forgot her name.

Outside the club drunk office people staggered all around. Pete and I talked about how we were glad they kept walking past us. We knew most of them were trouble.

We had been slow so far this night. I was worried about being able to pay the staff at the end of their shifts. I was hoping for a rush; just not a rush of bombed Christmas Party people.

"If those backward-eyed-forward-glared drunks stopped to come inside. I'd probably let them in. We need to make payouts for the night," I told Pete.

He looked down on me through the bottom of his glasses, "You know that's trouble man."

Every night people took the subway to Greenwich Village to listen to comedians and musicians. They got off at The West 4th Street Station. A hub for the A,B,C,D,E,F and Q subway lines at the time.

At The Lion's Den, a door guy's attention would most be drawn to noise coming from people walking from West 3rd to get to Bleecker Street. The West 4th Street subway station is actually on West 3rd street a few hundred yards from The Lion's Den. Being Christmas Party season the streets were extra heavy with revelers.

I was inside the club when Pete gave me two blinks with his flash light from the front door. Two blinks of a flash light means he has to take a leak. I walked to the front of the club outside. Pete went inside. I began to watch the door.

I was outside for maybe five seconds when I heard the undistinguished sound of a street sign getting punched and the roar of a mob. I looked toward the commotion. Thirty people dressed as Santa Clause were marauding onto Sullivan Street from 3rd street. They were running and screaming. They were pounding their fists into stopped taxis. They were kicking garbage cans into the street and going ape-shit berserk. The mob was sprinting right at me. Loud hooting and hollering overtook the block. They quickly were upon me.

"Keep going. Please God! Let them keep going!" I said out loud for no one to hear.

I backed myself up against the front door of The Lion's Den so no rampaging Santa would be able to sneak past me. The mob had a full head of steam. Most of them were blowing by me fast heading toward Bleecker Street. They didn't seem to notice me. Three huffing and puffing Santas were straggling behind.

I thought, 'Just these three dicks left and I am in the clear. Yes!'

If you didn't know The Lion's Den was there you could run right by it in a marauding holiday frenzy. I willed physics to make myself and the club invisible.

The second to last drunk Santa stopped to catch his breath. He had his hands on his knees sucking wind. He was five feet from The Lion's Den. After a big breath he noticed me standing in front of our green neon Pilsner Urquell beer sign. He started waving and calling out to his Red suited pillagers.

"Hey! Hey! There's a club here! We got to go in! You know the rule! We don't pass any bar!"

"Fuck!" I said to myself.

The huffing bombed Santa approached me. The other thirty drunk Santas stopped like they were on Army orders. They all turned around. In a full sprint they ran over surrounding me. They were all panting from running in a fury.

"How much is cover?" A giant Santa asked.

"Ten dollars," I said.

I should have said it was fifty dollars. In actuality, there was no cover. I needed time to assess the situation. The giant Santa leader began to haggle.

"We got thirty people that want to drink. We only want to stay for one round. We don't want to pay cover. We're on a bar crawl. Come on! Let us in for one drink. It's Christmas time! We have on Santa suits!"

I looked at the mob of drunk panting Santas. They were mostly guys but I could see a few naughty Misses Santas mixed in. I calculated a round for all these people. I realized I could make payroll for the night.

I thought to myself, 'I'm probably going to regret this. But I have to let them in'.

"Ok. Show me ID for over 21. I'll let you in."

They all got out their ID's. They were all in their mid-twenties.

I let all the drunk Santas enter. I went inside the club to watch them from the front door. Pete came out of the back room. He walked through the club dumbfounded. He was astonished to see thirty big time drunks in Santa Suits going to town. Pete was annoyed.

"What the Fuck is this!?"

"I know it looks bad. I had to let them in. We need to make payouts tonight. I had no choice. They're only staying for one round."

"One round! I've heard that before. It's only a matter of time!" Pete said shaking his head. He began stretching out his shoulders in anticipation for a fight.

The drunk Santas slammed to the bar. Everybody bought something. Some bought beers. Some bought shots. Some bought beers and shots. I did a calculation in my head. I figured we had payouts for the night. Now it was time to make some money.

Alejandro was a great bartender. He was moving fast. He was ringing the register hard. The waitress was selling booze like it was going out of style. The band was happy to have a crowd to play for. I watched the action from the front door.

Pete went back to the outside of the club. I decided to go outside and have a conference with Pete.

If people see crowds in your club, they will pay to get in. We were busy. The club had an opportunity to make money. The key to the strategy is to never let anybody walk away. If they don't want to pay, let them in anyway. Take the negotiation until they turn away. Then tell them to come in for free. I was about to tell Pete to go into cover charge mode when Kahn the porter came running out.

"They're going crazy. The waitress is fighting Santa Claus. Santa Claus grabbed her ass!" Kahn yelled in a panic.

I looked at Pete. He looked at me. "Let's Go!"

I had been outside the bar for maybe twenty seconds. When I got back into the club anarchy had overtaken it. Ten Santas were on stage trying to grab the bands instruments. Two Santas were on the mic singing 'Santa Clause is coming To Town", while the band played an original song. Five Santas were gyrating and grinding on the bar. A girl Santa laid on the bar as a guy Santa dry humped her. Alejandro was trying to push them off. Bryan the soundman was shoving Santas off the stage two and three at a time. The new waitress was swinging wild at everyone.

I yelled to Pete, "They've taken over! First things first! Let's get the ass-grabber!"

Pete nodded affirmative.

We rushed up to the arms flailing waitress.

"Which one grabbed your ass?" I yelled to her.

"That one!"

She pointed to a Santa that had his beard ripped off and scratches all over his face. The waitress did a number on him when she fought back. Pete and I looked at each other. The 'Ass grabbing Santa' got an automatic punch in the face. Pete got a hold of his head. I grabbed his feet. And out the door he was going.

Six or seven Santas saw us bum-rushing the ass-grabber Santa toward the front door. They started a charge at us. The 'Ass Grabber' was wriggling to escape our strong hold. Pete held his head tight. I fought holding his squirming legs. He tried to kick his feet. I held on like a rodeo cowboy. We were ten feet from the front door as the six or seven charging Santas grew to ten or twelve. They hit Pete and I full force knocking into us like a battering ram. We dropped the "Ass Grabber'. The fight was on.

Pete and I started swinging haymakers. More Santas joined in attacking us. Every shot we threw connected because Santas were everywhere. Drunken Santas tried jumping over the bar. Kahn, the waitress, and Bryan pulled them back. Alejandro slammed Santa heads into the wet wood bar like he was killing ants.

I was proud of Alejandro for staying behind the bar and fighting. If he would've come out from behind the bar, for sure, all our booze and the register money would have been looted.

I ran over to the electrical breaker board. I hit on the very bright end-of-the-night-clean-up lights. This always stuns a rowdy crowd. Bryan, Kahn, the waitress, myself, and Pete started herding the drunken Santas out the door. They were all so stewed it was easy. Before you knew it the club was empty.

Outside the club The Santas didn't even do the normal yell at us after being ejected. They didn't call us, "Losers!" Or, scream, "You suck!" They simply straighten up their bloody beards and continued their sprint toward Bleecker Street.

Pete looked over to me with his hands on his knees. He was huffing and puffing out of breath, "I hope we made payouts".

"So do I!" I huffed back.

The next year the Santas returned. I didn't let them in the club.

I Heard The Dogs Talking 1998

CHAPTER 24

I HEARD THE DOGS TALKING TO ME 1998

In spring of 1998, I was managing and bar tending at The Lion's Den on Sullivan Street in the heart of Greenwich Village, New York City. I was living in downtown Jersey City on 9th Street now.

It was about a year since my old band *The 4th Floor* broke up. It took a few months, but I put together another great band called *Weedkiller*.

Weedkiller wasn't a happy band like *The 4th Floor*. It was angrier. I was not in a happy head space. Two band members shared my mindset – Laurent "Frenchy" Cosani on guitars and Eric Czar on bass – They were maniacs. I loved it.

Kenny Kramme *The 4th Floor* drummer was also The *Weedkiller* drummer. He loved playing drums and didn't care whether it was angry or happy.

Captain Al from *The 4th Floor* was also in the band on vocals with myself.

Peter May from *The 4th Floor* was in the band but thought we were to loud and angry. He only stayed in the band a few months. He was out of the band by the time this story happened.

Frenchy, Eric, and I were always together either writing, practicing, recording, or hanging out. We were doing real well.

My daily routine was waking between noon and 2pm, getting the newspaper, eating, then working on music for a few hours. I would leave for The Lion's Den or the rehearsal studio around 5:30pm. Most days I would be back at my house in Jersey City around 6am to go to sleep.

I loved living on the other side of the night. I was happy in the early mornings on my way home to sleep. My ten minute train ride heading out of Manhattan to Jersey City was always empty, except for a few other night owls. I would get a kick out of all the morning trains I passed heading into Manhattan crammed packed with solem face commuters.

I was very lucky because I loved my job. Every night I worked in a great club serving drinks and watching bands. If I wasn't working at The Lion's Den I was in the city either playing, writing, or recording music. Life was good.

One staple to start my day was getting the Jersey Journal newspaper with my breakfast at lunchtime. I would go to my local deli a block away to buy it.

The Jersey Journal was Jersey City and Hudson County, New Jersey's local newspaper.

This particular day the headlines were extra big. A local teenage girl had been hit by a car and was in a coma. The family asked for prayers from the community.

I was a guy who prayed every day. It was a trait I obtained from my Irish Catholic mother mentally beating it into me. Most of my prayers were for thanking God for the safety and well-being of my family and friends. I added the girl to my daily prayers, like her family asked.

For about two weeks her status was updated daily on the front page of the Jersey Journal. Seeing the headlines reminded me to keep her in my prayers, which I did.

Then one day the headline was horrible. She had passed away. I didn't know the girl, but I was terribly sad. I remember thinking about her on the way to the city that night. I stared at the dirty floor of the train. I thought about the girl's parents. How sad they must be. I said prayers for them. I got to my stop at 9th street. I went about my night working at the Lion's Den. I went home after work. I was in bed around 6am.

I woke in the afternoon happy. I had the next three nights booked in the recording studio. Weedkiller was recording our first songs ever. Six tracks of what we called trip metal. We were set to record from 6pm to midnight the first two nights. The third night was an all-night session that started at 8pm. It was scheduled to end whenever we finished the six tracks.

The two days past to the final session. The work load this night was recording a few tracks, mixing, and finishing the record. We wrapped up at almost eight in the morning. All of us went our separate ways. The record was finished and sounding great. I got to my apartment in Jersey City about 8:45am.

I walked up my block. The sun was out and shining bright. Up ahead I saw a line of six or seven yellow school buses parked in front of the Church two doors from my apartment. School buses never park on my block. There is no school. Outside the church three or four hundred teenagers were crying. Right away I knew what was going on. It was the funeral for the girl I had been praying for.

My neighbor was out front of his building. He confirmed my thoughts. The happiness I had from recording a great record evaporated fast. I stood in front of my building looking at all the teenagers in front of the church. I put my bag of lyrics inside my apartment. I then walked to the church eighty feet away.

I looked at myself in the reflection of a parked car. I was wearing purple pants and a wife beater. I stopped myself from going in and saying a prayer.

Across the street from my building and the church was a park. I walked into the park. People were enjoying the sunny morning jogging, biking, and walking dogs. A park bench faced the church from across the street. I sat down. I stared at the church. I felt so bad. I watched hysterical women wailing, watery eyed tough Jersey City teenage boys trying to hold in their tears. Young girls cried out loud. I said one last prayer for the girl to be taken into heaven. I also said a prayer for her parents to get through the sorrow.

I sat about a half hour outside the funeral watching. I could hear the mournful songs from the organ.

I suddenly heard a young sounding voice talking to me from the ground.

"Hey, how ya doin'?"

I looked down expecting to see a child. There was a large-bright-orange dog sitting on the pavement facing me. The dog had no leash or collar.

I looked around for a person the voice might be coming from. Not a person for fifty feet. People jogged by with headphones on. I put my eyes back on the giant-orange dog. It looked me direct in the eyes and stood up on all four legs. The dog walked up to me. It began nuzzling his head on the knee of my purple pants. I looked at the dog. I heard the voice again, "Hey! How ya doin'?"

The voice was coming from the dog. Its lips didn't move, but a human English speaking voice was most definite coming from the dog. I was in disbelief, though I felt at ease. I didn't feel shocked. I felt normal. I answered the dog back, "I'm ok."

The dog laid down at my feet. I then heard another voice speak, "What's up, buddy! Nice day."

I looked to the other side. Another dog was standing there. It had a sheen gray coat that was almost glossy. He was big also and had no collar too. I looked down at the orange dog lying at my feet. The gray dog walked toward me. He sat facing me two feet away. I heard a voice coming from him.

"What's up? How ya doin'?"

"I'm good," I answered back.

A feeling of peace came over me.

"Good," the gray dog said.

The gray dog sat on my right. The Orange dog was to my left. I thought to myself, 'I got two huge dogs sitting next to me. I think they're talking to me.'

I heard another voice.

"All right. Good day, Huh?"

The new voice was coming from another dog. This one had a color I had never seen before. It was a reddish-blue-brown. All the dogs were solid colors. No spots. No markings. No leash. No Collar.

I now had three dogs sitting at my feet staring at me. The park was sunny. I started to contemplate, 'Did I have special powers. I have attracted a pack of dogs that are talking to me'.

A woman walked by with a German Shepard on a leash. As they walked by I looked at the German Shepard. I tried to talk to it in my mind. Nothing. The German Shepard walked by not even noticing me. My pack then stood up. Another man walked by with a beagle on a leash. I tried to talk to it in my mind. Nothing.

I looked down to my pack. They were gone. Not a sign of them anywhere.

I sat in awed silence. I wasn't drunk, or high. I was exhausted from being up all night. But, I was up all night every night. I thought to myself, 'Did it really happen? Three giant dogs of the most spectacular colors I've ever seen, talked to me. I heard them. I saw them.'

The funeral let out. I watched the coffin be put in the hearse. The procession was at least fifteen blocks long. It took a long while for everybody to leave. I waited until the last person attending the funeral was gone. I sat quiet on the bench for a good minute. I went inside my building. I said another prayer for her parents. I went to sleep.

I had that night off. I didn't do anything but watch TV. The girl I was seeing came over. The next day was Sunday. I had no work that day either. I told my girl what happened with the dogs. She laughed and asked if I was smoking crack.

I said, "I know it sounds crazy, but I swear to God I heard dogs talking to me."

My Girlfriend lived in Manhattan. She spent a lot of time at my place. She knew about the teenage girl. I talked about her every day while I read the paper for the last few weeks.

I had to work Monday night bar tending at The Lion's Den. Mondays were always slow in the beginning of the night until about 11pm. Monday was 'Jerry Adams Metal Night'. Famous Metal bands and movie stars were always on hand until the wee hours drinking.

I arrived at the bar at 6pm. The doors to the public open at 7pm. At 6:30pm I heard a knock on the window. It was Eric from *Weedkiller*. I let him in. He sat at the bar.

I decided to open the doors. The bar was ready for business. Eric was the only person sitting at the bar. I began telling him the story about the dogs.

"I swear to God I heard the dogs talking to me. They

were these weird and different colors. Colors I have never seen before."

Eric was laughing at me.

"Did you go out and smoke dust or take mushrooms after our recording session," he asked.

He saw how serious I was. He got quiet. He chugged his beer.

"Hey, Man. Things like that happen. When you're on a hallucinogenic," Eric cackled. "Give me another beer, Doctor Doolittle!"

"I don't do hallucinogenics. You know that!" I said.

I grabbed him another beer. I rang it up. I moved on from the dog talking story. Eric didn't believe me at all.

About 7pm people started trickling into the club. About 7:15 a woman walked in. I saw her talk to the singer of the 8 o'clock band. She approached the bar. She ordered a club soda with a splash of cranberry. I thought to myself, 'This crowd doesn't seem like the boozing type. It's going to be a slow start'.

I put the drink in front of her. I grabbed her money. I rang it up. As I put her change on the bar she reached out and touched the back of my hand. It was a light graze. I became alarmed. People don't reach out and touch people unless they know them. The woman looked me in the eye and spoke.

"Dogs want to talk to you."

I stopped in my tracks. Thinking I didn't hear her right. I spoke.

"What did you say?"

"Dogs want to talk to you. Right?" She asked.

I didn't say anything. I told only two people the dog story. My girlfriend and Eric. I just told Eric. He hasn't moved from his seat. Nobody was around to overhear when I told him. My girlfriend was embarrassed by the story. I knew she wouldn't tell anyone. I asked her if she knew my girlfriend.

"No. I don't know her. You must excuse me. Sometimes I say things I should keep to myself," she replied.

"Why would you say, 'Dogs want to talk to me'? Right after you touched me?" I asked, kind of tough.

"I'm a psychic. When I saw you. The force in me was overwhelming to tell you what I said. I don't really know what it means, because that was all I heard."

I was quiet. I looked at this woman. For some reason I trusted her. She had a nice vibe. I told her the story of the dogs talking to me, of the funeral, of praying for the girl for weeks.

The woman looked at me. Something was going on in her head. I was mesmerized. She spoke.

"While you were sitting on the bench outside the church. The girl who died was there. She noticed you. She saw how sad you were for her family. She wanted you to know she heard all your prayers. Even the ones you said when she was in the coma. She wanted to thank you. She wanted to let you know she was safe, and all right, and at peace."

Tears welled in my eyes. Eric, at the other end of the bar, noticed my emotions watering my face. He raised an eyebrow. His tough guy singer was misted behind the bar.

The woman continued.

"She sent the dogs to let you know she was fine and safe. It's ok. You're not crazy. Those dogs were from the other side, but very much real. She doesn't want you to worry. She wants you to know she's ok."

I stared at the ladies eyes. I felt light. I felt the other side tugging.

A group of people came into the club. They walked up to the bar. I had to break the eye contact with the lady and do my job. I got the costumers orders.

Mike Lawler the soundman walked up to the bar to get a soda. He asked me, "What were you talking to the psychic lady about? You looked pretty intense."

"You know her?" I shot back at Mike.

"I know who she is. She's a psychic. I've seen her on TV. She writes books. She spoke at a book store I did the sound for one day."

I didn't want to get into the story with Mike. The Lion's Den was starting to fill up.

"Nothing. I wasn't talking about anything," I said to Mike.

I went over to Eric.

"What was with the water works before? You going soft?" he asked.

"That lady I was talking with is a psychic. She asked me from out of nowhere, 'Do dogs want to talk to you?' She told me the girl having the funeral sent the dogs to let me know she was all right."

"Why would she send the dogs to you? You didn't even know her."

I knew the answer. I didn't want to tell Eric about my other side. That I pray. In his eyes, I'm just a loud pissed off rock n' roller. That's the way I wanted him to think. I wanted to get off the subject.

"Want to do a shot to our record?" I asked Eric.

"Hell Yeah!"

I poured two shots of cheap rot-gut house bourbon. We drank to our recording.

Weedkiller Wednesdays 1998

CHAPTER 25

WEEDKILLER WEDNESDAYS 1998

In the fall of 1998 it was almost a year and a half since The 4th Floor broke up. My new band *Weedkiller* was a doing real well. We had a 6 song CD and had been playing shows with like-minded heavy bands. Our fan base was growing.

Weedkiller was a mix between *Tool, Black Sabbath*, and *Korn.* Our line-up was solid with Laurent "Frenchy" Cosani on guitar, Eric Czar on bass, Kenny Kramme (from The 4th Floor) on drums. Myself and Captain Al Batenko (also 4th Floor) were on vocals.

One night on Bleecker Street I was approached by my promoter friend Rachel Martinez to do a residency at a club in the Saint Marks section of The East Village. A residency is when a band has an ongoing day of the week to perform. Rachel wanted us to play every Wednesday Night at midnight.

The last residency I had was with *The 4th Floor* at The

Red Lion on Bleecker Street two years earlier. It was for every Friday and Saturday night at 1am. That residency lasted a couple years and made us very tight as a band. It was also the place that got us a record deal.

Besides writing songs people want to hear, a great location to perform is very important for a band to get exposure. Along with writing good songs, *The 4th Floor* had fans from all over the world because of The Red Lion's Bleecker Street tourist location.

The tourists who saw *The 4th Floor* perform on Bleecker Street would buy our shirts and tapes. They would go back home to Europe, or Brooklyn, or South America, or the midwest, or New Jersey, or where ever they were from and play the tapes for their friends. Our fan base was pretty big and worldwide.

Saint Mark's Place was very similar to Bleecker Street. It was a tourist destinations. I knew *Weedkiller* would have a great chance to grow the fan base if we did a residency at this club. Except for one thing. The owner was a jerkoff.

I told Rachel, "If we do the residency you got to keep that prick owner away from us. I've been to shows at his club. I see how he treats his staff and the bands. He's a complete douchebag. We are not going to work well together."

There wasn't a band in New York City the owner of this club didn't piss off. Why should we be any different?

Saint Marks Place in the 90's was a Bohemian mecca. The building on *Led Zeppelin's Physical Graffiti* album cover is at 98 Saint Marks place a few minutes' walk from this club. Tourist flocked from all over the world to see it. They also visited to experience live music and real New York City artists. Thousands of people walked around all day and night long.

Rachel and I talked about a door deal. Most deals in New York City, the first ten people that pay to see a band go to the promoter. Whatever money comes in after that goes to the band. The club usually does not get involved. Rachel was one of the few promoters I trusted. She ran an honest door.

I asked Rachel to not do a cover charge for *Weedkiller* Wednesdays. Let our show be free.

Rachel stood quiet for a second thinking. She knew that meant no money in it for her.

I knew the door money generated at midnight on a Wednesday wasn't going to be that big. It wouldn't be worth the hassle. I needed to exploit the location of this club and grow our fan base. Thousands of people walked by this place hourly.

I pitched Rachel, "I'll put my own flyer guy on the street to hand out free admission flyers. Weedkiller will print and pay for it all. We'll exploit the Saint Marks walk around crowd. That's the plan. What do you say?"

Rachel was calculating in her head. She thought deep and hard for a minute.

"You know what? Let's go for it," Rachel said. "I'll make my money from the earlier slots in the night. If the bar does good after midnight, the owner won't bust my chops. He'll leave me alone and that'll be a win."

"Good deal! You know the owner there is an idiot. He should be packed every night. He has the best location in the city. He could rival CBGB's but he's an ass."

Rachel nodded in agreement.

I continued my rant, "He could develop music the world would want to hear from his spot but he doesn't. He chooses to bully his staff and shit on bands!"

"I know. It's such a shame. I wish I owned the club," Rachel said.

"Don't worry about nothing. I got the best flyer guy in the city," I told Rachel.

Monk was my flyer guy at The Lion's Den. He worked the crossroads of Bleecker and Sullivan Streets like a silky smooth charm. Monk was absolutely fantastic. He had a happy stance and was sincere in his desire to let people know about good live music.

I knew if Monk was out on Saint Marks he would zone in on the tourist crowd. He was the best direct marketing tool in the New York City street world.

Monk wouldn't worry about just handing flyers out to any and everybody. He was a quality over quantity guy. His goal would be to expose the band to as many new Japanese, German, Swiss, Long Island, New Jersey, Brooklyn, Queens, and anywhere fans. He would zone in on the walk around people looking for live music and a good time. Monk had a 6th sense.

"My flyer guy will get this place packed. I know *Weedkiller* will keep the crowd," I told Rachel.

"Ok. Wednesdays Midnight! It's on!" She smiled.

We shook hands.

With the handicap of the dick owner, the Vegas over/under odds line for Weedkiller Wednesdays was for five Wednesdays.

Day one of Weedkiller Wednesdays.

The only way *Weedkiller Wednesdays* would go wrong is if the owner spoke to me or any band member. This owner talked down to everybody. I knew it was only a matter of time before he acted the ass. My job was to keep the night going for as long as possible. If the owner talked to me. I needed to bite my tongue. If I couldn't. The residency would be over. I knew *Weedkiller* could get a bunch of new fans every show at this club. I planned on being quiet.

I met Eric and Al at the Lion's Den to have a few cocktails before the first show. We met at 9 O'clock. We left two hours later feeling good. Eric and I were pretty good drinking buddies since the day I met him. Al and I had been drinking buddies since the 8th grade. Frenchy and Kenny were at the club when we walked in.

Frenchy had our free drink tickets in his hand. He dealt them out. Each band member got two tickets. About fifteen minutes later Monk showed up. He was smiling. He was happy to be there. I knew his good glow and happy stance would attract people. I handed him a stack of flyers.

"Don't go out until 11:45. The flyer says midnight but we are going on at 12:15 sharp. Let people know that. These flyers are for free admission. Hand them only to people looking to see music," I said to Monk.

At 11:45pm we went to set up. Monk went outside to drum up new heads. We had a draw of twenty or thirty regulars that always seemed to show up when we played. I knew they would come. Those people were very important but we still needed new people to experience the band to grow our fan base. That was Monk's job. Pick out new fans.

Monk saw *Weedkiller* many times. He loved us. He really thought we were great. He will have that sincerity when he speaks to the tourists. It will attract people.

We hit the stage at fifteen minutes after midnight. The club was doing well. There was our regular crowd of twenty five mixing in with the previous band's crowd. Monk's flyer flow was starting to roll in. I saw about fifteen new faces with flyers in hand entering the club. I figured by the time we played our third song this place would be packed.

We opened with "Coffee", a violent song about the decay of society's moral compass. A small pit formed with our regulars. I looked at the club's front window from the stage. I saw heads peering in. They had flyers in their hands. I could tell they were deciding to come in or not. We were jumping all over the place going crazy. The energy coming off the stage was hazardous and hard. We played our second song "Bucket", a groove filled anthem about 'Sometime you got to choose to be happy'.

The crowd grew in front of the stage. Two groups of five were getting ID'd at the front door. Monk was kicking ass. I decided to stop thinking about the door and get lost in the music.

The third song was called "Poking". It was a trippy song with heavy riffs. I looked at the crowd toward the end of the song. The place was packed. People were dancing in the pit. It was great. The owner, wearing the stupidest looking rice patty field hat, stood behind the bar like a douche.

We played for an hour and a half. The show was great. The bar made money. Monk got thirty or forty keepers that stayed for the entire show. The people Monk brought in drank allot. The bartender and the club did well. Rachel wasn't gonna get her balls busted.

I jumped off the stage into the audience. I saw the owner. He was still standing behind the bar looking like a dick. He wore a hat that an eighty year old Vietnamese grandmother would wear. I avoided any eye contact with him. If he came near me I planned to look off like someone was calling me, then run away.

When you pack a good bar owner's place they throw beers at you when you come off stage. Our drink tickets were long gone. We packed this club from midnight to 2am on a Wednesday. We were not charging the club any money. We also came out of pocket for fliers and a flyer guy who filled the bar and I was still nervous about this owner acting like a jerkoff. I couldn't complain because I willingly made the deal. But, if he didn't offer to comp us a round of beers for doing the great job we did, I knew I wouldn't be able to keep my mouth shut. There would be no tongue bite.

The best strategy to keep the residency going was to not put this guy in a position to act the ass, because he will. I knew it wasn't worth the gamble to ask this prick for a beer. I didn't want to give him a chance to charge me. I would flip out if he did.

Over and over again I said to myself, "Keep heart for this place as long as you can. It's the first night. Don't get thrown out. We need to grow our fan base."

I decided I had to leave the premises immediately. I took a step toward the front door. I was going to take off. At that instant two Japanese guys came up to me.

"Can we get on your mailing list? We are from Tokyo."

"Of course. Thanks. Let me get it."

I went to get the clipboard on stage.

Eric was wrapping his cables. He was staring at the bar while he wrapped. He spoke, "Hey, look at that dickhead behind the bar wearing his stupid hat. I swear! If he charges me for a beer I'm going to be pissed. We packed his place."

"I know," I said.

Eric was about four minutes from having all his gear packed up. Then it would be on. Eric would go to the bar for an after show beer. If the owner asked for money, it wasn't going to be pretty.

"Hey Kev! Eric!"

Someone was screaming our names. We looked over. It was the "Three Romanians". The "Three Romanians" were three immigrant Romanian guys living in New York City. They always came to see Weedkiller. Their giant hands were filled with beers and shots. They were walking over to us.

I said to myself, "Thank the Lord."

Frenchy, Kenny, and Al were waved over. The "Three Romanians" bought a beer and a shot for the whole band. I loved those guys. They always supported us and made the band feel great. We were safe for this round. But I knew we had to get out of the club as quick as possible.

I did the shot with the band and the Three Romanians. I thanked them. I grabbed my beer. I went back to the Japanese guys to get their names and addresses. I chit chatted with them for a minute then I put the mailing list at the front door by Rachel. People lined up to sign it. I saw Monk. I paid him. I went back to Eric.

"Let's get out of here after these beers. I'll tell the Romanians and everybody to go to The Red Lion," I said.

"Ok!" He replied.

Minutes later most of the crowd was gone. We left too. I felt a sigh of relief once I had the band and our friends out on the street. Weedkiller, The Three Romanians, The two Japanese guys, and a bunch of other new people walked the ten minute stroll to the Red Lion on Bleecker Street. We hung out until closing. Weedkiller Wednesday number one was a success.

Two Days Later:

Two days later Eric and I were walking up 8th avenue in midtown Manhattan on our way to rehearsal.

I could tell Eric had something on his mind. He was quiet. He was never quiet. I said nothing until he spoke.

"Do you think we drank too much before the show the other night?"

"No? Do you?"

"We drank for three hours before we stepped on stage."

I scrunched my eye brows, perplexed.

"Yeah. So? Some bands can do it. Some bands can't. We can do it. Kenny doesn't drink that much. Frenchy usually keeps it in check. We play clubs and bars. Drinking goes hand in hand. You, me, and Al have the gift. We can hold it together after a few beers."

"I know man. I just don't want to get in the habit of drinking before shows. We should try not to drink before next week's Weedkiller Wednesday."

"Not drink!?" I said, aghast. "Not drink anything before

a show? Why would you want to do that? Look man! I can play drinking, or not drinking. I've done it hundreds of times. I don't think we have a problem. We always show up early. We always kick ass. We never-ever have fucked anything up because of drinking. If we ever did. I would be the first to put a stop to it!"

At the corner of 29th street and 8th avenue we waited for a light. Eric's convicted eyes stared at me over the top of his wire glasses.

"We should do it. At least not drink for three hours before a show," Eric said.

"Ok, what do you want to do?"

"How about we don't drink until 11:30 this Weedkiller Wednesday? We are billed for midnight. We can't get in that much trouble," Eric said.

I was annoyed and defiant that I was listening to this. The light changed. We started walking again.

"I don't care Bro. Fine with me. I don't think we have a problem with our live show. I would never let booze, or anything fuck us up. We are big boys. This isn't a pussy band," I said.

Eric stopped walking. I stopped too. He spoke, "Ok. No drinking until 11:30 on Weedkiller Wednesday next week. Deal?"

He put out his hand. I nodded affirmative.

"Deal!"

We shook.

Weedkiller Wednesday show #2:

I arrived at 11 O'clock. Rachel was at the front door smiling. The club was busy. It was already a good night for the house now it was our turn to add to the pile. Monk was lined up to hand out flyers again. I knew we would do well this night.

Al, Frenchy, Eric, and Kenny walked in sporadically over the next ten minutes. Eric came up to me.

"Did you get the drink tickets?" He asked.

"Whoa! You got twenty minutes before you can use them. Remember?"

"Of course I remember. We got eighteen minutes though. Do you have the tickets?" He asked again.

I pulled them out of my pocket, "I got them."

Eric reached out grabbing his tickets, "We need to do this. We have been getting out of control lately. It's the right thing."

"What are you 'High Horse Magee'?" I asked him.

"No. You'll thank me. The band will be tighter."

"I got no problem. I've always paced myself. Most times I don't even drink for shows and we're tight as hell."

"Tell whatever you want to yourself," Eric said. He turned to the digital clock behind the bar and continued, "We got seventeen minutes."

Eric walked away. The crowd was filing in. I knew most of last week's twenty five regular fans wouldn't be there. I knew another twenty would take their place. To keep the show fresh for those repeat people we planned a totally different set list.

Between our regular fans, the new tourist crowd Monk would wrangle, and the leftover people from the band before us, we would be in good shape for a nice audience. Things were good.

A few more minutes past. Eric walked up. Frenchy was with him.

"Eleven minutes," Eric said.

"Let me ask you," I replied. "You haven't had a drink since last night. Nothing at all today?"

I made a drinking motion like I was sipping a bottle from inside a coat and questioned, "You weren't Sneak Pete'n in the corner somewhere? Were you?"

Eric stuck out his chest proud.

"Nope! Nothing all day."

Frenchy was shaking his head the whole time while he listened. He was holding a beer. He took a sip making sure Eric and I saw it before he spoke, "You guys are fucked up. Why you waiting until 11:30 to drink? You guys are idiots."

Frenchy was right, but this had nothing to do with him or anybody else in the band. It was between Eric and me. Kenny and Al came over smiling and giggling. They were holding beers. They took big sips also making sure Eric and I saw them.

"What's up? You guys still waiting until 11:30 to drink?" Kenny laughed.

"We got ten minutes," Eric answered.

Al decided it was time to give one of his speeches. He directed it at Eric and me.

"You guys should look deep, man! What the fuck do you think you're trying to prove? As long as it doesn't affect the show, drink! If it affects the show! Don't drink! Fighting yourself to wait until 11:30 is stupid," Al said, speaking like a disgusted football coach.

Some friends and fans came over interrupting Al's speech. We all started chit chatting. Another few minutes crept by. Eric was talking with the soundman twenty feet away from where I stood. In his mid-conversation Eric looked up from the soundman. He yelled across the bar toward me.

"Six Minutes to go!"

I have to admit I was watching the clock too. At 11:27 Eric slid in beside me at the bar. He waved the bartender over and ordered, "Two Long Island Ice Teas, Please."

"Hey whoa! You have three minutes to go!"

"I'm going to wait the three minutes. I want the drinks here when the clock strikes booze. No waiting around."

The Long Island Ice Tea is one of the most powerful

drinks. It has a shot from five different liquors in it, gin, vodka, rum, tequila and triple sec. Eric just ordered two.

"I don't want a Long Island Ice tea. Why you ordering one for me?" I asked.

Eric was leaning over the bar watching the bartender pour the drinks. He turned to me to answer, "I didn't order one for you. I ordered two for me!"

I called the bartender over, "Two Long Island Ice Teas for me too, please." If he was going there, so was I.

My drinks arrived at 11:29pm. Eric and I stared at the clock like we were waiting for New Years to ring in at midnight. It seemed like forever until the clock struck 11:30. When it did we tapped glasses. Eric chugged his first ice tea down in two gulps. I decided, 'Fuck it'. I chugged my ice tea down in two gulps. After all, we had to be in the same mindset for the show I figured.

I called the band over. The bartender walked past. I stopped her, "Shots of Jägermeister for *Weedkiller*."

The bartender poured the shots. We all cheered to a great show and to Weedkiller Wednesdays having a long and prosperous run. Once the empty shot glasses hit the bar. Al called out, "Fill'em up again! Another shot for the boys in *Weedkiller!*"

The bartender filled the shot glasses once again. We raised a toast to being alive. We downed the second shot. Eric called the bartender over. His second Ice Tea was finished, "Two buds please."

I politely chimed to the bartender, "I'll take two buds too."

The boys from *Weedkiller* threw our money in a pile for the bartender to work from. I chugged my second ice tea. The buds came quick. Eric and I knocked bottles. I said to him, "It's probably almost midnight. We should set up."

We looked at the clock. It was 11:36. We were only drinking for six minutes. In six minutes Eric and I had two Long Island Ice Teas, two shots of Jägermeister, and we were now working on beers.

More people started arriving. Two of the "Three Romanians" showed up. They came over and bought shots and beers for the band. I was done with my second beer. So was Eric. The Romanian's round came at a perfect time.

I felt all the booze hit me at once. It made me feel invincible. We had five more minutes of drinking until we had to set up. Eric called the bartender over, "One more Long Island Ice Tea, two buds and a shot of Jägermeister. I need to stock up for the stage. We have a long set."

"Me too. Same thing," I echoed.

We got on stage at 11:55 to set up. Our first song was 12:15. We played like total madman that night. The crowd was a lot like the one the week before. Monk did his job. A pit broke out. Eric jumped into it at one point. He was all over the stage. So was I. It was a nasty hard-hitting energetic show. The crowd was happy.

After the show we were all drenched in sweat. We played for over an hour again. All the booze had sweated out of us.

The night was a success. Eric and I didn't have a drink until 11:30. The crowd got rocked. The register was hit hard with money again. The show was crazy, fun, and great. We got thirty new people on our mailing list. Rachel wasn't gonna get her balls busted. A success all around.

The crowd emptied after the show. I wanted to get out of there. The dick owner was standing behind the bar menacing his staff. He had his stupid hat on. I wanted no interaction with him.

A lot of my waitress, bartender, and bouncer friends from Bleecker Street were at the show. Steve the new owner of

The Lion's Den came to the show too. He was a good guy and a friend. He also knew how to run a club. He was one of the good bar owners. Steve and I were drinking buddies.

He called over the bartender, "Get everyone here a drink, please. And shots if they want."

There were five band guys and ten Bleecker Street people at the bar. That was a big round of booze.

The bartender was good. Everybody had their drink within two minutes. She was adding up the round in her head. Those who had shots cheered and drank them. The round came to seventy four dollars. The only good thing about this place was drinks were cheap. Steve handed her the money. She rang the register. I heard the clanking. She put the money in the kitty. She gave Steve the change. Steve tipped her. She said, "Thanks."

At the same millisecond the bartender said, "Thanks", I heard the register clang three times. That is the sound of a register being zee'd out. That means the night is over. I looked over to see who hit it since the bartender was standing right in front of us. It was the jerkoff owner in his Vietnamese Grandma hat. He grabbed all the money out of the register. He made a snickering-obnoxious face. He then looked toward the ceiling and yelled, "Drink them up! Let's go! Closing time! Drink 'em up!"

I couldn't believe what I heard. Steve just bought a seventy four dollar round of drinks less than eight seconds ago and this prick was throwing us out. Everybody got real quiet. We were all bar people.

I heard the voice in my head, "This is the test. Be quiet and leave. Be quiet and leave right now!"

Steve snapped, "What the fuck is that! We had the drinks five seconds!"

Steve was pissed. He shook his head but he wasn't going to start a fight in someone else's club. I chugged my beer. I did my shot. I walked as fast as I could out of there.

"Come on! Let's go! Drink up!" I heard the dick owner yell again as the door closed behind me.

In front of the club I was alone with the street traffic. People started to trickle out. It took about three or four minutes before everybody was outside. I looked around for all of the members of Weedkiller. Everyone was present and accounted for, except Eric.

I looked in the window of the bar. The bouncer was standing in front of Eric a few feet from the front door. I knew the bouncer very well. I knew he wasn't going to hurt one of my band guys. Eric was walking backward screaming. The bouncer was walking face front of him. The bouncer had his arms out-stretched herding Eric to the street.

Eric gave one final outburst before he stepped outside, "Who the fuck do you think you are? A guy pays seventy four dollars for a round of drinks and you throw him out five seconds later! Fuck you!"

Eric walked over to me still screaming, "I want to punch that guy in the face."

I knew Weedkiller Wednesdays were over. I did what I set out to do. I bit my tongue. Eric on the other hand didn't promise himself that. Stone-faced, I spoke calm to Eric.

"Go for it. Punch that prick in the face. I'll get you back in there. I know that bouncer."

"Get me in there. I'm going to punch that owner in the face."

I walked over to the bouncer. I had worked with him at different places over the years. He hung out with Big Rob my buddy from the Lion's Den. He knew all of the Bleecker Street crowd I was with. He saw me coming. He spoke first, "I'm sorry Kev. He's a dick. That was wrong what he did to Steve and you guys. That round was a lot of money."

"Listen that guy has no respect for anybody. Eric wants to tell him so."

"Fuck it Kev! I don't care. I hate that guy. He paid me for the night already anyway. He's always getting screamed at. So many people hate him he will forget it ever happened. See ya around!"

The bouncer walked away. I pointed to Eric.

"Let him have it."

Eric stormed past me into the club. I watched from the window. The dick owner was still by the register. Eric rushed up to the bar. Lucky for the dick owner the bar separated Eric from him. I could hear Eric yelling faintly through the street sounds of buses and cabs through the window. The dick owner put on an 'I-don't-give-a-fuck-I-am-the-boss-here' look.

I could clearly hear the words, "Cocksucker! Mutherfucker!" hollered by Eric.

Another clearly audible set of words were, "Everybody hates you! Nobody likes you! You are a piece of shit. I will never play here again!"

The dick owner never took the snippy look off his face. Eric was screaming at the top of his lungs. He grabbed a bar stool. The dick owner finally got nervous. His snippy look disappeared. He threw his hands up in surrender. Eric threw the barstool across the bar toward the stage. He grabbed another one and flung it against the wall. On his way outside Eric knocked over every barstool.

Everybody had walked over to the Red Lion except Frenchy, Kenny, Al, and I. We waited for Eric to unload his rage. When he came back out to the street I asked him, "You feel better?"

Eric smiled, "Yes I do! Now let's go to The Red Lion and celebrate."

Official length of Weedkiller Wednesdays: Two Wednesdays.

Al won the pool.

Yogi Berra Is A Great Guy 1999

CHAPTER 26

YOGI BERRA IS THE GREATEST PERSON

The Yankee World Series Parade October 29, 1999

Weedkiller was recording allot during 1999. I had picked up extra work as a sound operator for TV crews to supplement my income at the Lion's Den in order to pay for studio time. I tell this story of my meeting the baseball legend Yogi Berra on October 29th, 1999 all the time. My friends make me tell this story again and again. In a New York City bar if you bring up the name Yogi Berra everyone will smile. He was one of the coolest people I have ever met.

For those who don't know Yogi Berra was responsible for some of the greatest linguist sayings in American history. Coming up with gems like, "It ain't over, til it's over."

"The future ain't what it used to be."

"Always go to other people's funerals, otherwise they won't go to yours."

"A nickel ain't worth a dime anymore".

"Baseball is ninety percent mental. The other half is physical."

"I always thought that record would stand until it was broken."

"It gets late early out there now."

"It's déjà vu all over again."

"Nobody goes there anymore, because it's too crowded."

In April of 1985 Yogi was the manager of the New York Yankees. Sixteen games into the season Yankee owner George Steinbrenner fired him. Yogi Berra was disappointed at "Not getting a fair shake" in his words. Yogi vowed to never go to Yankee Stadium, a place he had been a part of for 40 years, as long as George Steinbrenner was owner of the team.

The feud lasted fourteen years until George Steinbrenner apologized to Yogi in January of 1999 for the firing. Yogi accepted the apology. A few months later Yogi Berra threw out the ceremonial first pitch at Yankee Stadium.

Later in that 1999 season George Steinbrenner proclaimed July 18th,1999 "Yogi Berra Day" at Yankee Stadium. It was a Sunday afternoon. David Cone was pitching for the Yankees. Yogi was honored on the field before the game. I call it "Yogi Magic" because David Cone pitched a perfect game that day.

A perfect game is the hardest and most prized accomplishment a pitcher can achieve. It is an extremely rare occurrence. The only time a perfect game was pitched in World Series history was by Yankee Don Larson, Yogi Berra was the catcher. It was on October 8th, 1956 at Yankee Stadium.

In a twist of fate Don Larson was in attendance for David Cone's perfect game, because it was 'Yogi Berra Day' at Yankee Stadium. Don Larson was there to honor Yogi. That

1999 season was a championship season for the Yankees. They won the World Series. "Yogi Magic" once again.

On the morning of Friday, October 29th, 1999, a parade was scheduled down the 'Canyon of Heroes' in New York City for the Yankees. Yogi Berra was asked to join in the parade to celebrate the victory as one of the greatest living Yankees.

On the day of the Yankee parade Friday October 29th, 1999 I had a sound tech job for a TV production company. Being a recording musician I was happy to have this extra means of making money. Our assignment was to go to *The Yogi Berra Museum* in New Jersey to film with Yogi.

We were at the Museum in Montclair by 6:00am to set up for the 8:15am taping. Yogi was going to do a sit down interview and a walk and talk around the museum. The shoot was scheduled from 8:15 to 8:45am. Yogi had to be on the road to the parade in lower Manhattan by 9am.

We had a good team of TV people. My childhood friend Captain Al (also 4th Floor and Weedkiller member) was on the crew too. He was the camera guy. Al changed from bar business and music to TV production at this point in his career.

We hung lights all around the museum for the walk and talk. We lite the set for the sit down interview. There were no glitches, no problems. Yogi showed up at 8am. Everything ran well.

Yogi was a great interview. He talked about everything, especially Mickey Mantle. It was a great day and a great interview. We were done on time at 8:45am. We did our job. Yogi had plenty of time for the nineteen mile trip to make the 11am parade.

With no traffic you could be in Lower Manhattan from Montclair, New Jersey in less than thirty minutes. The Lincoln and Holland Tunnels into New York City are a few miles from Montclair. It was a weekday morning. There would be traffic.

They gave Yogi two hours to make the parade. Should be no problem.

After the interview was over my sound mixing job was done. I packed the audio gear up. It took about fifteen minutes. Once my audio equipment was packed away, it was time to help take down lights and wrap cables.

I was told to take down the lights in the farthest room we had lit in the museum and work my way back to the interview base. I got moving. We had a ten foot ladder with us to hang our lights. When you film a walk and talk interview you don't usually want to see light stands and cables. What we do is hang lights from ceiling beams, tops of shelves, or whatever you can get the light to grasp onto with your "grip" gear.

In the room I was dismantling we hung lights from ceiling beams. I climbed to the top of the ten foot ladder to reach the first light to take down. My feet were on the second to the top rung of the ladder. About eight feet up.

I was in a precarious position stretching out over the floor unhinging the light from the beam. The ladder was in the best position to get at the light. It was still precarious. I was extending my reach as far as I could on the ladder. The ladder was shaky. I was turning the nut from the light to remove it when I felt the shaky ladder stop moving. Someone grabbed it. I thought I was the only one in the room. I figured it was Al.

I look down to see what was going on. It wasn't Al grabbing the ladder. It was Yogi. I was in a precarious position holding a giant steel light. I felt immediate danger for Yogi underneath me. He saw me look down. He spoke, "I got ya kid. Don't worry."

I had a six pound red hot thousand watt metal light barely in my hand, and barely attached to the beam. It was dangling fifteen feet right over Yogi Berra's head. I thought to myself, 'If I drop this. Yogi is going to get creamed. I don't want to be the guy that skulls Yogi Berra. I would be the most hated man in New York City history'.

I spoke back to Yogi, "I got it Yogi. I'm ok. I don't want to drop this light on you."

"You won't drop it. You got it kid," Yogi said with encouragement.

I realized Yogi wasn't going away. Like a brain surgeon I began to unfasten the piping hot light. I gripped it as if I was saving the world. Thank God my gloves kept the heat away from my hand. One false move and Yogi was going to get it.

Yogi kept talking to me while I unhinged the light, "You know kid? I don't like Little League baseball."

I didn't answer Yogi. I concentrated on the task at hand. I was too worried about dropping this molten object on his head to respond. It took a minute until I got the light off the beam. I breathed a sigh of relief. I had the light secure in my hand. I gripped it hard. I looked down at Yogi. He was still talking.

"Little league is just not good for kids," Yogi continued.

I climbed down the ladder careful with the light in one hand. I wasn't going to attempt to remove the other lights that were right next to the one I just took down. Not while Yogi Berra was underneath me. Besides, Yogi Berra is talking to me about Little League baseball. I have to hear what he has to say.

When I got to the bottom of the ladder I was standing facing Yogi. I was taller than him. He was in his 70s at the time. I was in my early 30's. I sat on the second from the floor rung of the ladder. I was a little below Yogi's eye level. I wanted to show Yogi Respect.

There was nobody in the room. Just me and one of the greatest baseball players ever. I wasn't star struck at all. Yogi was just like the old World War II guys I grew up with. I loved listening to those guys stories.

I finally responded to Yogi's earlier statement, "Why don't you like Little League baseball, Yogi?"

Yogi had no hesitation in his answer.

"You don't get to build confidence," he said. "You don't get to get the at-bats in Little League baseball. A kid who could be a great hitter will get two, maybe three at-bats in a Little League game. If he doesn't get a hit at first. The coach would think he's no good and he'll get less at-bats. A kid who doesn't do good at first in Little League baseball could be ruined. He could think he's no good."

"I never thought about that, Yogi."

"Yeah. We didn't have Little League baseball where I grew up on *The Hill* in Saint Louis. We played in the street or we played in empty lots. We would get up twenty-five or thirty times in a game. That's how I learned to hit. I wasn't any good at first, but I got the at bats and then I got the confidence. A kid could be a great future hitter, if he don't do good at first, he'll never get the confidence in Little League baseball."

"You're right Yogi," I said. "I could see what you're talking about."

"It's like that in anything kid. Confidence. You got to build confidence. It doesn't matter what you do. You got to have confidence."

For the next fifteen minutes Yogi Berra talked to me about life, about timing, about making your own way, about confidence. I sat on the second rung from the floor of this ten foot ladder, and I listened. Yogi was in the middle of speaking when Al came in the room.

Al saw Yogi talking to me. He walked over and sat on what space was left on the second rung from the floor of the ladder. He pushed me aside with his butt to fit. I grew up with Al. It felt like we were eleven years old again.

Yogi spoke to Al, "You know kid. I was just telling your pal here that I'm not a fan of Little League baseball."

"Oh yeah. Why Yogi?" Al asked.

"Confidence. It can ruin a kid..."

For the next twenty minutes Yogi Berra spoke to me and Al about life. He told us stories about the Yankees in the 50's. He talked to us about Don Larson's perfect game. He talked to us about Jackie Robinson and Mickey Mantle. Every story Yogi told he related it to life. He related it to always doing your best. Listening to Yogi was like having an audience with the Pope. Al and I were so captivated we forgot about packing up our gear. We didn't care about the owner of the company in the other room wondering where we were. Neither of us wanted this time to end.

After almost a half an hour of listening to Yogi. I heard a woman's voice calling, "Yogi, Yogi? Where are you?"

Yogi heard the voice too.

"That's my wife," Yogi said.

The voice got closer until Carmen, Yogi's wife, found us in this back room.

"Yogi we're going to be late for the parade. We've been looking for you everywhere," Carmen said.

Carmen turned to us in a consoling manner, "Sorry guys but Yogi's has to go. They're waiting for him in the city."

We nodded humble.

"Ok guys, I got to go the parade now. I'll see you around. Nice talking to you."

Yogi shook our hands, turned, and walked out with his wife.

I had been hanging out with Al since we were children. We were now in our thirties. We played hundreds of shows together as well as worked together many nights. We both were silent in the same room for the first time ever.

"Do you believe that? Yogi was talking to us and I think he forgot about the Yankee parade," I said.

"He's a good guy. For some reason he wanted to tell us

about life," Al said as he began climbing the ladder to get the rest of the lights.

I looked at the clock. It was almost 10am. "If there's traffic. He's not gonna make the parade."

"He'll make it," Al replied. "He's Yogi Berra. They'll shut the tunnel down to get him to the parade on time. He would never ask for it but they would do it in a heartbeat."

"Yep. Presidents, Popes, and Yogi Berra closing the tunnels down. Wow! What a great guy," I shook my head in amazement.

It took about an hour to wrap up and pack the truck. We always had WFAN sports radio on while we drove from job to job. This day was no different. The announcer Susyn Waldman, who legend has it, was responsible for George Steinbrenner apologizing to Yogi earlier that magical year, was on the air. The first words we heard when Al clicked the radio on were from Susyn, "Has anyone seen Yogi? There's no sign of Yogi yet."

I spoke while staring at the radio, "Because he was talking to us about confidence Susyn."

"Oh wait! I think I see Yogi," Susyn said over the radio, "Yep it's Yogi! He's here. Yogi is here!"

Yogi made it in time for the start of the parade.

I ran into Yogi many times over the years on jobs at Yankee Stadium and other TV events. For some reason he always tried to help me with carrying and moving my equipment. I always told him, "I'm ok Yogi. I got it."

He always told me, "I know you do kid."

Yogi Berra was a great human being! God rest his soul.

The 4th of July Staten Island 2000

CHAPTER 27

JULY 4, 2000 STATEN ISLAND, NEW YORK

The Fourth of July in 2000 was on a Tuesday. I had plans to attend a party at my friend's house on Staten Island. Staten Island is one of the five boroughs of New York City. It sits in the middle of New York Harbor along with the Statue of Liberty.

My girlfriend at the time, my friend Wayno Draino, his wife Sharon, and I took the twenty-five minute ferry ride from Manhattan. We went looking for a bar by the ferry terminal when we arrived in Staten Island.

The sunlight reflected hard off the water as we walked along Bay Street looking for a bar. On the corner of Slosson Avenue and Bay Street stood a one story building painted like an American flag, everything red, white, and blue. It was like a flowing river in the desert. The bar had a lit neon Beer sign in the window. It was the bar of our 4th of July dreams. The perfect place to have a drink on Independence Day. The doors were open. We went inside.

The place was busy. A bunch of Navy guys in their whites were whooping it up. I was happy to see them having fun. They were all singing along to Bon Jovi's "Living on a Prayer".

I called my friend from a pay phone to tell him where we were. He said he would pick us up in about an hour.

We got a booth and ordered drinks. I noticed all the Navy guys were Japanese. I said to Wayno, "I can't believe how many Japanese guys are in the Navy. Look! All these Navy guys are Japanese."

Wayno giraffe necked his sight around the bar.

"Yeah. You're right. That's weird," he said.

My girl talked with her hands, very demonstrative, like she was swatting at flies.

"They're all Japanese! Because they're all from Japan!" She squawked.

"Yeah, we know their families are from Japan. Like I was born here, but my family is from Ireland," I answered.

I looked around to see if anyone was listening. I waved everybody to lean in close. I didn't want anybody to hear me, "I can't believe they still segregate people in the Military. That's fucked up."

My girl's head was in close with the rest of us. She whispered, "There's no segregation anymore. At least I hope not," she gave an inconspicuous point, "Look knuckle heads!"

We turned our heads trying to be invisible. We looked to where she was pointing.

She continued whispering, moving her hands like she was catching bubbles in the air. Her voice giving a cadence insinuating Wayno and I were dunces, "Look at the Japanese Flag on their shoulders. They are not Japanese-Americans in the American Navy. They are Japanese-Japanese in the Japanese Navy. They aren't Americans."

I looked at the shoulders of the Navy guys. The Rising Sun flag was on all of their white uniforms.

She continued, "There's an Operation Sail thing going on today in the harbor. There are Navies visiting New York City from all over the world. Why do you think we saw all those war ships in the harbor? The Japanese Navy must be here for it."

Sure enough thirty sailors from the Japanese Navy were getting loaded in a bar painted red, white, and blue on the 4th of July in Staten Island, New York USA 2000. It was great. They were having a ball.

I thought to myself, 'Our Grandfathers were killing each other 55 years ago. Now we're drinking and listening to Bon Jovi together'.

Our drinks came. I proposed a toast.

"Let us remember our Veterans who fought and died for us so we can live in this peace enjoying this moment to-gether. Happy 4th of July. I love America."

We cheersed and started drinking. We had an hour to kill. I walked across the bar to the jukebox. I pulled money out. I put three dollars in the machine. I started looking through the songs. Six drunken Japanese Sailors staggered over to me.

"What you song play?" They asked in broken English.

"I don't know yet. Probably some AC/DC," I replied.

"Yes! Yes! Yes! AC/DC! AC/DC!" They chanted, nodding in cheerful unison.

I looked at these guys. They were having the best time. They were so happy. I moved out of the way.

"Here you go guys. Play whatever you want. It's on me," I said.

I pointed to the numbers in the juke box. I backed away.

"Go ahead play whatever you want," I repeated.

The Japanese Navy guys were joyous. They were nodding, bowing their heads, and smiling. They looked at the song list punching in numbers. The Japanese Navy guys played AC/DC, Journey, Bruce Springsteen, Black Sabbath, The Beatles, The Stones, and Credence Clearwater Revival. They had wonderful taste.

By the third song everybody in the bar, American and Japanese, stood together arm to arm singing Piano Man by Billy Joel. It was like we had known each other forever. An unforgettable Day. A great 4th of July moment I will never forget.

An hour passed. The singing never stopped. Steve picked us up. We hugged the drunken Japanese sailors on our way out. We high fived the Staten Island regulars. We went to the Party and had a great time.

28

The Secret Service At Kenny's Castaways 2003 or 04

After many years of late New York City Nights had caught up to me in the beginning of 2000. I left the bar industry. I was working as a freelance sound tech for the major tv networks national news broadcasts. Weedkiller was on our 3rd record.

After 9/11 - I was everywhere there was a story to cover about that horrible day. I spent many days at ground zero doing reports. The self-imposed bar industry exile lasted about a year. I missed working in the clubs and the nightlife. But, in reality, I couldn't take all the sad stories I was doing. I couldn't take the sorrow I was exposed to on a one on one daily basis. I was getting seriously depressed. I was becoming immune and cold and feelingless. So, I left my sound job.

In late 2001, I went back to Bleecker Street to find a

job. My old clubs The Red Lion and The Lion's Den were fully staffed. I would have to wait for someone to leave.

Keeping the faith I walked into the legendary Bleecker Street bar Kenny's Castaways to see if I could get a job. A guy named Pat Kenny was the owner. He opened Kenny's Castaway in 1967. He was a legendary New York City bar figure. He loved of all types of music. He called the Village musicians who played his club castaways. Hence the name Kenny's Castaways.

Pattie Smith, Bruce Springsteen, Aerosmith, Yoko Ono, The New York Dolls, The Fugees, and The Smithereens were among the many notable performers that took the stage at Kenny's Castaway over the years.

I knew Pat Kenny for over ten years at the time. I was in the right place at the right time because the door guy just quit. Pat hired me on the spot.

In the early 1990's Pat Kenny taught me a lot about the bar business. Even though I worked for other clubs on the Bleecker Street strip, Pat would give me advice when I asked. I would hang out at Kenny's Castaways a lot after my shifts at The Lion's Den. I also performed there many times in impromptu jams and with *The 4th Floor*.

Pat was a fan of *The 4th Floor*. He put our Cd in the Kenny's Castaways jukebox. It was great to listen to it late at night. When *The 4th Floor* broke up Pat pulled the CD out of the Jukebox and threw it in the garbage. He was pissed off at us. I remember him giving me a speech about holding things together and we were on our way to the top. Despite that scolding he gave me that day Pat Kenny was always very, very good to me. Pat died in 2002. When he left us so did a huge piece of New York City's musical heritage.

Kenny's Castaways sat next door to another long time Village mainstay The Back Fence Bar. It was also two doors down from The Red Lion Pub. The Pub where I began my Bleecker Street music and club career over a decade before.

Just Another Night On Bleecker:

It was about twenty minutes to eight when I arrived at Kenny's Castaways this night in 2003 or 2004. I don't remember the exact year. As soon as I walked in the club the daytime bartender Lori flew toward me with a worried look.

She spoke rushed, "The police have been calling all day. They've been asking for you?"

"The police! What the hell do they want with me?"

"Well, he asked for the Head of Security. So, he didn't really ask for you by name."

Lori made a face like she was sorry. I knew something was up.

Lori continued, "Ahh, I gave him your name by accident."

My jaw dropped, "You gave him my name by accident!"

I loved Lori. I knew her for years. She was a great person and the best coworker, but we all knew not to give out names over the phone. I wanted to be mad but I couldn't ever be mad at her. She was too nice of a human being.

"Come on Lori you know the rules. Never give out real names."

"I know. But, he was so official. I didn't think."

"Ok Lor, I'll deal with it. But the next time anybody asks for the Head of Security at Kenny's Castaways, tell them it's Santa Claus!"

"Ok, I will Kev. I told them that you came in at 8pm. He said he would call back. It sounded important."

"By the way Lor... I didn't even know we had a head of security? Did they give a name? Are you sure it was the police?"

It sounded like a cop. The guy sounded important and official. I forgot the name he gave," Lori responded.

I started thinking about what might have happened the night before. I didn't work. I also thought I never knew I had the title "Head of Security". I didn't get paid like a "Head of Security".

"Who worked last night? Do you know?" I asked Lori.

"Andrea and Vanna worked the bar. Jerry worked the door."

At that second Andrea walked in for her 8pm bartending shift. I bum rushed her, "Did anything happen last night? A fight? A robbery?"

Andrea paused for a second taking a step back, "Woah! No! Nothing... It was quiet! Ahh! Hello Andrea would be an appropriate greeting before you jump down my throat Dingbat!"

Andrea was always swift on her feet with quick remarks. She was also a good friend of mine and a great person. By her tone I realized I wasn't cool.

"I'm sorry I jumped on you with questions," I said.

"Don't worry about it Kevin... Oh! Yeah! One thing did happen."

My eyes widened. Lori turned her ear toward Andrea. We both listened for the breaking news.

"The bass player of the second band got really drunk. He wound up puking on stage. Jerry made him clean it up. Nothing out of the ordinary. Why?" Andrea asked.

"The cops have been calling asking for the Head of Security."

"Do we even have a Head of Security?" Andrea replied, sipping on her coffee.

"I guess I am for tonight. Because they're calling back at eight. I got to find out what happened last night."

I walked out in front of the club. I saw Gordon the door guy for The Back Fence Bar next door. I went over to him.

"Hey Gordon! Did you work last night?" I asked.

"Yeah, Why?" Gordon questioned.

"The cops have been calling over to Kenny's all day asking for the Head of Security."

Gordon put a look of shock on his face.

"You guys have a Head of Security?"

"We do now! And it's me. Did you see anything happen last night? A fight? Or, a bust? Or, anything?"

"I didn't notice anything. I gave Joey Lemma a fifty pound bag of onions last night. He got drunk and left it at the bar. I got it in the basement for him. By the way, you want a bag of onions?"

Gordon was from another place and time. He was a hippie from the 70's. He worked The Back Fence door for decades. He had a little farm in upstate New York. He would visit it when he wasn't staying in Brooklyn.

Gordon was always trying to give away onions. Not just a few onions; but fifty pound bags of onions. Gordon was another Village character that was wise beyond his years. He was there for me on Bleecker Street many times when shit went down and I was there for him. And shit always went down on Bleecker Street back then. I loved to listen to Gordon tell stories at the front door of The Back Fence Bar.

"I'm good with the onions Gordon."

I thought about how I would carry a fifty pound bag of onions on the train home.

"So nothing happened that you know of?" I asked again.

"Not that I know of. I was out by 2am last night. Nothing as of 2am. You know anything can happen out here in the witching hours til closing time at four."

"Believe me I know. Thanks, man! Be safe."

I walked the few steps back to Kenny's Castaway's. I saw my sandwich I bought in with me sitting at the bar. I was starving. I had a few minutes to eat before my shift started. Pat Kenny never liked staff eating at the door, or behind the bar. It created an unprofessional atmosphere he said. Pat was right. I always hated walking into a bar when a bartender would be eating not paying attention to their customers. So did Pat Kenny.

I sat at the end of the bar. I threw the semi warm ham and cheese down my throat. It was two minutes to 8pm when I finished. I took a quick leak. I was on the door at thirty seconds to eight.

At 8:01pm the phone rang. Lori answered it. She walked it over to me.

"Hey, Kev! It's him."

She handed me the cordless phone at the door.

"Hello."

"Is this Kevin?"

'Yes," I replied.

I looked at Lori. I gave her the 'Why'd you tell him my name' eyes.

"This is Captain (Blank) from the United States Secret Service."

"The Secret Service," I laughed. "Pete is that you?"

Pete Puma was my buddy from The Lion's Den. He always was playing pranks on me.

"This isn't Pete and this isn't a joke. I am from the Secret Service. In ten minutes two agents are going to approach you and identify themselves. Chelsea Clinton is going to your club tonight to watch the 9 o'clock band. I want to make sure that nobody will bother her."

"I don't let anybody bother anybody when I work! Not just Chelsea Clinton," I replied. My voice taking offense to his questioning the way security is run on my watch.

"Good. I am glad you said that. The agents will be in plains clothes. They will approach you in ten minutes. They will ask for Kevin. Will you be at the door?"

"Yes. I'm always at the door," I replied, offense in my tone. "I'm always at the door."

"Thank you Kevin for your cooperation. Over and out." Click.

While I was speaking Lori and Andrea stood two feet from me watching and listening the whole time. I handed Lori the phone.

"Well, Chelsea Clinton is coming to the club tonight. That was the Secret Service. They wanted to know if I was going to let anybody bother her while she's here."

"What did you say?" Lori and Andrea spoke at the same time.

"Didn't you hear me? I said I don't let anybody bother anybody when I work! You know that anyway."

"Nice!" Both Andrea and Lori spoke again at the same time.

I went back to my post at the front door. I started taking the five dollar cover charge, proofing for ID's, and keeping away the miscreants of downtown New York City.

Bill Clinton had not been President for a few years. Bush number two was President on this night. I hoped there would be no problem while Chelsea was here.

Ten minutes later two men, one black, one white, each about thirty years old walked up to the door. They were carbon copies of the other, except for the skin color. Each guy was about 6-feet tall. I was a little taller than them. They wore normal clothes. Both had on jeans and sneakers. The black guy had on a polo collared shirt with a gap jacket. The white guy had on a t-shirt with a zippered type sweat shirt. They were in shape. You could tell they could kick ass. Before I could ask them for ID. They had theirs out.

"Are you Kevin?"

"Who are you?" I replied.

I never say who I am when working the front door of a New York City club.

"Agent (Blank) and Agent (Blank) United States Secret Service."

They showed me their badges. I looked extra hard. They were official. Or, the best knock off ever. I was sold.

"Yes. I'm Kevin. How can I help you guys?"

I shook their hands. This was for real. This wasn't a joke by my buddy Big Pete.

"Can you show us around?"

"Yep. No problem."

I opened the door. We went inside. I waved for Lori. She walked over.

"Lori, can you watch the door for a minute. It's a five dollar cover."

I gave her the door money.

"Ok," she said.

Lori looked at me like she knew something was up. I spoke of nothing.

I gave the two Secret Service guys the lay of the land. It took about three minutes. They looked at each exit. They looked at the bathrooms and the stage. They were very business-like. They thanked me. I went back to the front door.

I stood outside the club looking in the window. I could see the entire inside of the bar from that vantage point. Kenny's Castaways was a straight shot. Once you walked in the door the bar was on the left. It was about a fifty foot bar. Straight ahead was the stage. The stage was about a little over a hundred feet from the front door. You could see the stage through the windows from the street. I noticed one secret service guy posted up at the end of the bar section right before the beginning of the stage area. The other secret service guy was just inside the door watching who was coming in and out of the club.

They mingled in like chameleons. No one knew that two Secret Service guys were in the club. I didn't tell anyone. Not Lori, not Andrea, not anybody. There was no way any bar customers knew either.

People started arriving in groups of four and five to see the band. It was a yuppie crowd. Before I knew it the place was filling up. About 8:40pm a group of four people walked up with their money and ID's in hand. Chelsea Clinton was one of them. The black Secret Service Guy came outside. He got behind Chelsea's group. Chelsea had her five dollar bill and ID out. Chelsea stuck out her hand and introduced herself.

"Hi. I am Chelsea," she smiled.

"I know who you are, Chelsea. I'm Kevin."

"Glad to meet you, Kevin."

I didn't take her ID. I knew she was just of age from the news. I hesitated taking her money. I was going to comp her but she insisted, "Thanks Kevin. But I want to pay."

"OK," I said.

I took her money.

A local Bum was walking past when I grabbed her money. He noticed Chelsea. He became excited. He started yapping, "Hey, Hey, that's Clinton! That's Chelsea Clinton."

The white secret service agent magically appeared behind the Bum.

I opened the door to let Chelsea and her group inside. The black Secret Service guy followed right behind them.

The Bum walked up to the window. He looked in the bar.

"Was that Chelsea Clinton?" He asked me.

"No. She just looked like her. Didn't she? Her ID said she was from New Jersey. I thought it was her too."

"Man, you telling me!" The Bum said, amazed.

I knew if I told the Bum it was Chelsea he would've never left my doorway.

The white secret service agent made his way inside the club. He gave me a slight affirmative nod as he went past me. The Bum walked down the block shaking his cup of jingle change.

The band Chelsea came to see went on stage at 9:15pm. Everybody was having fun. The Secret Service guys mingled in like fans. They never stopped being nonchalant looking around with their cranberry juices in hand. About 10pm the band finished. I was in front of the club by the door when a small group came outside to smoke after the show. Chelsea came out too.

She wasn't smoking but her friends were. They stood outside the club. Chelsea walked over to me, "Hey Kevin. How you doing tonight?"

"I'm good Chelsea. How are you?"

"Good. The band was great. You must see a lot of music here on Bleecker Street?"

"I do."

While her friends smoked Chelsea asked me questions about the Village and the crowds I see. The Secret Service guys were both outside blending in with the smokers. Some people walking on the street noticed Chelsea. They pointed as they went by whispering, "Look that's Chelsea Clinton."

I never took my eye off the street while Chelsea spoke to me. I would look her in the eye for a blink or two, then scan the street, then look a blink or two, scan Street and so on as I listened. I thought Chelsea was a nice kid.

She was very curious about the history of Greenwich Village. I knew all the answers to her questions. A crowd started gathering noticing Chelsea outside the club. Chelsea and her friends went back inside. I was relieved.

Some of the crowd tried to follow her. I stopped them at the door.

"It's a five dollar cover," I said.

I knew they wouldn't pay. I also knew they weren't going to drink if I let them in. I didn't want gawkers in the club. Especially, non-drinking gawkers. The white Secret Service guy went in with Chelsea. The black secret service guy stood out with me for a few minutes. When the crowd of gawkers dispersed he went inside.

Everybody was having fun in Kenny's Castaways. I was happy there were no problems, so far.

An hour went past. Things were going smooth. I almost forgot Chelsea Clinton and the Secret Service were inside. I decided to go in the club to check on the crowd. When I do this, I go right inside the front door. Always an arm's length from the street and any maniacs that might think no one is watching the door. I looked at the crowd. Chelsea was at the front of the club about ten feet from me. She walked over and spoke.

"Thank you so much for the night, Kevin. I had such a good time. Your club is great. The bartenders and waitresses are so nice. I really appreciate it."

"No problem Chelsea. It's what we do here."

"Well, thank you. I am going to be leaving now."

She stuck out her hand. We shook. She walked outside the club. I went with her. So did the blending in Secret Service guys. Chelsea stood waiting in front of the club for her friends. It was two minutes before they were all outside. It seemed like forever. A new crowd of gawkers walking by noticed Chelsea. The Bum from before came by jingling his cup. He saw Chelsea. He started to get excited. Chelsea and her group got into a car and they were gone. I was extremely relieved.

The Bum rushed up to question me, "That was Chelsea Clinton wasn't it?"

"Yeah, it was." I said like I was busted in a lie.

"Damn! I knew it! Why didn't you tell me before, Kev?"

I thought of what to say. I felt bad. I couldn't tell him the truth.

The Bum was sad. He shrugged his head. He continued speaking, sounding like a three year old, "Dam Kev! Why didn't you tell me Man? That's not right!"

The truth of why I didn't tell him would have hurt him.

I knew he would have been yapping and screaming like an ass. I knew he would have never left the front of the club. I knew he would have made the secret service guys uneasy and who knows what they would have done to him.

I started thinking of a lie to tell the Bum. He was a lost soul, not a bad person. On slow nights I'd talked to him outside the club for hours.

Allot of weekday nights after 2am would be slow. He and I would be the only ones on Bleecker Street. We would chit chat till 4am. We had deep conversations. I liked the guy. He was a good guy. He was just on the wrong side of the edge for now.

"I really didn't think it was Chelsea. I just found out right now that it was her," I lied.

I heard my name called.

"Kevin."

It was the two Secret Service guys.

"Thanks for everything. You guys run a good ship, Kevin." The black Secret Service guy said.

They both shook my hand and off into the night they went. Thirty seconds passed. The Bum was staring at me with a sad puppy face the whole time. I looked around pretending he wasn't there. He knew I knew it was Chelsea from the start. He also knew I felt bad. I knew within five seconds he was going to ask me for money. Two seconds went by, a guy with a newspaperman's type camera hanging around his neck walked up. It broke the sad pouty stare I was getting.

"I hear Chelsea Clinton is in there?" He asked.

"Nope," I replied, ice cold.

The Bum was watching.

"Was she here tonight?" The photographer asked.

"I didn't see her," I said, blank faced.

The Bum was about to speak. I gave him the "Shut the fuck up" look. He ate his words. The photographer asked if he could come in.

"Sure, if ya got twenty dollars. It's a twenty dollar cover charge to get in," I said.

You never want paparazzi in your club. Celebrities will never visit if you get a reputation for letting them in. And paparazzi don't drink. So what bar would want them in just clogging seats and space?

The photographer walked away. The Bum came up to me.

"You got a dollar?" He asked.

"You see me out here every night. Can you remember me ever giving you or anybody else any money?"

"No. I know. I figured I'd try because I caught you in a lie."

The Bum started walking away. He walked about ten feet down the block jiggling his cup. I called after him.

"Hey Calvin! Come here."

He turned around. I reached in my pocket. I took out my wallet. Calvin almost twisted his ankle running over when he saw me pull out money.

"Tomorrow we go back to normal. Don't ever even think about asking me for money again. Cause you're not getting any. I'll go broke out here with all you guys."

I looked him dead in the eyes when I spoke. I handed him two bucks.

"Ok, Kev. Thanks," Calvin said. He walked away.

I watched him head toward the Back Fence bar. I saw Gordon walking out carrying a giant fifty pound bag of onions over his shoulders. Gordon noticed me looking toward him. He shouted, "Hey Kev! You sure you don't want a bag of onions?"

"No. I'm good with the onions Gordon. Thanks though!"

My world was back to normal.

29

The Hug 2003

CHAPTER 30

THE HUG 2003

In 2003 I was working four nights a week at Kenny's Castaways. This particular night working was a weekday. My music life at the time was playing gigs and recording with Frenchy in Weedkiller as a duo. Eric and Kenny were asked to play with an internationally touring blues band. They were gone and out of the picture for this time. We were all still close though. Al was fulltime working in the TV business. Weedkiller was in a never ending search for a bass player and a drummer. It was Frenchy and myself in the band for that moment in our history.

There was a gorgeous bartender who worked a few doors away from Kenny's Castaways. She conjured desires of everything filthy. She walked like she was holding a potato chip in her butt cheeks. She always wore Yoga tights. Her body was fit. She should have been on magazine covers. She never acknowledged me. Ever.

Beside the Irish and Mexican immigrants, most bar

workers on Bleecker Street were artists, actors, musicians, poets, writers, and creative types.

Bleecker Street people were friendly to each other. We all drank together, fought rowdy patron's together, dated each other, and performed shows together. We supported one another and said, "Hi" or "How's it going" when walking past. Not this uppity girl. She exuded an 'I am better than everybody and too good for this block' vibe.

I once asked some other door guys on the block if she ever acknowledged any of them. They all said the same thing, "She puts her head down and walks by. Never says, 'Hello'."

It wasn't just me getting the cold shoulder from her. The entire block got it. I felt better after hearing that.

This summer night at Kenny's Castaways it was late, The Michael Packer blues band had finished playing and loaded out to go home. They were great. Real deal New York City blues. Michael Packer (R.I.P.) was a living legend. It was always busy when he performed. He would start around 8pm and play for four hours without a break sometimes. Every once in a while Michael would call my name up to freestyle some blues with them. It was an honor to do it.

My friend Vanna was the bartender. I was the bouncer. With Michael Packer gone, Vanna was at the jukebox calling out to me. There had to be music playing at Kenny's Castaways every second. Silence was death in a bar we were all taught by Pat Kenny.

"Kev, what do you want to hear?"

"Master of Puppets by Metallica," I replied. One of my favorite songs.

It was about 1:45am. Two hours until last call. We were busy earlier but now the night was slow. Vanna punched the numbers on the jukebox. 'Master of Puppets' by Metallica began to blast. I turned to give Vanna the thumbs up when I got hit by the front door. It opened hard right into my shoulder. The slam sounded and felt of trouble. I turned ready for anything. It was the uppity-hot-tight-wearing Bartender from four doors down. She was in a panic.

"Help me! Help me! There's a Marine trashing my bar. He just attacked a musician on stage. I have no bouncer! Help me, please!" She pleaded.

I thought, 'This Bitch got to be kidding me. Coming in here, finally acknowledging my presence, because she needs help with a drunk Marine'.

I was going to tell her to 'Fuck Off' but something held me back.

"Ok. Let's go," I said.

I fast walked the four doors to her bar getting mentally ready for confrontation. You never want an agitated person seeing you running toward them. Especially, a Marine. It gets people defensive. It makes people more dangerous. You walk with purpose. No running out of control.

I stepped into her bar. I saw a musician holding his jaw. His lip was bleeding. I knew him. I couldn't stand this guy. He was a dick. He played music for chicks, not to move people. He was a pompous ass much like the hot bartender of this club.

In the back of the bar I saw a crew cut Military looking guy in street clothes. He was probably around twenty-three years old. He was in a fighter's stance. He was jumping in place - shadow boxing - ready for anything. Almost every table and chair in the place was overturned. A crowd of people huddled on the fringes of the club. I took one look at this guy. I knew he was very dangerous. I spoke to him in a peaceful manner.

"What happened, man?" I asked.

"I am a United States Marine. I just got back from Iraq. I saw my friends die for this country. And this prick wants to say, 'It's all stupid' from a stage. This guy don't know shit! Who is he to put us down?"

Seeing this musician in action before, knowing his history of mouthing off from the stage, I was on the Marine's side automatic.

The Marine continued, he pointed to the musician, "He was talking to the audience. He asked me where I was from. I say, 'I just got back from Iraq'. He says, 'Bush is an asshole. It's stupid that we're there, and anybody that is there, is stupid'... I couldn't give a shit about Bush! I care about my guys! He wouldn't let up saying, 'We are stupid'. So, I got up and punched him in face."

I wished he did more than punch this jerkoff in the face, but I had to get this situation right. This one musician was an asshole. Everybody on Bleecker Street knows, "No politics on stage. It causes fights."

"Ok. Look. It's over. You're going to have to leave now," I said.

The Marine never took his eyes off mine. I looked back at him. I continued.

"All you have to do is leave and everything will be cool," I said.

There was silence for five long seconds before he whispered in an eerie tone, "Ok."

He put his fists down and calmly walked out to Bleecker Street.

I followed a safe distance behind. He stopped right outside the doorway on the street.

I stood just inside the doorway a few feet away. I was not on the street yet. I did not want to get to close to him.

I have had fights with bikers, rappers, frat boys, gym rats, goons, skin heads, metal heads, West Point cadets, Navy guys and many different types of people. Active duty Marines are the scariest of them all.

The marine began to stare at the sky. I was still just inside the doorway. His head was up for ten long quiet seconds when he started to tremble. I watched. Everybody in the club stood in the windows, silent. Then the Marine began to cry. A sadness came over me for him. I became engulfed in it. This guy was in pain.

It was late. This club had their garbage on the street out front. Another few seconds past. I watched the Marine's trembling body be overtaken by a shaking rage. It was like the devil just jumped into his body.

I watched as he snapped. He lets out a loud roar and suddenly sprints at the garbage. He attacks it with kicks and punches. He picks up a giant bag of empty bottles. He swings it around three times, like the Olympic hammer toss. He launches the bag in a line drive that skids across Bleecker Street. He follows like a tracer round after the skidding bag.

I stepped out to the street. I watch the Marine catch up to the bag. He began swinging punches with a furious flurry when he reached it. I heard bottles breaking with each punch. After twenty or thirty rage filled haymakers he stops punching and falls to his knees.

I looked at his hands. It was a miracle they weren't a bloody mess.

He began crying and sobbing again. The cry quickly turned to a scream at the top of his lungs, "My friends were killed! My friends were killed! Why am I here!? Everybody's dead! Why am I here!?" He wailed out.

I stood looking. My heart was bleeding for this distraught man. I heard the sounds of sirens in the distance. I knew they were for this poor guy. He was over the edge. Someone called the cops. Probably the stuck up bartender. I knew I had to calm him down before the sirens were upon us. I didn't want him going after the NYPD because some bigmouth on stage set him off. I began to approach the Marine very slow. I talked at him with a peaceful tone.

"Hey buddy. Its ok man. You're going to be Ok."

When he heard my voice he looked at me suspicious.

"You're gonna be ok," I repeated, looking into his eyes.

"How do you know?" He asked like a child.

"Because you're a good guy," I replied in my most consoling tone.

The Marine, still on his knees crying in the middle of Bleecker Street, held up his fists toward me. I eased with caution closer. I stretched my arms out with open palm hands to the side, like the pose of the Statue of Mother Mary. I slow stepped toward the Marine. His eyes were wild in sadness.

Speaking soft and sincere I inched closer, "It's gonna be ok. You're a good guy. I can tell. You just went through some rough stuff. This pain that you're feeling right now, it's not going to last forever. You're gonna be better."

In the Mother Mary pose I slow stepped closer to the troubled Marine. The sirens got louder. Over his shoulder I saw a cop car turn the wrong way onto Bleecker Street. Then I saw another one turn right behind it.

Bleecker street ran one way west to east. The cop cars were hauling ass east to west the wrong way. They were flooring it with lights flashing. I could hear the engines strain from five blocks away. Whoever called them must have been in a panic.

The Marine rose from his knees and faced me. I never took my eyes off his. I kept slow stepping toward him to almost a foot away. I never stopped whispering in a consoling manner to him, "It's gonna be ok."

In my thoughts I prayed, "Please God, don't let this guy attack me. He's hurting and he needs us right now."

The hardest tears I had ever seen were teeming from his eyes. His body shook with weeps. I reached out slow. I stared direct into his eyes and once again said, "It's gonna be ok."

He stared at me. I saw a trust drop into his watering eyes. He breathed in deep sucking tears into his nose. He tried to regain composure. He put his fists to his side. With a hard caution I reach out slow putting my arms around him. He grabbed me back. We embraced in the middle of Bleecker Street. I held him tight and sincere.

"It's gonna be all right, Buddy. It's gonna be all right," I soft whispered while watching the cop cars hammering toward us.

The Marine squeezed harder, hugging me. His entire lungs filling with air in every breath.

"Why am I here? My friends are all dead," he sobbed.

"It's gonna be all right man," I repeated, "It's gonna be all right."

The cops pulled up screeching. Each car had two guys. Both cars sped down Bleecker Street the wrong way. The Marine was oblivious to it all. These cops were ready for anything. They jumped out of their cars. I knew them from the block. I held onto the crying man. The cops were assessing the situation from a few feet from me. I spoke to them very calm.

"This is a Marine who just got back from Iraq. He's having a rough night. He's Ok."

The cops walked closer towards us. I lighten my grip on the Marine. I moved my hands to his waist like we were slow dancing. If he was going to make a move on the cops, I would be able to stop it. I showed no sign of stress for the cops to be weary of.

The first cop to walk up, also spoke very calm. It wasn't an act.

"It's Ok Buddy. My brother is in Iraq right now. I can't stop thinking about him. You want to get something to eat. We're going on lunch. Come on with us. I'll buy you a cup of coffee, or a burger, or something."

The Marine was perplexed about the compassion from the cop. I could see his distress ease down a little.

The cop looked him direct in the eyes and spoke again, "We're on your side. It's Ok. Are you here with anybody?"

"No," the Marine sniffled, "All my friends are dead..."

"Well come with us to the diner. You're safe with us."

The Marine was surprised at the cop's sincerity. He fought his sobs, "Really?"

The cop nodded affirmative.

"Ok. I'd like some coffee," the Marine's voice sounding like a child.

The cop put his arm around the Marine.

"It's ok. We're on your side. Marines huh? What's your name?" The cop cheerfully asked.

The cops walked and talked with the Marine to the squad car like one of their own. The musician who got punched in the face came running over.

"That guy should get arrested, not a cup of coffee," he wormed out load.

I got in his face.

"Don't worry about him. The cops are taking care of it. You're a fucking dick! You get everybody else in trouble with your big mouth," I screamed, anger dancing in my tone.

The musician contemplated having a go at me. I saw it in the back of his eyes. He was not a small musician. He was in shape. He decided against it. The cops pulled off.

I walked back to my post at Kenny's Castaways a few feet away. 'Master of Puppets' by Metallica was still cranking on the juke box. I began to head bang along. The hot-tight-wearing Bartender from four doors down walked in. She approached me.

"I want to thank you for helping me with the Marine," she said.

"No problem. Anytime you have a bigmouth screaming politics from the stage. Shut them down immediately. It'll stop the problems from starting," I said.

"You're right. Thank you again."

The hot Bartender turned and walked out. From that time on when she walked past me she always said, "Hi."

About The Author

CHAPTER 30
ABOUT THE AUTHOR

Born December 28, 1963 at Margret Hague Hospital in Jersey City, New Jersey. Kevin Patrick Corrigan has been a fixture in the New York City Irish bar and music scene for over four decades.

Spending his early years in Jersey City. Kevin and his family moved to Old Bridge, New Jersey the "Heavy Metal Capitol Of The World". Where he was raised.

At 19 he moved back to North Jersey spending most of his adult life between Jersey City and Greenwich Village in Manhattan. He currently has been residing in Queens, New York since 2006.

Corrigan spent the 1980's hanging out in the rough Irish bars of Hell's Kitchen and Times Square areas of Manhattan. He also was a mainstay in the dingy clubs of the Lower East Side. It was in these crack plagued pre-Giuliani New York City streets he found inspiration for many of his stories and song writings.

From 1987 to 2004 Corrigan spent his time working, hanging out, and performing in the Rock Clubs of Greenwich Village, New York City on world famous Bleecker Street.

The Red Lion Pub, Kenny's Castaways, The Lion's Den, The Back Fence, and The Bitter End are venues where he worked both as a bouncer and performer. He witnessed first-hand the change of New York City from a perilous mom and pop city to a corporate mall.

Corrigan estimates he has been in about two hundred street and bar fights. He joking claims his record is 143 wins and 72 loses.

"Working and hanging out in New York City in the 1980's and 1990's was an outrageous and magical time. Allot of great music and deviant behavior was everywhere. I was all in." Corrigan says.

Corrigan is currently the lead singer and bass player of New York City Irish American band *BEGORRAH*. Their 2011 album "MOLLY B'GEE" was voted album of the week on VH-1's "That METAL SHOW".

BEGORRAH has played Monmouth Park Racetrack, The New Jersey Irish Festival, The Bitter End, as well as many New York Irish Pubs, and Rock clubs. Their second album "Tough Guy Prayer" was released in 2017.

Google "Begorrah Band Youtube page" to watch the many Begorrah videos and listen to songs. Also, available on all major download sites and iTunes.

Family and The 4th Floor Photos

Corrigan Family from First Chapter
L to R: Patricia, Kevin, Shelia, Brian, Eileen,
Mary

4th Floor band and crew backstage KISS
Meadowlands N.J. 12/31/96
Back L to R: Sasha (crew), Peter May (guitar), Howie,(crew), Al
(vocals), Antonio (crew): Front – Marcello (guitar), Lee (bass),
Peter Cav (vocals), Kenny (drums), Kevin (vocals)

4th Floor Pictures

**Kevin Patrick
Corrigan with The
4th Floor**
*At 'The Limelight' NYC
1994*

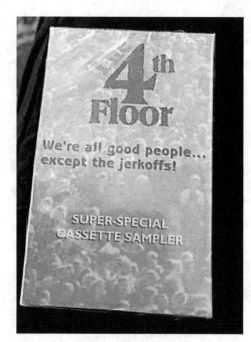

The 4th Floor
Cassette Sampler

The 4th Floor 1996
L to R: Kenny Kramme (drums), Alex "Captain Al" Batenko (vocals), Kevin Patrick Corrigan aka Bocko (vocals), Peter May (guitar), Marcello Capparelli (guitar), Lee Matheson (bass), Peter Cavanagh (vocals)

4th Floor Press Photo

The 4th Floor (Peter Cav with mic L Kevin with mic R band swallowed by crowd).
Live at The Lion's Den In The Village NYC 1995

4th Floor Motto

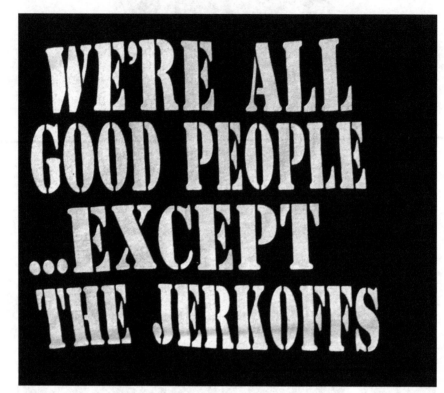

Back of 4th Floor t-shirt
Our album title

The New Underground 1989 (Chapter 7)
L to R: Kevin Patrick Corrigan aka Bocko with skull, Dave "Roadhog" Ryan with knife, Wayno Draino with axe, Jim Florentine with hair

The New Underground

L to R: Kevin Patrick Corrigan, Oderus (Gwar), Wayno
Draino (from Chapter 7), Gwar Woman (Gwar), 1990
Photo credit: Frank Forcino

The New Underground And Gwar

Weedkiller

WEEDKILLER 1998
*L to R: Frenchy (guitar), Captain Alex Batenko
(vocals), Eric Czar (bass), Kevin Patrick Corrigan
aka Bocko (vocals), Kenny Kramme (drums)
missing from photo*

**Kenny Kramme Weedkiller and The
4th Floor Drummer 1995**
*Red Lion Building's Rooftop Twin Towers in
Background*

Pete Puma 2020
*Kevin's Bouncer buddy from Chapter 23 Ass
Grabbing Santa Gets His Ass Kicked and Chapter
29 The Secret Service At Kenny's Castaways*

Bouncer And Club Friends Nowadays

Club Friends Photo taken 2015.
*Jerry Adams Chapter 22 La La Paluuza and
Rachel Martinez Chapter 25 Weedkiller
Wednesdays*

Newspaper Announcement

NEW YORK'S 4TH FLOOR TOURS WITH KISS

NYC - New York's **The 4th Floor** were hand-picked by **Paul Stanley** to open for Kiss on select dates of their tour, including the New Year's Eve show at The Meadowlands. The 7-piece punk-funk, rock & roll band are infamous in the NY/NJ area for fun, outrageous live shows, and have previously opened for **Alice Cooper** at the Garden State Arts Center. Besides the Garden show, 4th Floor opened for Kiss at the **Worcester Centrum**, **Long Island's Nassau Coliseum**, and **Hartford's Civic Center**.

THE 4th FLOOR

Newspaper Clipping 1996
Opening For Kiss

Memorabilia

**Newspaper Ad: The 4th Floor at
Nassau Coliseum**
NY Local Papers December 1996

**Backstage
Lamanent**
*KISS Tour Northeast Leg
1996 Tour*

The 4th Floor live at The Lion's Den 1995
L to R: Peter Cav, Peter May, Captain Al, Kevin, Lee, Marcello, Kenny on drums

Bryan (Sound Man), Kevin on bus Chapter 16 Lee Defies Gravity 1995
Bryan appears in chapters 15, 16, 20, 23

Live Shots

Smith's Bar Times Square 44th Street 8th Avenue
(2021)
Chapters 2, 5

Smith's Bar Times Square

Google "Pictures Times Square 1970's" and "Show World Times Square 1970's" for photos of the Chapters 1,2,3,4,5 era.

The Red Lion Greenwich Village NYC 2021
Corner of Bleecker and Thompson Streets

The Red Lion Bleecker Street

The Red Lion was *The 4th Floor* band's headquarters. The normally packed street is empty because of Pandemic in this photo. This is the exact spot where Kevin met Alan Whelan (Chapter 8) to play Rugby for a job at *The Red Lion*. Where Peter May told Kevin he should be on stage (Chapter 10). Third window from right - on first floor above bar - is Kevin's old room. The fire escape by it - is the one Kevin ran up in his underwear to Kenny the drummer's room to tell him they were opening for KISS (Chapter 19). Also, where Chapter 9, 11, 13, 14, 17, 18 took place.